Betty Hornbeck's
Whirligig Stories
Tales of the Sixties in a West Virginia Town

To Ann (Little Mother)

To David (Son No. 1)

Betty Hornbeck's
Whirligig Stories
Tales of the Sixties in a West Virginia Town

Buckhannon West Virginia – Howard Hiner Collection

Compiled and Edited by Son No. 2
William R. Hornbeck

DenHoorn Publishing   Leesburg VA

Whirligig Stories

Tales of the Sixties in a West Virginia Town

Copyright © 2014 by William R. Hornbeck

ISBN: 978-0-615-91550-0

First Edition 2014

Published by:

WRHORNBECK, LLC.

DenHoorn Publishing
38782 Mt. Gilead Road
Leesburg, Virginia USA
703.777.6840
info@wrhornbeck.com

Order online www.WhirligigStories.com

This work is licensed under the Creative Commons Attribution-NonCommercial-ShareAlike 3.0 Unported License. To view a copy of this license, visit http://creativecommons.org/licenses/by-nc-sa/3.0/ or send a letter to Creative Commons, 444 Castro Street, Suite 900, Mountain View, California, 94041, USA.

Whirligig, n., 1. Any of various child's toys that whirl or spin. 2. A merry-go-round. 3. Something that seems to whirl, or revolve in a cycle. 4. A whirling motion.

Webster's New World Dictionary, 1967

Rainbow Restaurant 1963   Howard Hiner Collection

Contents

Foreword

Introduction

1	Coming Home
3	April Daze
4	Antique Newspaper
7	The Bogerts
8	The Tag
9	Kindergarten
13	Bloopers
14	Trees
16	Ham Supper
17	Strawberry Festival '59
20	Swimming Pool
22	Bull Money
23	Mouths of Babes
24	County Statistics
25	City Statistics
27	Salk Vaccine
29	Coal Economy #1
30	Antique Delta
32	Getting Paper To Press
34	Traffic Fatalities
35	Sure Is Hot
36	Airline Dinners
37	Traffic Lights
38	Civil War Facts
40	Courthouse
41	Newsboys
42	Take Home A Student
43	Coal Economy #2
44	The Fabulous Fifties
45	Cigarette Sales
46	1849 Auction
47	Magic Closet

48	Where Are The Birds?
49	Miss West Virginia
50	Distinguished Students
51	Snow Storm 1960
53	Bandmaster Harold Fultz
57	On The Bus To Bluefield
58	Mt. State Visitors Bureau
59	Eye Bank
60	Bob Ours & Others
61	Doctors and Medicine
63	Election Results
65	Polio
67	Strawberry Festival – 1960
68	June Potpourri
69	Newsmen
70	Our Children
72	Political Slogans
73	Boy Scout National Jamboree – Colorado
74	Janet Cosgrove With The Queen Mother
75	Republican National Convention
77	Hay Fever
78	David Plate
79	Homelife With Teenagers
80	Funds For Athletic Programs
81	Athletic Funds – Follow-Up
82	New Year's Resolutions
83	City-County Progress
85	Civil War & Stonewall Jackson
87	Civil War – 100th Anniversary
89	Winter Is Wonderful
90	Executives Can't Write
91	Executive Writes Reply
92	Coffee Breaks
93	I'm A Giggler!
94	History Notes
96	City Image
97	Introduction To Civil War Feature

99	West Virginia's Birthday
100	Feeding The Boys
102	Man Will Conquer
103	Pearl Nutter and Civil Defense
104	Please Buy My Book #1
105	"The Girls" – After 20 Years
106	The Salesman
108	Cleanup Campaign
109	Career Diplomat
111	Sunday At Home
113	Main Street
116	Football Season's Over
118	Welfare Letters
120	Births and Deaths
121	How To Raise Delinquents
124	Bowling
126	Just What Me Wanted
127	Merchant Sales Up
128	Innocence of Childhood
130	John Scott
131	Free Groceries
132	Bottle Caps For Education
133	Youth Center / Forbisider
135	Ken Phillips – Strawberries
137	Little Mother Ann
138	Grade School Basketball
140	The Coming Centennial
142	The Birth Of WV Wesleyan
144	Spring Cleaning
146	Self Image
147	I Am West Virginia
150	Letter From Mary Harman Carl
151	W. W. Wimer Roadside Stop
152	Spring In The Yard
153	Strawberry – Vegetable or Fruit?
154	The Flag – The Trees
155	Fractured Nursery Rhymes

Page	Title
157	Upshur County Forgotten
158	Ban The Bikini
160	Entering The First Grade
161	Watching "Lunch Eaters"
162	Folks at The Delta
165	Cuban Missile Crisis
166	History Of Voting
167	Election Notes
168	Weekday Holiday
169	Housewife Reply
171	Gumperson's Law
173	Santa Myth
174	Tele-Sacroiliac-Itis
175	Womanless Wedding
178	City-County Growth Projections
180	Howard Hiner and The Centennial Bear
181	Grade School Centennial Songs
182	Uncle Sam & The Sutton Dam
183	Welfare Tab
185	Antique Newspapers #2
188	Letter To Dean Q. Wilson – WVU
190	Ready For School
191	Prejudice
193	Saturday Morning
194	Letter To Bill Evans – Re: Zopp
197	Welfare
198	Government Regulations
201	Football Champions
202	Death of J.F.K.
203	Resolutions
204	Margaret Kyle's Rose Thief
205	Tucked In Bed
206	Welfare and Birth Control Pills
207	B-U Students on TV Toss Up
208	Gibson Library
210	Whirligig by Herb Welch
212	Mental Illness

214	Vote For School Levy
215	Zopp Resigns
216	Summer Camps
217	Welfare & The Pill – Part #2
218	Topless Bathing Suits
219	Transient Aid
220	How To Cook A Husband
221	Neighbors
222	Welfare – Commissioner Report
224	Not Raising Hogs
225	I Remember Buckwheat Cakes
226	Little League Football - #1
228	Little League Football - Rebuttal
231	Little League Football - Reply from Fred Boyles
232	"Little Girls" By Alan Beck
234	"Little Boys" By Alan Beck
236	Babysitting The Iguana
237	The City Plan
240	New St. Joseph's Hospital
242	The Great Society
244	The Monkey, The Bird, The Jerk
246	Mental Health & Retardation
248	Libraries
250	School Lunches – Freight Costs
253	Forming The YWCA
254	Putting In The Garden
255	Summer Job For Kids - Protesting
256	Merchants Remodeling
257	Aboard Ship With Sis
259	I'm Worth $329 Per Week
260	Baxa Restaurant
262	Buckhannon-Wesleyan Swim Team
264	Welfare – Free Contraceptive Foam
265	See Cass Railroad
266	City Traffic Problems
268	Welfare – Physician Ratios
269	Creeping Socialism

270	Men & Women 1882-1966
271	Timber Industry
273	Whirligig by Son No. 2
274	Federal Funds
275	New Décor at St. Joseph's Hospital
277	Mental Health Clinic
278	Big Money In Poverty
279	Killed In Action - Vietnam
280	Grandmom Dutton
281	Foreign Exchange Student
283	I Can't Cook
284	Beautification Going Sour
285	Instant Housing
286	Jennifer Is Born
287	YWCA Events
289	Trimble Hill
290	School Budgets
292	Overworked Doctors
293	Trouble With Kids
294	Mrs. H. M. Darley
296	Babysittin'
297	Instant Schools
299	Pearl Harbor
300	The Ant & The Grasshopper
301	Tales of Fantasy
302	United Fund – Little Angel
303	New Job Ideas
304	Letter From A Foxhole
305	The Big Flood Of 1967
308	Telephonitis
309	The Jackson Cemetery
310	High School Guidance Counselors
311	Loud Music
312	Traffic Problems
313	City Police
314	That Darn Dog!
315	Great Society Goofs

317	One Sewing Machine For Sale
318	Please Buy My Book - #2
320	Welfare & The Pill #3
321	WBUC Radio
322	World Evolution
323	Off The Paper Spike
325	Pumpkintown, WV
326	Miss Whirley
327	The Bowl Games
328	Statue of L.B.J.
329	Income Tax Laws
330	West Virginia Ranks Low
331	Mental Health Clinic - #2
333	Moonshining
335	Secretary's Prayer
336	Teacher Pay
337	Jim Knorr
339	Jim in Vietnam
341	The Future of Medicine
342	What Subscribers Want To Read
343	Delinquent Notice Reply
345	Upshur County Educational Ranking
347	Central West Virginia
348	Bill, Barb & The Agnews
349	The Chicago Convention 1968
350	Governor George Wallace
351	Cleaning Out My Drawers
352	Short Skirts
354	The Great Society Has Arrived
355	The Value of a Vote
357	Christmas Crafts
358	Juvenile Crime – The Penalty
360	Hospital Expenses
361	Student Demonstrations
362	Spray Cans
363	I Hate That Spade
364	Man On The Moon

365	Miss Alta Ice
367	A Football Dream
369	Middle Age
370	SNAFU
371	Epilogue – Stop the Presses!
372	Howard Hiner – A Tribute
373	Acknowledgements
374	About the Editor

FOREWORD

Stephen Coonts

In the years after World War II, Upshur County, West Virginia, had two weekly newspapers: *The Republican-Delta* owned and published by Herb Welch, and *The Record*, the democrat newspaper owned and published by Richard Ralston. These two friends bickered endlessly in their editorial pages about every conceivable social and political issue. Consequently everyone in the county read both papers. In 1959 Welch hired Betty Dutton Hornbeck, a Buckhannon native who had been working on the *Bluefield Daily Telegraph*, to be his Number Two. She was soon writing a column, the "West Virginia Whirligig", which quickly became a *Delta* staple.

Betty was a smart, articulate, professional journalist and a keen observer; she could have found a job on a big-city daily that paid her twice the money Herb Welch did, yet she stayed in her hometown to raise her three children with all the advantages that a good small town provides, including having her parents right down the street to grandparent her kids. She wrote thousands of news stories through the years, most without a by-line, but it was her column that gave her a voice in the community. In the "Whirligig" Betty wrote about any subject that interested her, including city, county, state, national and international political issues and events. Like most educated women, she had opinions that she wasn't shy about voicing. Whether you agreed or disagreed with her, her columns shaped conversation and public opinion.

Her son Bill has put together some of her best "Whirligig" columns in this collection. Not all, for heavens sake, or this book would be a tome. Betty wrote about darn near everything, from the Cuban Missile Crisis, the death of JFK, the 1968 Democratic Convention in Chicago, to welfare reform, treatment of neglected, abandoned, and mentally-ill children, school bond campaigns, The Strawberry Festival, floods, fires and civic improvements. If she was interested, she assumed everyone else would be too, so away she went.

I was fortunate because I got to know Betty professionally and personally. I was the same age as her eldest son; she knew how to talk to boys. Like hundreds of kids through the years, I sold copies of the *Delta* for pocket money, lining up in the office every Thursday to get 25 copies, then pedaling away on my bicycle to hawk them. Yes, it was an age when a 12-year old on a bike could ride anywhere in town, indeed, anywhere in the county, and parents didn't fret.

The summer I turned 14 I got another opportunity. Herb and Betty decided to let me try my hand as a summer sports reporter, and gave me my own column, "Steve Coonts' Sports Specials." The *Delta* paid me the magnificent sum of five bucks a week. I covered the county sports scene for three summers while the regular sports editor, John Scott, took his summer break from attending Wesleyan. No doubt the opportunity came about because Betty and my mother, a high-school journalism teacher, were friends. Mom was my first editor and Betty was my second, on every story, every column. I learned more English grammar from those two than I ever did in school.

I liked to hang out in the pressroom on Thursdays watching the linotype operators set stories in type and assembling the page forms. I helped proof for typos. Then the pages were put on the press and the continuous rolls of newsprint began to feed through the press with a deafening roar. Newspapers poured off. The process of converting typewritten words to a printed newspaper was endlessly fascinating. I quickly found I liked writing and seeing my words in print. Many years later I became a professional novelist. Holding a new book in my hands with my name on the cover still gives me the same kick I got as a boy holding a copy of the *Delta* containing my stories and column, smelling the warm ink, listening to the roar of the press.

The world has changed profoundly since the 1960s and early 1970s, as has West Virginia and Upshur County. Reading Betty's "Whirligig" columns will take you back again to that wonderful place, that American small-town, where many of us spent our youth or a portion of our adult years. You will once again be charmed by the humanity, wit, keen observations and opinions of that delightful, articulate lady, Betty Hornbeck, who graced our lives with her talent.

~Stephen Coonts

Betty Hornbeck ~ Assistant City Desk Editor, Bluefield Daily Telegraph ~ 1958

INTRODUCTION

The year was 1957 or so, and those early childhood memories of mine are centered on the crossing of paths as I came home from elementary school just as my mother was leaving home for her evening job at the Bluefield Daily Telegraph. After all, morning newspapers are produced in the dark of night and there was nothing unusual to me that she worked different hours than most of my friends' parents.

In fact, even at my young age, I had a certain sense of pride in knowing that the rewards for her efforts were visible each day in tangible, smudgeable black and white; a timely source of news that was an important part of everyone's daily lives. Upon later reflection, I have surmised that it must be this daily deadline, this incessant and unrelenting marathon to complete each day's edition that accounts for the fact that long-term newspaper people have evolved printer's ink for blood.

She wrote under the byline of Betty Hornbeck. She wrote hundreds of thousands of words, more likely millions, over the course of thirty-five years in the newspaper business. Most of the time, those words were the mechanical assembly of information relating to countless anonymous facts and figures so necessary to the daily production of "the news". I have heard her refer to that role as being a production writer. That is undoubtedly true when you consider the effect of deadlines on creative writing. Nevertheless, her writing had a particular style that generated consistent readership and a regular vocal response.

Following the dissolution of her young marriage in early 1959, she accepted a position with her hometown weekly newspaper, The Republican-Delta, and moved the family to Buckhannon, West Virginia.

She spent the following twelve years with The Delta and, during that time, she raised the three of us kids (David, Bill, and Ann) successfully, wrote numerous feature articles, pounded the streets as the paper's advertising manager, filled in as Editor on multiple occasions, wrote a history book on the Civil War, _Upshur Brothers of the Blue and the Gray_, was a guest lecturer at innumerable clubs and college classes, served as an officer in the local Chamber of Commerce and the local Historical Society and, in general, was either an advocate, antagonist, activist, or participant in just about everything that went on in that small town.

During those days in Buckhannon, she wrote a weekly feature column that steadily became the most familiar item in the newspaper. Indeed, it was synonymous with the paper's masthead.

Occasionally, she filled the space with community growth statistics, sometimes with the commentary of other scribes and pundits, but mostly she wrote the personal anecdotes that reflected the period's attitudes toward life in a small town such as life in the family, community happenings, or national, regional, and global concerns. As a humorist, she could bring out more chuckles than Erma Bombeck. As a patriot, she could generate more waves in the flag than Paul Harvey.

She had a defining sense of logic and a passion for commitment. The words she wrote during those years were timely and meaningful. And those of us who participated in the societal evolution of that period can be assured that we all played an integral role in her enlightening and irreverent transcription of The Sixties.

Please note that the composition style of the period has been retained in this compilation and no edits were made to match the original narratives with current capitalization styles or grammar usage. What you read is what it was.

Further, as you read certain stories in this collection, you will most likely attempt to align your current sense of "political correctness" with some of Betty's words. I urge you not to do that. These are the stories of the mid-twentieth century, full of the vigorous opinions of the day. Oh, what a time that was…

Please share my pleasure in remembering those incredibly defining yet confusing days when life was spinning like a *West Virginia Whirligig*.

William R. Hornbeck
Son No.2

THE REPUBLICAN DELTA

89th YEAR. NO. 27.   BUCKHANNON, W. VA., FRIDAY, JULY 10, 1959

WEST VIRGINIA
Whirligig

West Virginia leads the nation again—this time, in the ratio of illegitimate births—and just when we were feeling pride in the state's first woman judge, the rise in personal income and the strides toward better and bigger schools.

And to add insult to injury, no other state was even close, District of Columbia came in second, followed by Tenn.

Betty Hornbeck But while some Mountaineers were cavorting in the hills, others were showing another spirit by boosting state personal income after the recession scare of 1958.

Locally, according to the recently released West Virginia Business Index, Buckhannon valuation of building permits jumped from $8,800 in 1958 to $10,600 in 1959. And to prove that Mountaineers believe in their state, a gigantic surge of building valuation permits was noted with an increase of from $3,637,366 in May, 1958 to $15,725,372 in May, 1959.

In a survey of county indexes of retail trade in West Virginia, indications show Upshur county rose from 136 in April, 1958, to a high of 184 this past September and dropped again to 142 in April, 1959—still more than the year previous.

Buckhannon bank debits to individual accounts in West Virginia show dollar comparisons as follows: May, 1957, $4,629; May, 1958, $4,497 and May, 1959, $4,395.

In the survey of post office receipts for 24 largest cities, the state noted an upward swing of $732,126 as against $565,774 in May, 1958. Buckhannon is also up with $4,779 as against $4,148 in May, 1958.

All of which proves, this county isn't standing still or even holding its head above water, but moving forward—a shot in the arm for many optimists, like me.

Thieves Loot Stout's Gulf Station, Atlantic Drive-In

Public Is Invited to Attend Wheeling Symphony Concert

Music enthusiasts in the Buckhannon area are looking forward to next Wednesday's appearance of the Wheeling Symphony Orchestra at West Virginia Wesleyan college.

The orchestra, conducted by Henry Mazer, will perform at 8 p.m., July 15, on the lawn in front of Pfeiffer Memorial Library on the Wesleyan campus.

The concert, patterned after the successful "Music Under the Stars" program presented each summer in Wheeling's Oglebay Park, will be free to the public.

Dr. C. Buell Agey, head of Wesleyan's department of music, will serve as guest conductor for the English Folk Song Suite by Vaughan Williams.

Mrs. Howard G. Oliver II, a Wesleyan alumna, will play with the orchestra, performing the Third Movement of Mendelssohn's Piano Concerto in G Minor.

The program will consist of light classical and popular selections, designed to blend with the outdoor setting and summertime mood.

Although the program has been planned as a special project, its success may spell the future of a series of similar programs.

Included in the program are the following selections; Verdi's Grand March from "Aida," Mendelssohn's third movement of the Piano Concerto in G Minor, Mrs. Howard Oliver, piano, Williams' English Folk Sing Suite, C. Buell Agey, conducting, Strauss' Emperor Waltz, Willson's selection from "The Music Man," Song of the Moulin Rouge, Anderson's Trumpet Jubilee Promenade, and Loewe's selection from "My Fair Lady."

HENRY MAZER

Money and Beer Are Taken in Early Morning Entering

Stout's Gulf Station and lantic Drive-In, both on the burg road, were entered and sometime Wednesday night early Thursday morning in a of breakings and entering continue to plague local and police.

Paul Stout, owner and op discovered the service theft around 7 a. m. Th morning when he arrived up for the day's business.

Patrolman John Slaugh swered the call and an hou Gus Quertinmont, owner erator of the Drive-In jus the street, found that his lishment had been enter the second time in the p months and the fourth tim the past year.

Both businesses were through a back window. was robbed of between $35 taken from a cigarette m At Quertinmonts between $100 in dimes was taken juke box aong with 15 quart sorted brands of beer a cases of regular bottle be taken was approximately a jar containing money for

State Trooper H. H. M assisting local police in vestigation.

Chief of Police Paul Thursday issued a new wa an attempt to crackdown
(Continued on Page

City Employes Are Rehire Wage Hikes Are Granted

3 New Councilmen Are Seated at First   **Fight Ends**   *Frenchton Man*

COMING HOME

March 27, 1959

Moving day has come and gone. The curtains hang fairly straight, the windows have been cleaned inside and out and even a picture has been hung here and there. And the only thing I've learned in the process of moving is that there is no way to pack a pogo stick or a hula-hoop.

I'm returning to Buckhannon after an absence of almost ten years. This is home! This is where I graduated from high school, where I married and where my second son was born. I feel that my roots are here and I'm looking forward to a new phase in life that so far has been a busy but interesting one.

With my return to work on a weekly paper, I've completed a circle. Many people here will remember me 16 years ago when I started in the publishing business in 1942 with the Buckhannon Record. I worked as a cub reporter for the East St. Louis, Ill., Journal during the waning months of World War II, worked briefly on city desk of the Parkersburg News and was society editor for the Clarksburg Exponent before accepting a position with the Bluefield Daily Telegraph as assistant city desk editor.

During these past three years I worked from 4 p.m. until 1 a.m. copy reading, editing local, state and wire copy, and "making-up" pages that left my desk for the composing room.

No one person can make a newspaper – it is formed by a group of people, working together to unify facts that are presented to the reader. In leaving Bluefield and that newspaper, I've left people that almost seemed like part of my family. Around my wrist I wear a sterling silver bracelet with 13 discs that constantly remind me of that newspaper family.

This, perhaps, can be my way of thanking them as no profession is more closely knit than those who work together in compiling the news.

On one disc is the name Mr. Shott, the publisher, whom I must thank for his patience and tolerance when many times he must have wondered how confusing one newsroom could get.

On another disc is written the name of Stubby, the managing editor who, after more than 30 years, never let any situation quicken his tempo, and stood as a rock when the deadline neared.

On the third disc, is the name of Jerry, the city editor, who more than anyone else taught me to keep a level head in the whirly merry-go-round.

On the other discs are the names of Jim, who taught me not to become a cynic as I read of the turmoil and human misery night after night; Jeanne, who is proving that a whole new profession can be learned without prior experience; Jack, the Associated Press correspondent who taught me cooperation; Fitz, the society editor and close friend who provided the wit needed in an air of tenseness; McHone, who stood in "ad alley" night after night and was a friend; Pooch and Raymond, the boys on sports who totaled all my wrongly added box scores; Shaw, another in the composing room who caught those mistakes of mine so cheerfully during make-up; Vernon, the photographer, who never turned me down on a picture assignment though many times the snow laid deep or the rain ran in rivers; and B. Yost, the composing room foreman, who had the ability to lash out in a fiery temper yet taught me all in the operation and procedure of the printing world.

These are my kind of people, my 'family'. They will be found in any publishing business – I will find it so here with the Republican-Delta.

April Daze

April 3, 1959

We won't be the first or the last columnist to write of the number of observances marked in one month and we are as puzzled as most as to how one person can possibly observe a total of 32 such 'red-letter' days in the 30 days of April.

We'll admit many days and weeks are worthy projects, some for fun and some just plain ridiculous. For instance, for the benefit of all husbands who want to get in the good graces of their mother-in-law, "National Mother-In-Law Day" is scheduled for April 19. The ridiculous angle comes in though when the next day April 20, begins Good Human Relations Week. Many husbands will contend they can't possibly be in the mood for good humor after a day spent spreading cheer for mothers-in-law.

The entire month of April is devoted to Cancer Crusade, Diamond Month, National Hobby Month and Clean-up, Paint-up, Fix-up Time and just for your edification you are now in the midst of a week that calls attention to Let's All Play Ball Week, Cereal & Milk Week, National Noise Abatement Week and National Boy's Club Week.

We have a suggestion – quietly crunch that breakfast cereal while gaining strength to play ball in the interest of boyhood! And, as if enough coffee weren't already consumed by office workers and neighborhood wives at the kitchen table, we are asked to mark April 13 as Coffee Day. I presume we are to step up consumption as a tribute to the great American practice of 'coffee break'.

Of course, the 13th is an appropriate day as it precedes the deadline for the payment of income taxes on April 15, and where would the poor, confused taxpayer be if he couldn't bolster his strength and jangle his nerves with pots of coffee in his race against fine and imprisonment. Don't waiver, here's where the fun begins – right smack in the middle of the month with the observance of National Fun Day on the 17th. Be sure you make full use of the day, for you have much to face.

In the next two weeks you must be kind to your secretary, your retail creditors and all babies and at the same time mark Bike Safety Week, National Conservation Week…

Antique Newspaper

April 24, 1959

Garner M. Groves, personable young owner and manager of Shaffer's Jewelry, has in addition to the wealth of diamonds and rubies in his safety vault, a yellowed, faded and tattered newspaper published in 1800 during the administration of John Adams.

Dated Saturday, January 4, 1800 in Ulster County, Kingston, N.Y., the paper was bought 55 years ago for twenty-five cents by Grove's father-in-law, Daniel G. Simmons, then of Gassaway and now of Buckhannon. A merchant of Gassaway sold the paper after finding the four-page edition in the attic of an old house he was then demolishing.

Hand-set, of course, in Old English type, the paper is still very readable and as a safety precaution, Groves has put it under glass and anyone that is interested in looking at the publication is welcome to do so.

Published just 18 days after the death of George Washington, the paper carries a complete story on the funeral procession. And as now, the world was in the midst of war with Napoleon marching on Russia and the Austrians. Shipwrecks were in the news and Congress was in session, faced with most of the same problems facing the recent 82nd Congress.

One of the most interesting and unusual features of the paper were the advertisements, one of which was of a particular interest to me, a 'for sale' by one Lodewyck Hoornbeek dated Rochester, N.Y., Dec. 17, 1799, offering choice plots lying on the military track ranging from 50 to 550 acres. The Hornbeck families of Randolph and Upshur counties originally came to New York from Holland with the early Dutch settlers of New York and no doubt this is one of my ancestors.

Another most interesting ad is the offer for sale of one-half of a sawmill, …"with a convenient place for building, lying in the town of Rochester. By the mill is an inexhaustible quantity of pinewood. Also a stout, healthy, active Negro Wench…"

A boy 14-18 was wanted as an apprentice to a clothier's office and a stolen gun was being advertised with a reward of $2 offered.

The paper has two notices of bankruptcy suits, eleven sheriff's sales to "dispose of goods and chattels" and one Dry Goods and Groceries firm was offering cash paid for wheat and fur while a "most elegant well-furnished pleasure sleigh" was for sale. The law firm of Hasbrouch and Jansen was issuing notice of the dissolution of partnership, and a private sale of a pleasant farm, well-watered and timbered with an indisputable title was up for sale.

Before the House of Representatives was a statement of accounts for 1799 laid before the Secretary of Treasury, a ways and means committee had been appointed and a committee named to pursue a resolution passing on the revision and amendment relative to the judiciary system.

While over in the Senate, that august group was pleading with President Adams while lamenting the "arts and calumnies of factious and designing men who have excited open rebellion a second time in Pennsylvania, compelling employment of military force.

And in the same issue, "the House of Representatives met Thursday, Dec. 29 in deep sorrow on the occasion of Washington's death, paying honor to his memory in a resolution read by Mr. Marshal." In the meantime, the Senate was expressing deep regret and issuing a proclamation to that effect.

A part of the story on Washington reads as follows:

George Town, December 20   WASHINGTON ENTOMBED

On Wednesday last the mortal part of Washington the Great – the Father of his Country and the Friend of man was consigned to the tomb, with solemn honors and funeral pomp.

"A multitude of persons assembled, from many miles round, at Mount Vernon, the choice abode and last residence of the illustrious chief. There were the groves – the spacious avenues, the beautiful and sublime scenes, the noble mansion – but alas! the august inhabitant was now no more. That great soul was gone. His mortal part was there indeed, but ah! How affecting? How often this spectacle of such worth and greatness thus, to mortal eyes, fallen? – Yes! Fallen, fallen…"

On the ornament at the head of the coffin was inscribed

GENERAL GEORGE WASHINGTON
Departed this life on the 14th of December 1799

The funeral procession was formed in the following order: cavalry, infantry, guard, music, clergy, all with arms reversed, the general's horse with saddle, holsters and pistols and the pall bearers, Colonels Sims, Ramsay, Payne, Gilpin, Martseller and Little, the mourners, the Masonic Brothers and citizens.

And covering the highlights of world events was the story as follows: "Great variety of foreign news arrived by the last mails.

"French official account under the Bern…(missing) of October 8, states that on 4th Austro-Russians were defeated with several thousand killed wounded and taken.

"On 5th, Austro-Russians defeated at Giatus, with loss of 1200 persons and a great number killed. "At this place there were 1400 Russians wounded and 600 at Multen. French Army of the Rhine, 8th of October defeated Austrians with loss of 3000 killed and wounded. Their loss, 1000."

And, as a final coverage of shaking world events, and as proof that life was very cheap, there is a complete story on the "sinking of the British frigate Lutine of 39 guns, lost on 9th of October on the banks of outer Fly Island Passage; had on board nearly a half million, 200,000. Was insured and bound for Texel. She was to have proceeded to Hamburgh (sic) to clear the commercial failures in that city – the crew perished except two." Yes, life was cheap; what would now be a streamer headline with the number dead was only an afterthought.

If there are readers interested in buccaneers and pirates, the "Spanish frigates, bound for the Havanna (sic), having on board three million and a half dollars besides merchandise were taken on the 16th of October by four British frigates and safely arrives in Plymouth."

We found this publication interesting, and have barely touched on the highlights. There is a wealth of knowledge to be read in the issue and, like we said, Groves will have his valuable possession on display.

The Bogerts

May 1, 1959

The blue blood of royalty is running thick in the veins of the Bogert family this week. Strawberry Queen Barbara XVII can now claim descent from the Lord and Lady of May.

Raymond and Polly Bogert will do some retracting of memories tonight when Alderson-Broaddus College presents them to the student body in a pageant as honored alumni and this year's Lord and Lady of May Day.

Dr. Richard Shearer, president of A-B College, will make the presentation and also introduce Polly Bogert as a former May Day Queen of 1933. Here the confusion arises – like Polly says, time has passed swiftly and she doesn't exactly remember just what the pageant theme was in 1933, but she does remember wearing a straight, cheesecloth dress with a wide sash, and she knows somewhere in the story she was stolen by the villain, then recaptured by the prince and somewhere in the last act, crowned queen.

Raymond, who was sitting in the audience that day back in 1933 interrupted her to say she was an Arabian princess. He should know, we think, after all, it wasn't too long before Polly became Mrs. Raymond Bogert.

Mrs. Rex Pyles directed that pageant in 1933 and she and her husband are the only members of the faculty still on the staff of Alderson-Broaddus College. It was staged as now, on the grounds in front of the administration building overlooking the town of Philippi.

Along with the changes in personalities, several changes have taken place on the college campus too - $1,300,000 worth. Since 1933 there is a new hospital, this cost excluded from the above million and a half dollars, a new Women's Hall and the R. J. Funkhouser library and auditorium. In 1933 there were around 100 students enrolled compared to the present 350.

Yes, time passes. Raymond, a coal operator in Barbour county, and Polly, are definitely Lord and Lady of their Florida street manor, and parents of Queen Barbara, and twin sons, Raymond and Roland, fifth grade students at Central School and we bet Polly will feel just as queenly tonight as she did in 1933.

The Tag

May 8, 1959

I've played hide-and-seek with THE TAG, that elusive cleaning label, for the last time. For twenty years I've waged a fight and now I admit defeat. That tiny piece of pink paper, held solid in a grip of metal, I know, hides someplace on my freshly cleaned garment – but where?

What madman lies awake nights seeking seams and hemlines to clamp THE TAG?

I know it's there!! I go through the same routine each time. First – remove the outer plastic covering – that's easy! Secondly – remove the pins from the skirt. Yep, that's simple too.

Now – where's THE TAG. Waist band? Hemline? Left side seam? Right side seam? I find it – underneath the zipper seam.

Five minutes and two broken fingernails later I've removed the metal clamp that holds THE TAG tighter than welded steel. A sudden thought – surely they wouldn't put another tag on the jacket.

I'm late now! Hurried glance over jacket – back, front, no, it's not there.

Quickly button jacket – slap on hat – where's purse, gloves? Hurry. Hurry.

At last – in church. Hope outer appearances don't indicate my flurried battle with THE TAG.

Cautiously, I move my fingers around the jacket hem. Ah! Nothing. Slip fingers up and down seams from armpit to hem of the jacket. Whew – nothing. First hymn is over – no one titters! O, why, o, why can't I see the back of my collar.

Rearrange hair in back while actually probing for THE TAG. Nope, nothing.

There is absolutely no other possibility. Be calm. There is no TAG.

Collection plate is coming. Reach to deposit envelope. THE TAG is clamped securely at my wrist seam.

Kindergarten

May 14, 1959

With the end of the current school term in sight, we'd like to toss a couple of bouquets to Mrs. Helen Reger and Mrs. Alice Byrne for their outstanding work with the local kindergarten and the special school for exceptional children.

Upshur County we feel can be most proud of these two ventures and the accomplishments realized in what started out to be rather an experiment. Mrs. Reger teaches 40 students a day, 20 in the morning and 20 in the afternoon, in a little white cottage on Victoria street that has blossomed into a fairyland of adventure for her lively and healthy charges.

On the other side of town, in a little building that once was the North Buckhannon church, Mrs. Byrne shows the strength of Samson and the patience of Job in her teaching of 12 children, who through a twist of nature or by accident, find life a little unreal at times. These children arrive by bus for study from 9 a.m. until 2:30 p.m. receiving hot lunch at noon from the Academy school, also transported by bus.

Miss Ona Frum, the first teacher for the special school, and well-known for her many years of work with small tykes, also deserves special credit for her inauguration of a program that has proved a godsend to both student and parent in the classes for exceptional children.

These children have shown definite progress in their understanding of the world and their own surroundings, their adjustment to a routine and the habits and manners of their playmates, and a will to improve their ability even though it may appear small at first. Perhaps, the greatest progress has been shown in their fight to learn coordination in both speech and writing.

This program, now one of many in the state, was started five years ago and has showed definite progress throughout the years. One of the students is transported from Sand Run, the furthest point for any pupil. Here, too, we think Nuzun Garlowe, of the Hemlock community, deserves credit for his understanding and patience during long runs as bus driver.

On the other hand, Mrs. Reger's pupils have been under close scrutiny on local and state levels with over 300 visitors observing the work of the kindergarten, the first in the state since the county unit system was inaugurated in 1934.

Her work has been highly complimented by the state superintendent of schools and on May 25, she will attend a conference at the State Capitol aiding in the setting up of standards for other such public kindergartens in the state. The recent state legislation just passed a bill which would install such classes in the state school system. A scrapbook, itemizing work and study, will be on display at this conference.

Parents have been amazed that their youngsters could settle down to such a routine and seemingly progress in the pre-school readiness program. Emphasis is placed on creative work, not just copy. Youngsters learn to think for themselves and see for themselves.

Just Friday, Mrs. Reger, along with her vitally interested charges, toured St. Joseph's hospital, seeing the operating room, the sterile procedures involved along with the makeup of any hospital, tried on sterile masks, and viewed the oxygen tent, all that might be most frightening if not seen beforehand. With excursions of this type, Mrs. Reger has helped dispel any fear a youngster might have of hospitals, dentists, doctors, or even the shrill blast of the fire siren or train whistle.

Along with the many advantages, this program has tried to teach adjusting in play with other, independence, following of school routine, coordination, the using of the large muscles on down to the small muscles, setting up sharper means for writing and reading.

We've just touched lightly on the many advantages realized in these two special classes, but we hope that Upshur County residents understand the rich source of schooling these students are receiving.

Bloopers

May 5, 1959

Bloopers! Every newspaper makes them. We're no exception. Any paper not only tries to inform but also to entertain – but by entertainment we don't mean the glaring bloopers that suddenly loom after 4,000 papers run off the press.

Don't ask us how the awarding of a plaque suddenly becomes a plague or why the bride chose to carry a white Bible topped with white linen shoes and wear streamers!

Yep! That happened to us!

The gremlins or Kilroy take spells messing up our type. They may leave us alone for weeks at a time then suddenly go to work leaving "funnies" in their wake. How many readers caught the line that kindergarten was held in a white cottage on Victoria street. If you plan on a visit, go next door to the red brick – please!

Sure, we all do it. Consol for console, quality for quality, patent for patient – we could go on for several lines but you've read them before. Perhaps you'll get a laugh from those classics that we've enjoyed through the years. In the Bluefield, W. Va. Sunset News "The Friendship Class of Graham Christian Church will meet at 7:30 Thursday night at the church, slug slug slug slug."

Or the headline in a California paper, ROBERT G. TEFFS LIVING ON FIFTH AFTER MARRIAGE. And in Australia, a car dealer said: "Bring your present car in for valuation. We will offer you a proposition you cannot afford to accept."

From another California paper "We are not responsible for errors in Clafficied Ads."

Or in the California Register: "To Mr. and Mrs. Ben Smith, a son, 7 pounds, 12 ounces, more to kum more more more mor." And in an Ontario ad "You don't need cash! Instead use our revolting credit plan." In Augustine, Fla., someone was carried away with "These Dwellings will be for retired people and will be in moderate price racket."

Yes, newspapers can sure be entertaining!!!

Trees

May 28, 1959

Do 315,900 trees sound like a lot of trees to you? Well, exactly this amount of forest tree seedlings have been planted in Upshur county by 81 families, and just since March.

Plantings have ranged all the way from 300 to 3,000 trees planted by Dr. Leigh Lowman on Poverty Ridge, as he would like to call it, to 21,000 planted in the Land of Canaan by Myron B. Hymes, local attorney.

The practice of tree planting, now several years old, is available through the local office of the Conservation Commission of West Virginia and is strictly for the control of erosion, for shelter and protection, timber production and Christmas trees. Orders are not accepted at the local office for less than 300 trees nor less than 100 of a species.

Trees aren't sold either just because you'd like some shade in the front yard or your land newly landscaped – and only the thinnings may be sold for Christmas trees.

Ten different species of seedlings are offered, with the price ranging from $9 to $12 a thousand. Available seedlings are Scotch pine, shortleaf pine, Virginia pine, white pine, red pine, European larch, Norway spruce, tulip poplar, black locust and black walnut seed.

All of these seedlings come from the state tree nursery located at Parsons, and it must be several acres wide to keep these Upshurites in stock.

All together 1,715,000 trees have been planted in District 3 which comprises 11 counties. And we don't need to remind you that this is a lot of shade.

According to Mrs. Thelma Stewart, girl Friday to Charles R. Hall, local conservationist, the commission employs county foresters to provide technical assistance to forest owners in making simple management plans, marking trees to cut, estimating timber volumes, advising proper cutting methods, marketing forest products, making thinnings and protection.

Many, many county people have taken advantage of this conservation move and just a partial list of all the planters include: Ellis D. Zickefoose at Alton, with 80,000 seedlings; Tom Clawson with 15,000 on his Bushy Fork land; Mark Koon, popular Gulf operator at Ellamore with 18,000; Karl Arbogast with 10,000 on his farm at Kanawha Run and George W. Sturm with 13,000 at his farm at Sago.

Warren L. Turner on the Hall road has planted 7,000 seedlings; Carl E. Brady, of French Creek, 5,000; James Edward Zickefoose, 5,000 at his Alton farm; Dale Woody, 5,000 on the Elkins road; Forrest Stump with 5,000 at Fishing Camp; Russell Neely, 6,000 seedlings; Daniel C. Hinkle, 10,000 on Route 3; H. D. Potter on their land at Hampton, 5,000; Dr. Stanley Martin 5,000 trees at his farm in the Elkins road and Mrs. Jesse L. Musgrave, Hall Route 1, 9,000 seedlings.

And if you are visualizing each of these trees as being planted by hand, let us hasten to inform you that they aren't. One can rent a handsome piece of machinery called a tree-planter that takes the backache out of tree planting.

Ham Supper

June 5, 1959

There's nothing wrong with this world that a ham supper wouldn't cure! We've tried diplomacy, tact, and threats of annihilation, but has any envoy thought of sitting our enemies down to a hearty, country meal of soup beans, ham and cornbread?

We had the opportunity recently to eat such a meal at the Heaston Methodist church in Hodgesville and if this food wouldn't soothe the ache of bitterness and vengeance, we'll eat crow – baked.

Pity the city slickers who have lost touch with the art of country cooking. Even the finest artist can have no more pride in his work than the farmer's wife when she opens that glass of home-made pickles or jar of preserves. And don't tell me that sterile, plastic-wrapped bread tastes the same as that home-baked bread.

There was country butter and cottage cheese, green onions right from the garden, baked corn and fried potatoes that couldn't possibly harm any diplomat's ulcer. And you could go back for seconds or even thirds.

We certainly aren't trained in the field of foreign relation, but it does look like more good could come from talks around an oilcloth-covered table in a friendly, cooperative air of a village church than the damask-covered mahogany tables of palaces of kings.

Anyway, this nation has tried everything else and we might as well add our two cents worth to those of other sidewalk diplomats. A church supper certainly shows pride in one's work, cooperation and cheerfulness, work toward a common goal and the betterment of a community. Multiply this nation-wide and world-wide, and maybe for the first time in history countries could live together in peace.

Strawberry Festival '59

June 12, 1959

Two wagonloads of princesses, pulled by dapple-gray mares, and donated by the late M. C. Melton, superintendent then of the game farm, inaugurated the Strawberry Festival – a far cry from the pageantry and beauty now seen in the grand parade.

Like Topsy, it just grew – starting from a chance remark back in 1935, and developing into a strawberry exhibit in the First Presbyterian church in 1936 with the first coronation held on the steps of the county courthouse.

Perhaps, the first and only casualty suffered in any parade through the years occurred that first year of 1936 when Eloise Alkire, a princess, was thrown from one wagon when the horses lurched. She suffered a mild concussion and was confined to her home for some time. The next year, horses were out, and floats were pulled by trucks.

The procession both formed and passed in front of a judge's stand in the courthouse yard and a Grand Ball in Whitescarvers's Hall followed that night. Each princess held an armful of roses as she stood on the steps. Thousands saw the parade which had attractive floats, led off with the high school band and followed by the American Legion post, Boy Scouts, city officials and the fire department.

Others of the court were Helen Judson, crown bearer; Peggy Chrisman, and Mary Esther Fike, heralds; Pat Dawson and Dickie Talbott, train bearers, and strawberry bearers, Aleta Wise Heck, Peggy May Zickefoose, Mary Lee Rusmissell, Barbara Fish, Nancy Sander and Sue Billingsley.

A group of farmers, businessmen and professional men met May 13, 1936, and organized the first festival in Central West Virginia for June 3. The farmer's income back in the '30s then was just a few hundred dollars a year, and it felt at that time that the county farmer could be helped with the commercial growing of the berry. H. P. Stalnaker headed the first association at that meeting and again in 1937 with a W. A. Hallam serving as secretary. On the first committee were Kyle Reger, Dr. J. E. Judson, Dr. F. M. Farnsworth, Prof. R. H. Carder, Glen Ford, Russell Westfall, J. O. Butcher and J. M. N. Downes.

The first queen, Laura Jean Watson, had 30 local girls in her court, and the event was aired over the National Broadcasting hook-up by stations WJZ and WEAF.

That first parade and coronation were such a success that from then on the idea grew and blossomed and seemingly mushroomed into a huge event planned months ahead for the year of 1937. Throughout that winter of '36-'37, committees met with Wesleyan inviting the use of the college lawn for a pageant and the gym for exhibition room. Officials of the West Penn Power company, now Monongahela Power, offered help as did the extension division of the state. Leslie P. Brody, then general manager of the West Penn, announced at a January, 1937 meeting that he had contacted buyers for full carloads of berries and "dirt farmers" Kyle Reger and Russell Westfall accepted his challenge vowing to go into the business of raising berries in a big way.

Then in February, 1937, a general goodwill and get-together meeting was planned by boosters and strawberry producers from five counties with over 200 farmers invited to a luncheon in the First Methodist church. By then, the selling of strawberries had already been arranged and the problem was to get farmers interested in sufficient numbers to produce enough berries for market.

For the first time, the 1937 festival saw the association branching out to enclose three other counties, Barbour, Harrison and Lewis. A novel and unique plan for the selection of the queen was still a secret in March but each county had been told that princesses would be selected with each state senator selecting two; each representative, 1; Women's Club, Farm Woman's Club, the Lions, and Agriculture Committees each selecting two.

The National Farm and Home Hour, heard by millions, agreed to broadcast much of the event and Perce Ross was selected to direct the first pageant "Birthday of a Princess." A huge stage was built on Wesleyan's football field and 105 dancers performed to music from a 20-piece orchestra; and Miss Lela Huff directed a chorus of nearly 1,000 voices.

The first prevue for 55 princesses was set for April 20 at the Grand Opera House starting at 9pm. It was in the nature of a dress rehearsal and candidates were asked that hats not be worn and to be in evening dress if possible. That April night of 1937, Phyllis Curry reigned as queen and Joby Knight, of Lumberport, and Mary Alice Barlow were selected as her maids of honor.

This time the festival directors adopted a prize list for berries totaling $250 in cash. Not one, but two parades, marched that second year. "Story of the Strawberry" was used as the theme in the Children's Parade which started at 9:30 a.m. Over 700 students marched in the two-mile parade and by costume and posters revealed the various stages of the life of a strawberry.

Starting from tiny seeds, watched over by "Moonbeams", drenched by "Raindrops", warmed by "Sunbeams", the children told the story of the "Berry" in various stages of development, ending with the inevitable "Strawberry Short Cake" and "Ice Cream Cone." Thousands were attracted that first and second year to Buckhannon creating goodwill and opportunity for both farmer and businessman. Now, with hard-work perhaps we shall see the event become even bigger with the festival on a state-wide basis and the hope that all 55 counties will participate in 1960.

Swimming Pool

June 19, 1959

Who can say just how many lives of youths have been saved just because West's swimming pool is in operation. And who can estimate the value learned in the past 19 years from swimming classes taught thousands.

Sure, I'm plugging a private concern – why shouldn't I? Young people today don't have to swim in treacherous river water learning the hard way that a rock may project here or a tree branch there, gulping dirty water while learning to "dog-paddle". This county has a drowning every year, I don't deny that, but the ratio of such accidents is far down over neighboring counties. And it's my thinking along with many others that swimming is safer because of Garland West and his daughter, Lota Marie Wilfong.

The operation of the pool is no gold mine, very little money is made. And the budget isn't augmented by sale of candy bars or pop that is so often seen in other towns operated privately or city-wide. No danger of broken glass in the city pool or a slip on a messy chocolate-covered paper wrapper. It's incidental that West has always been more than generous with the use of his grounds and pool to private individual parties or organizational meetings – the important thing is that he has taught our young people to swim.

Garland himself for many years taught class himself. Later the instruction shifted to Lota Marie and now that her son and daughter, Jack and Jill, are practically grown, they have assumed much of the instruction, assisted in recent years by Bill Hall, Betty June Talbott Wilson and Jerry Hall.

Classes of some sort of swimming instruction run every week all summer long. In the beginners class alone, 100 youngsters from six on up, participate each summer. Then there is the intermediate group, and the American Red Cross sponsored classes in junior and senior lifesaving and every six or eight years the ARC instructors' classes, when instructors are taught to instruct.

Multiply figures like that by 19 years of operation and there's no doubt that Buckhannon young people can handle themselves well in any kind of water. Adults too for that matter – there's instruction available for grownup non-swimmers.

According to Lota Marie, a child of six can learn in two or three lessons to paddle and to keep one's face in the water. But after that it's up to the individual to learn strength and stamina through at least two years of practice.

So, we're applauding the Wests for maintaining a safe and sane form of summer recreation.

West's Swimming Pool   Howard Hiner Collection

Bull Money

June 26, 1959

Dick Young, Pruntytown supervisor, has been concerned with the sex of cattle in recent weeks. The Industrial School for Boys was allowed to spend $3,250 for bulls and boars. The institution, however, used $1,950 of the money to purchase six registered Holstein heifers. Auditor Edgar B. Sims turned the requisition down with a penciled notation "Plenty of bull money but no heifer money." It's alright now, the Board of Public Works revised the expenditure schedule.

Delta's Joyce Hornbeck, tele-typesetter and linotype operator, leaves this week for Akron, Ohio, where she will be employed by the B. F. Goodrich company.

Usually good-natured Harry Hall, local restaurateur, displayed a touch of sarcasm recently by displaying his cashed "rubber checks" in the window of his establishment for the world and all to see. They are disappearing one by one, we might add.

A little belatedly perhaps, but we ran across an item recently as to why the strawberry is so named. According to our information, the origin of the name is uncertain but "straw" may refer to the long straw-like suckers of the plant, or to the straw laid between rows to keep the berries clean or to an old custom of stringing these berries on a straw.

There is also the possibility that the "straw" was originally "stray" in reference to the way the suckers stray from the parent plant and lie as if strewn on the ground.

Mouths Of Babes

July 2, 1959

Out of the mouths of babes often come the unexpected and the truth. Perhaps it would be better if child psychology books were written by the young. Or, maybe adults should retain some of the childish imagination and the honesty possessed in early years.

Any mother remembers a particular incident that may have been unusual or amusing at the time it happened. Too, we ran onto some stories that weren't publishable in a family newspaper.

Brent Scott is now grown and married but his mother, Mrs. Harold Scott, of Tennerton, still often wonders what her answer should have been the day Brent brought home five kittens when he already owned three dogs. "Brent, why in the world would you bring home five kittens!" "Mother, they were a family – all brothers and sisters!" Another time the story of George Washington and the cherry tree impressed Brent to such an extent that he cut down Dad Harold's prize apple tree with the explanation that if Washington could do it so could he.

Mrs. Robert Stansbury of Meade Street has five youngsters and she could write a book about the many, many incidents which have thrown her for a loss of words. Molly, 4, just recently told her mother that God and the Chinese were something alike – "you can't see either of them". When Bobby, the five-year-old was very small, his applesauce was placed in a bowl with the comment "it might walk off his plate". Whereas, master Bobby with an impish look said, "Mother, you know applesauce doesn't have legs".

Alan and Brian Shreve, sons of Mr. and Mrs. Calvin Shreve of the Brushy Fork road, have been more than intrigued with their new baby brother, now 6-months-old and more than willing to help. Mary Avis recently asked "How would you like another baby to care for". After a moment of hesitation, Brian answered, "Well, not before we go camping".

Mothers were made to hold just such stories in their hearts.

County Statistics

July 10, 1959

West Virginia leads the nation again – this time, in the ratio of illegitimate births – and just when we were feeling pride in the state's first woman judge, the rise in personal income and the strides toward better and bigger schools.

And to add insult to injury, no other state was even close. District of Columbia came in second, followed by Tennessee.

But while some Mountaineers were cavorting in the hills, others were showing another spirit by boosting state personal income after the recession scare of 1958.

Locally, according to the recently released West Virginia Business Index, Buckhannon valuation of building permits jumped from $8,800 in 1958 to $10,600 in 1959. And to prove that Mountaineers believe in their state, a gigantic surge of building valuation permits was noted with an increase of from $3,637,366 in May, 1958 to $15,725,372 in May, 1959.

In a survey of county indexes of retail trade in West Virginia, indications show Upshur county rose from 136 in April, 1958 to a high of 184 this past September and dropped again to 142 in April, 1959 – still more that the year previous.

Buckhannon Bank debits to individual accounts in West Virginia show dollar comparisons as follows: May, 1957, $4,629; May, 1958, $4,497 and May, 1959, $4,395.

In the survey of post office receipts for 24 largest cities, the state noted an upward swing of $732,126 as against $565,774 in May, 1958. Buckhannon is also up with $4,779 as against $4,148 in May, 1958.

All of which proves, this county isn't standing still or even holding its head above water, but moving forward – a shot in the arm for many optimists, like me.

City Statistics

July 17, 1959

Buckhannon has a story to tell – a progressive story, one that is being repeated again and again in other small towns.

Building is on the increase, property is being bought and sold over and over again at a profit and the remodeling business is on the upsurge. You can prove it with a glance in the deed books recorded in the county clerk's office, you can check it with John Anthony and the building permits issued and approved by the city council and you can double check it by talking with home builders like K. E. Queen, Fred Iden, Virgil Hood, Don Woody, Tony Anderegg, Charlie Green and Kyle Reger.

Prices for 50 foot lots have tripled and in some localities here even quadrupled in value. Where a lot once brought $500, you now pay $1200 to $1500.

Modern homes sell easily. One real estate man told me this week, even the old homes are selling, those of 10 or 12 rooms, maybe not as fast, but they aren't being left to deteriorate. The old homes sell at far less than they could be built today. Native stone basements, redwood reception rooms, oak floors, hot air furnaces with radiators to each room would cost at least $60,000 today, but you're lucky to get $23,000 for such a home.

The trend is for modern, one floor ranch style brick construction. Easy living for the wife used to old stairs to climb and massive rooms to maintain.

Back 40 years ago, one's measure of wealth was gauged on the number of rooms in one's home – not so today.

The retired farmer, salesman, railroad worker, miner all demand the compact, convenient modern home. And the price goes higher every year.

In my talks this week – there is one big reason for Buckhannon's increase in property valuation. There are no more convenient choice lots left for the buyer. The best are gone and now the spacious acreage on the outskirts of town is rapidly coming into demand.

Once price-poor Tennerton is catching the boom with home construction on the increase and land valuation tripled over 10 years ago. Another reason for Buckhannon's boom is due to the central location. Retired people like it here, families with children see Wesleyan as an attraction, traveling salesmen use it as a focal point in contacting tri-state firms. It's a clean town, a progressive town, a comfortable town.

I saw figures in the city treasurer's office this past week showing home and business construction and remodeling costs. July 1957 to July 1958 was a remarkable year when the rest of the nation was suffering from a depression, but thanks to Wesleyan college, in March of 1958, a $604,275 building

Now let's forget that $604,275 and notice that the total for home and business construction was $221,150. Then from July 1958 until this very month, construction jumped to $262,750, an upsurge of $41,600. And the building weather is far from over this summer.

And there is no way of getting figures for construction outside the corporate limit.

Surprising enough, even with the hike in farm land valuations over the nation the past recent years, Upshur county land valuation is at a standstill, except in cases where a good highway threads nearby. Reason could be that the young people once reared on these farms, better schooled than in previous years, find work in the cities and other states, leaving the older parents unable to tend a large farm.

Then again, perhaps the government's help in paying farmers not to raise corn and not to raise hogs brings in a pretty good income without working – too, farmers are aided by old age pensions and social security benefits that make it easier to sit on the front porch instead of working daylight to dusk in the cornfield.

I'm repeating an old theme – Buckhannon has a fine future.

Salk Vaccine

July 24, 1959

Last year, doctors and health departments were destroying free Salk vaccine because it became outdated faster than the public would take advantage of the new, miraculous serum. This year, there is no free vaccine and still the apathy exists.

No doubt, in recent weeks Delta readers have noticed a more or less drive in the interest of public health for poliomyelitis vaccine for both adults and children. We could be hit any time because the incidence of polio is far and above over last year. During the week ending July 1, 1959, there had been 20 cases reported to the State Health Department.

The serum is available – what does a doctor have to do to get patients to take advantage to the preventive dose? Does a law have to be passed forcing parents to inoculate children? Ohio just recently passed such a law making it mandatory that children be vaccinated for diphtheria, tetanus, smallpox and polio prior to entering school. Maybe that's a solution.

Right now, Mrs. Myron B. Hymes, Jr., chairman of the Junior Department of Buckhannon Woman's Club, with the sanction of her executive board, is sponsoring a special $1 polio clinic, bearing the cost of the vaccine, making it available for all. At the same time, those persons unable to pay the cost of inoculation will find the service free. This idea has worked in Clarksburg and Charleston, with the neighboring county of Webster planning the same proposal.

I was impressed with the story behind the two-state polio epidemic of last year which hit hard along the border of Virginia-West Virginia. As a matter of fact, the Mountain State for a time led in the ratio of persons suffering from paralytic poliomyelitis with 6.2 inflicted per 100,000 population. Not that there is any similarity between Upshur county and the rural mining counties of Wise county, Va., but the story is interesting in the fact that complete apathy existed among these people until the situation reached epidemic proportions late in August.

The majority of cases in both the two-state areas were found to be members of families living in the poorest circumstances. There was a striking concentration of cases in the group under five years. This type of age distribution is more characteristic of an urban outbreak and the data from Wise county showed that the highest attack rates occurred in small communities where persons were living in crowded, unsanitary conditions quite similar to urban slums.

Families of these cases in mining camps were found living in very crowded, substandard housing, few had running water, some had flush toilets and some not even privies.

Apathy and ignorance was attributed to many inhabitants because of poor education. In the town of Pound, Va., for instance, only 2 percent of the students entering school are graduated from the 12th grade. Consequently, many had no concept of the importance of vaccination. But almost 90 percent of the Wise county people responded to the free doses of vaccine during the outbreak after much damage had already been done.

Surely, Upshur people can realize the importance of the prescribed recommended dosage. It takes money, so I suggest the Junior Women be supported in the upcoming drive and blanket the county with a protective wrap against crippling paralysis.

Coal Economy #1

July 31, 1959

At least for now, the national steel strike is not hurting the coal economy of Upshur county – it may in time. Fortunately, local mines do not depend on large industrial plants for consumption of coal but sell primarily to public utilities, who in turn furnish electricity to the steel mills – this will hurt if the strike is prolonged. Few miners in the county have been laid off, but in Barbour county, the entire operation at the Century is closed. The three bid union mines here are still operating – Peck's Run, Repper and Christopher hiring around 216 men, working a total number of days of 379, or averaging 126 days and producing 553,098 tons of coal, these figures for 1958.

I just learned recently through correspondence with T. E. Johnson, secretary-treasurer of the Northern W. Va. Coal Association, that an Upshur union miner earns on the average of $3,112.20 a year, for a total of around $850,000 in wages for the county. Counting the 38 non-union strip mine workers and the 196 non-union workers in the county, approximately $1 million and a half in wages flows through here every year if in full operation. And the number of days worked and the amount of tonnage produced have risen considerably over last year. Over a half million tons of coal will stoke a lot of furnaces! But home consumption counts little to the coal operator. The No. 1 user is public utilities, secondly, the cement mills, and thirdly, coal for space heating, meaning coal for institutions such as hospitals, prisons and schools. Peck's Run at Hodgesville ships coal even to New York for this type of consumption. Some coal goes to the small industrial users but probably less than 8% of a year's tonnage figures in the picture. Unfortunately, Upshur county does not have the metallurgical grade of coal necessary for steel plant operation. Figures mean little to the average reader but to add to your list of things "I never knew before", the three union mines employ 216 men producing 553,098 tons of coal; the 12 non-union mines hire 196 men producing 253,692 tons and 3 non-union strip mines hire 38 men producing 122,843 tons of coal – again, all 1958 figures. So, 450 families depend on the pick and shovel or the higher mechanism process for their bread and butter in this county alone. West Virginia is first in the nation as a bituminous producer with coal found in 44 of the 55 counties. There's enough coal to last another 400 years if anyone is worried. After that, someone else can worry about the substitute – I shan't be concerned at all.

Antique Delta

August 7, 1959

Turn backward, turn backward, time in thy flight…and that's exactly what I did this week after Ira J. Tomblyn brought in an issue of the Buckhannon Delta, dated March 12, 1898.

This sent me scampering to the attic to hunt early issues only to discover that the earliest copy in our possession was October 25, 1898 which was pretty well frayed around the edges. Tomblyn's issue was in remarkable condition, not a tear in place. F. C. Pifer was editor and publisher and W. H. Hilleary, local editor.

I found that sometime between September and November (many issues are missing), the newspaper's name was changed from Knight-Errant to Buckhannon Delta. There will be many residents who remember the Knight.

Top story in the March issue was the explosion aboard the Maine in Havana harbor. The naval board was accused of being unable to fix the cause for the explosion but senators were saying that the authors of the atrocity were Spaniards, acting under the Spanish government.

In the news letter from Alexander, Col. Abe Beckwith and Capt. Ed Bennett had about recruited a company of men to go to Cuba and fight the Spaniards.

Despite the war news, life was going on in a genteel way with bicyclists, both ladies and gentlemen, cycling each evening on the city streets taking advantage of the late fine weather.

A.G. Giffin had been compelled to put on an extra force at his planing mill plant and had received so many orders, a nightshift had become necessary.

Ex-Sen. Thos. J. Farnsworth, accompanied by his daughter, Mrs. Anna Edmiston, left on the noon train Tuesday for the Hot Springs in Arkansas, to be absent for several weeks.

In Sago the grip (sic) seemed to be the prevailing epidemic in the community and Norval W. Loudin, superintendent, was inspecting the free schools of the area.

Eugene Montgomery had sold his house and 12 acres of ground at Alexander to a Mr. Stutzman of Selbyville for $250.

N. W. Hooker was advertising hardware, stoves, cutlery and tinware.

In going over early issues on file here at the office, I found few copies for the year of 1898, and those mainly for October to December. Of course by December a treaty of peace had been negotiated between Spain and the U.S.

Published in the Pifer Building under the company name of Lorentz Press, the Knight-Errant announced that Miss Jessie Gilmore, local editor for two years, had resigned, and by then W. H. Hilleary was city editor with E. W. Martin as manager. Subscriptions were only $1.25 a year with no notice made of the amount of circulation.

The biggest advertiser was Simon Levinstein, proprietor of the Enterprise Clothing Store operating in James L. Smith's building opposite the Traders National Bank, where now is the C&A Gas company. O, yes, and Castoria was good then for infants and children. Casto and Clark, photographers, were doing business opposite the Buckhannon Bank over Shinn's Store. The firm of Hodges and Smith at Peck's Run had shipped over 20,000 pounds of poultry.

The Knight-Errant of December published the first letter received by "our soldier boys in Cuba", from Pvt. John Watkins who had written to his brother saying he had left Camp Cuba, Libre, Fla., on a 7-day trip to Manzanillo, Cuba.

Typhoid fever was prevalent in Selbyville striking George Van-Gilder, Mrs. Andrew Wolf and William Chevuront.

David Pew had been stabbed by two men as he worked in his stable near town and Miss Alta Heaton won a gold lined silver cake dish in a speaking contest at the Opera House, competing against Nellie Chidester and Edna Brown.

On December 8, 1898, cold weather had set in and Florida street was frozen allowing pedestrians to use the sidewalks. Before that, the street had been a lake of mud and teamsters driving too close to the sidewalks had been scorned for throwing mud over the payment.

Dr. Will T. Dailey, of the 2nd W. Va. Volunteer Infantry, was spending the Christmas holidays with his parents, the James Daileys. Rabbit hunters of Hinkleville had been quiet for a couple of weeks, it was reported, and Mrs. L. W. Bartlett was receiving at her home on Kanawha street from 2 to 5 o'clock Thursday, Dec. 29, 1898.

So, 61 years ago, life wasn't so difficult – just a different disease or two, a different mode of travel and a different war.

Getting Paper To Press

August 14, 1959

Our editor was on vacation last week – and though I had been here five months and in this business for a good many years – I panicked!!! What had appeared so routine to Mary Liz was chaos for me.

I got a paper to press and within the deadline on Thursday and when I had time to look back, there were things I might have done differently and some things that weren't done at all – and then I got to thinking, just how many people realize the amount of time and energy and the long hours put into a single issue?

In recent years, thanks to movies and television, the "country" editor is usually pictured as a quaint old character with more than the normal amount of curiosity, knowing everyone's business and telling all. 'Tain't true.

As a matter of fact, newspaper people take their jobs seriously and try hard to find the truth in every story, oftentimes making a dozen phone calls merely to clarify one point. A day-by-day history is made of Upshur county with every issue and it must be correct. This paper lies in your home from one issue to the next and no one wants a mistake in print for approximately 16,000 readers to see. There's a saying somewhere about a dentist can pull his mistakes, and a doctor can bury his, but a paper's mistake is there for the world to read.

This is the time of year when many young people are entering college for the first time and still undecided as to just what profession to pursue. We like to think of journalism as a profession – one in which you'll never get rich but one in which you'll find many friends and a satisfaction in reporting the history of your town, your state and even the nation. If you like competition, you'll find that, too, whether beating out another reporter or the opposition sheet, story-wise or advertising lineage.

And it most certainly is a versatile field. An editor must not only know how to write a clear, concise story, but he must sell himself and his paper to his advertisers, bread and butter in this work. He must be able to write headlines, know the value of the news that comes across his desk every hour of the day, and the worth of pictures inserted. He must work always in mind that there is a deadline and at the same time make sense out of another's writing, coordinate between the newsroom and the composing room – all the time working with the three ABC's of journalism – accuracy, brevity and clearness.

For those who are considering entering this field, there will never be a job more exciting or yet one more routine and once that printer's ink invades the bloodstream, you'll never be happy doing anything else. Something to think about while you nurse those ulcers in later years.

Welcome back, Mary Liz, we feel those ulcers developing.

Traffic Fatalities

August 21, 1959

Driving at excessive speed on a straight, level road in daylight hours and in good weather – these were ideal factors leading up to traffic fatalities in West Virginia last month.

The superintendent of W. Va. State Police, Col. Hazen H. Fair, this week released figures pointing to 53 more fatalities in West Virginia in the first seven months of 1959 than recorded in 1958 – 232 to 179. Twenty-nine fatalities were chalked up in July with 14 drivers killed, 8 passengers dying, 6 pedestrians killed and one bicyclist.

"If we value the dignity of human life," Colonel Fair said, "we will show it in our respect for road signs and pavement markings, which are designed to protect the lives of highway users."

Drinking drivers and pedestrians were involved in eight fatal accidents during July. Why accidents occur in good weather on a level road in daylight hours can only be attributed to bad driving manners and carelessness. State Police have been ordered to crack down and crack down hard on any infraction of law. The state slaughter on roads is causing much concern.

Upshur county this week marked up its second road fatality of the year.

Colonel Fair also pointed out that August is an appropriate month in which to be reminded of the importance of signs and marking for this is a month of heavier travel.

With increased traffic on the road, the chances of accidents are increased for drivers and pedestrians who ignore stop signs, speed limits, cross-walk markings, no passing zones and traffic lights.

"Signs of Life", that's the description Colonel Fair used in urging highway safety this month and every month.

Sure Is Hot

August 28, 1959

Sure is hot. Yea, hot enough to fry an egg on the sidewalk. How long has it been hot like this? Dunno, wondering when it'll end. Is it hot like this every summer? Naw, seems like summers get hotter and the winters colder.

Yea, maybe it's because we're getting' older.

Hi, how are you? Hot. If one more person asks me that today, I'll scream. Yea, sure is hot. You got air-conditioning? Naw, you have to work in a restaurant to rate that. Yea, guess that's why so many people are going out for coffee breaks nowadays, you suppose?

Tried swimming? Yea, even the water is hot. It's low too. Suppose we'll have a water shortage? Dunno. I was tempted to stand under the sprinkler the other evening. Grass sure is brown. Guess we shouldn't waste the water that way.

Hate to think of kids sitting in those hot classrooms next week. Kids? Pity the teachers. Guess that's right. Kids will be out of Mabel's hair though. She sure is short-tempered, days like this. Can't blame her. I'm getting a little sick of cold salad and sandwiches. Can't blame her. Yea, guess it's too hot to cook. Heck, she could cool off if we'd eat outside. Yea, who's got strength to swat the flies. Yea, it sure is hot.

Smitty taking a vacation? Naw, too hot. Gertie said she was darned if she was baking in that car with five kids what with her sister's three after they got there. Yea, can't blame her. Sure is hot.

Hey, why don't you go to camp this weekend? Aw, Mabel said by the time you lug all the food and clothes, it isn't worth it. Double the cookin', you know, friends and relatives. Yea, guess that's right.

Hi, how are you? Hot. See what I mean – habit I guess. Well, back to the sweat shop. Yea, sure is hot.

Airline Dinners

September 18, 1959

With an appetite for food and with a vicarious interest in flying, particularly now when it looks as if Upshur county may develop a first-class airport, it was a perfectly natural question I popped at personable Jim Bunn, the West Virginia manager of American Airlines, when he dropped by the newspaper this week. I asked him how the hostesses could possibly serve dinner to a plane-load of passengers on one of the new jet airliners. Jim's eyes gleamed. He dug into his briefcase and came out with two typewritten pages of answers. I found them interesting and perhaps, you will too. Check me:

Americans are a hungry lot. So says American Airlines, the nation's number one airline, which has just released some startling figures on the amount of food consumed on its airplanes. Aboard one of its 600 mile-an-hour 707 Jet Flagships, the airline noted, it takes an average passenger about 300 miles to finish one meal. That's about half an hour. And what he and his fellow passengers put away is staggering. For example, the nearly 25,000 daily passengers on American eat nearly 11,000 meals. Every month the airline serves in excess of 326,000 meals.

Broken down during an average month, American's passengers consume: 1,565,000 cups of coffee, 169,500 servings of ice cream (or more than 6,000 gallons), 48,000 quarts of cream, 130,000 glasses of milk, 130,000 eggs (almost 11,000 dozen), 101,000 pounds of meat and poultry, 81,500 pounds of vegetables, 40,000 pounds of bread and rolls, 4,500 pounds of butter. Approximately 8,600 hens are required to provide breakfast for American's passengers every day. In addition, it takes about 72,438 pounds of chicken feed per month to supply the airline with 130,000 eggs it needs.

American's requirements on a daily basis call for cream from 1,164 cows, butter from 179 cows, ice cream from the milk of 115 cows, and milk from 81 cows. That's a total of 1,539 cows to provide the airline's daily dairy requirement. This is in addition to the vast quantities of dairy products used by the airline in preparing other foods. America transports more than eight million passengers a year. About 50 percent of American's passenger's are flying the line at meal time. That means the nation's number one airline serves some four million meals annually. Coffee served over a 12-month period amounts to nearly 19 million cups.

Traffic Lights

September 25, 1959

Frank Williams, Sr., one of the nicer people in this world, made a special trip to this office on Monday to point out an irregularity in the stop light at the intersection of Locust and Main streets.

Realizing what a headache it is each week for me to find and write about something new and of interest to many (I hope) Frank, Sr. bubbled in here and gave me an unusual lesson in traffic semaphores, whether they be mechanically synchronized or operated by police officers.

Did you know that as a rule, and of course, there are always exceptions to the rule, traffic lights usually have the red signal at the top and the green at the bottom? More than anything else this is an aid to color-blind drivers, who though unable to distinguish colors can tell at a flash of light whether to go or stop at a given signal.

Well, I didn't know, and lo, upon checking Williams' statement, here I've been passing the Main and Locust intersection a hundred times a week and never noticed that the light is uniform as one rides up and down Main street.

But, you notice the next time you drive up Locust toward Clarksburg or pass this office coming from Clarksburg down Locust – the green signal is at the top and the red at the bottom.

Just to do a little checking, not that I'd ever doubt Frank Williams' word, I phoned Ramus Holtz, who operates the dual-control car and teaches driving at the high school along with holding various offices in the national AAA, and he confirmed the fact that traffic lights in the U.S. generally conform to the red at the top and green at the bottom. And, he says, many states are passing legislation making it mandatory that signals be uniform. As a special salute to color-blind drivers, Holtz also said that such drivers seldom have accidents according to national statistics. This is attributed both to the conformity of signal lights and secondly, they observe traffic more closely than the normal driver.

Pity a color-blind motorist if one ever passes through here.

Civil War Facts

October 2, 1959

One of the most interesting brochures I've thumbed through in a long time is a pamphlet recently released by the Civil War Centennial Commission on "Facts About the Civil War".

Never before have the pertinent facts concerning the Civil War been brought together in a handy little compendium that could be examined quickly as in this little booklet. Beginning with the starting line-ups and ranging to recommended Civil War reading, the brochure contains every sort of information especially vital to any student of the Confederate-Union upheaval.

One of the most interesting to me was the "firsts" of the Civil War. The American Civil War was the first war in which railroads were extensively used for the rapid movement of military supplies and of large bodies of troops from one theatre of operation to another.

Aerial reconnaissance was first effectively used from anchored balloons in military operations. The electric telegraph was used in the strategic control of military operations in widely separated theatres and in the tactical direction of troops in battle.

A multi-manned submarine sank a surface vessel. Opposing ironclads engaged in naval battle. Naval "torpedoes" (mines) were widely used. Medical care of the wounded was systematically organized.

Participants, sites and equipment were photographed on a large scale. Nationwide conscription was used to raise armies in North America. A practical machine gun was developed. Voting by soldiers and sailors in service was provided for by national laws. Rifled artillery came into general use.

Mobile railroad artillery was used. Large-scale coverage was carried on by recognized news correspondents at the front. The repeating rifle was used by large troop units. Wire entanglements in field fortifications were used. The Medal of Honor was awarded.

Some pertinent facts about the Civil War heretofore little known lists the chance of surviving a wound in Civil War days as 7 to 1; in the Korean War, 59 to 1. About 15 percent of the wounded died in the Civil War; about 8 percent in World War I, about 4 percent in World War II and 2 percent in the Korean War.

The diseases most prevalent were dysentery, typhoid fever, malaria, pneumonia, arthritis, and the acute diseases of childhood such as measles and malnutrition.

Most wounds were caused by an elongated bullet made of soft lead, about an inch long, pointed at one end at the base, and called a "minie" ball, having been invented by Capt. Minie of the French Army. Of the 364,000 on the Union side who lost their lives, a third were killed or died of wounds and two-thirds died of disease.

Many doctors who saw services in the Civil War had never been to medical school, but had served an apprenticeship in the office of an established practitioner. In the Peninsular campaign in the spring of 1862, as many as 5,000 wounded were brought into a hospital where there were only one medical man and five hospital stewards to care for them.

In the battle of Gettysburg, 1,100 ambulances were in use. The medical director of the Union army boasted that all the wounded were picked up from the field within 12 hours after the battle was over. This was a far cry from the second battle of Bull Run, when many of the wounded were left on the field in the rain, heat and sun for three or four days.

During the Civil War, one small section of Virginia became America's bloodiest battle ground. In an area of barely 20 square miles and including Fredericksburg, Chancellorville, The Wilderness, Spotsylvania and Cold Harbour, more than half a million men fought in deadly combat.

Here, more men were killed and wounded during the Civil War than were killed and wounded in the Revolutionary War, the War of 1812, the War with Mexico and all of the Indian wars combined. No fewer than 19 generals – 10 Union and nine Confederate met death here.

A high price was paid to keep the states united.

Courthouse

October 9, 1959

This time 61 years ago the county was in a turmoil with the courthouse in danger of collapsing and a vote due in November to decide if a new building should be built by bonding the county.

The old Upshur county courthouse was built in 1853, burned in 1855 and demolished in March 1899 when the bond issue was approved. The cornerstone was laid in June 5, 1899. In October, 1898 the courthouse was described as a miserable dangerous firetrap, ready to collapse at any moment with the court records in constant jeopardy.

According to the Knight-Errant, editors were saying the iron safes did not afford adequate protection for records and although the old building, charred by fire, had been condemned as dangerous, assemblies of people continued to congregate in the old building to the imminent peril of their lives. But all turned out well. The levy passed, the old courthouse was leveled and a new structure was completed and furnished at a cost of $40,000. Imagine building the same structure now at that price. The light gray sandstone was taken from quarries near Hampton. Completely fireproof, the building was constructed of steel with floors of steel beams. Height of the building from ground to top of tower stands at 105 feet.

At the same time and just to do the job right, a jail and the sheriff's residence were also under construction and paid for in cash, the funds having been provided by a levy the previous November. Upshur county held its courts in nine houses and has had two courthouses since formation.

The first courthouse was in the home of Andrew Poundstone, 1851; second, Methodist Episcopal church, 1851; third, Court House, 1854; fourth, Baptist church, 1856; fifth, John Maxwell's shop, 1856; sixth, Baptist church, 1857; eighth, Pifer Building, 1899 and ninth, the new Court House, 1901.

The building still stands proudly with time erasing only the trees that once stood in the courtyard. Now one sits on the broad steps on Saturday to hear the latest news from friends and to barter. Time can never erase the need for congeniality.

Newsboys

October 16, 1959

This week we mark the National Newspaperboy Day with a salute to Jackie Ware, 14, son of Mr. and Mrs. Clarence Ware, of the Weston road. October 17 has been established that we may give proper recognition to the more than 700,000 newspaperboys in the United States and Canada. The building of proper moral and business foundations in the youth of our nations can certainly be ranked in importance with the foundations supplied by any single subject in school. Jackie is the epitome of just what the late Paul G. Lawson had in mind in 1939 in designating Newspaperboy Day. Then, Paul was chairman of the committee on Newsboys of the International Association of Circulation Managers. It was Paul who obtained the presidential proclamation designating one day a year be set aside to honor the newsboys of the nation.

The association embraces all metropolitan dailies in the world and prior to his death, THE DELTA was only one of two weeklies in the United States belonging to this association. The other weekly was, and is, the Pennsylvania Grit. Lawson was co-owner of THE DELTA coming to Buckhannon in 1947. Several years previously he served with the two dailies in Clarksburg. We have chosen Jackie Ware this week as our typical newsboy because of his dependability and long term of service. He has sold between 60 and 80 DELTA's a week for the past four years. A seventh grade student, Jackie averages $1.50 a week in spending money in addition to winning show passes, the number depending on the amount of papers sold each week. One week a few years ago during a special promotion, Jackie sold 380 editions of THE DELTA.

Sometimes he is ably assisted by his sister, Jean, 12, and his brother, Delmas, 10. What little money Jackie brings home is appreciated for his father is confined mostly to a wheelchair. Mr. Ware was hurt four years ago while working on the construction of a new men's dormitory on the campus of West Virginia Wesleyan college. He fell several feet from an elevator, crippling him for life. Jackie stands this week in the spotlight of American youth, because early in life he is an example of this country's system of free enterprise. He is learning, through on-the-job training, the important basic principles of business – serving to satisfy, collecting with courtesy and selling with personality. Let's help Americans remember the Newspaperboy!

Take Home A Student

October 30, 1959

Buckhannon, with its reputation for friendliness, is again demonstrating its friendly air this Sunday with "Take Home A Student Day".

Inaugurated last year, the idea is for Methodist families to take freshmen Methodist students into their homes for a day – making a home away from home. The Student Work committee of the Woman's Society of Christian Service, under the chairmanship of Mrs. Wayman Bennett, has worked a good many hours planning a family day for 270 new transfer students from the campus of West Virginia Wesleyan College.

Last Wednesday the student names were drawn at the six circle group meeting throughout the city.

A friendly idea, the plan has worked in both large and small college towns and last year 89 local Methodist families cooperated by entertaining 302 students.

Other members of the committee working for Student Day are Mrs. H. S. Cummings, Mrs. Patton Nickell, Mrs. Frank Hartman, Sr., Mrs. Heyward Williams, Mrs. Perce J. Ross and Mrs. William Willis.

The idea was adopted on a smaller scale here during the war years when members of the armed forces invaded the college as air cadets in training.

Realizing that the airmen were often homesick for their families and knowing that their own sons in service were possibly homesick, too, Buckhannon townfolks started taking servicemen into their homes for Sunday dinner.

The success of the idea was proved when these same airmen returned following the war to make their homes in Buckhannon – the town with a friendly air.

Coal Economy #2

November 6, 1959

What this district will produce in coal in the remaining three months of 1959 will depend mainly on two factors, namely, the settlement of the steel strike and the railroad car supply.

This statement came out of a meeting two weeks ago in Fairmont when representatives of the press, radio and television, together with leaders of the coal industry, the UMWA, public utilities, equipment manufacturers and various railroad officials heard Joseph E. Moody, president of the National Coal Policy Conference, preside.

Northern West Virginia, District No. 3, is comprised of 22 ½ counties, including Upshur, which depends greatly on the economy of coal. This district is served by three main railroads, the B&O which goes into practically all of 22 ½ counties; the Monongahela Railway which only operates in two counties – Marion and Monongalia; and the Western Maryland railroad, which moves into Harrison, Marion, Randolph and Webster counties.

In the past several years it is interesting to note that river movement of coal from mines in Marion and Monongalia has been rather heavy. This coal is destined to Pittsburgh, Pa., intermediate points and beyond and to Ohio River destinations.

According to the information released out of Fairmont, distribution statistics of Northern W. Va. coals have not been complete in recent years and comparisons cannot be made that would give a true picture of the movement of our coal.

However, it is known that well over half of the production of our district moves into the eastbound markets. In the year 1958, just under 50% of our production was shipped to electric utilities; approximately eight percent moved to the Lakes and overseas exports amounted to a little over three percent.

In the past 20 years, the coal companies in Northern W. Va. have spent over one hundred million dollars for capital investments, including new plants, mechanical mining machinery, cleaning plants…

The Fabulous Fifties

January 1, 1960

Dad, this pad ain't swinging. The world is faking! These wee cats seem on some frantic kick – heck of a world for me to take over.

The turbulent fifties? Big words, man. Way out in left field, that's what these day people are. Maybe I should let you keep this place, old man with your crazy goatee!

Playing soldier with pop guns earlier this decade weren't these hipsters? Gassin' like a B-western movie through those years!!

I don't know, man! Think maybe I better conk out for a longer snore! This old world seems draped in this black band routine – ain't right!

These peepers see things real queer!!! Hipsters taking to their skids, knocking them away out – faster than Gabriel can open these gates. Real frenzied, these hot pilots.

From pad to pad, cats called politicians, jawing and flashing signs, "My old man can lick your old man". Yeah, comin' on real big!!

Maybe they should tune in on "Sugar Blues", get in the groove, get rid of some of those hopped-up drivers – don't be no drag!

Sound off – make yourself heard! This world is sizzlin'.

Man, I dunno know. You're cutting out – leaving a mess for this be-bopper. You're dragging old man, bone-tired I can see. I'll see what I can do.

Cut out, old man, let this old Dad tune in on the action, can't do no worse. I'm coming on real cool. Gonna make the scene. Go on, split!!!

Cigarette Sales

January 8, 1960

Cigarette sales soared last year despite the frightening reports linking lung cancer and smoking. All sorts of methods are being employed to break the cigarette habit, but if fright won't do it, what will?

Even a leading magazine recently devoted several pages to a 21-day cure based on a withdrawal method used for drug addicts and alcoholics. The system worked exactly two days in this office, but then we are hardly the strong type.

But the surest cure I know is to face 34 different brands of cigarettes displayed on a store counter. Facing that minute of indecision, my conversation usually goes something like this:

Clerk: Do you want the soft pack or the crush-proof box?

Me: Soft-pack.

Clerk: King-size or regular?

Me: King-size.

Clerk: Filter-tip or plain?

Me: Filter-tip.

Clerk: Menthol or mint?

Me: Menthol.

Cash or carry? Forget it…I've broken the habit.

1849 Auction

January 15, 1960

Upshur county farmers will undoubtedly be interested in this auction sale which was printed in the Anderson, Kentucky News in 1849. We are indebted to a local resident for leaving the clipping but he failed to leave his name.

The sale bill indicates, more than any amount of statistics, the fabulous change in the course of history, our wants and our needs.

"Having sold my farm and am leaving for Oregon territory by ox team, I will offer at public sale on March 1, 1849, all my personal property, to wit: All my ox team except two teams, Buck and Ben and Tom and Jerry. Two milk cows, one gray mare and colt, 1 pair of oxen and yoke, one baby yoke; two ox carts; 1,000 feet of poplar weather boards, plow with wooden moldboards, 800 to 1,000 feet of clapboard; 1,500 tenfoot fence rails.

One 60 gallon soap kettle; 85 sugar troughs made of white ash timber; ten gallons of maple syrup; two spinning wheels; 30 pounds of mutton tallow; one large loom made by Jerry Wilson; 300 poles; 100 split hoops; 100 empty barrels; one 32-gallon barrel of Johnson-Miller whiskey, seven years old; 20 gallons of apple brandy; one 40 gallon copper still; one dozen real books. Two handle hooks; 2 scythes and cradles; one dozen wooden spikes; bullet mold and powder horn, rifle made by Ben Miller; 50 gallons of soft soap; hams, bacon, lard; 40 gallons of sorghum molasses; six head of fox hounds, all soft-mouthed except one.

At the same time I will sell my six Negro slaves, two men, 30 years and 50 years old; two boys, 12 and 18 years old; two mulatto wenches, 40 and 30 years old. Will sell all together to same party but will not separate them. Terms of sale – cash in hand or note to draw four percent interest with Bob McConnell as security.

My home is two miles south of Versailles, Kentucky, on McConn Ferry Pike. Sale will begin at 8 a.m. Plenty to drink and eat. J. L. Mess."

To which I can only add, Well, well!

Magic Closet

January 22, 1960

Ever hear of a "Magic Closet"? I hadn't until this week. This closet is unique – unlike Fibber McGee's closet – it isn't bulging. In fact, the shelves are pretty bare right now.

But residents of Buckhannon can remedy that in a hurry. United Church Women for the past two years have sponsored the Magic Closet in order to warmly clothe needy children of Upshur county.

Clothes are stored in the little white house on Victoria street, used for a fourth grade classroom and distributed every first and second Saturday to those children deemed worthy by Upshur county teachers.

About two years ago, Mrs. E. C. McCoy of Barbour street, saw the need of several schoolchildren for good, warm clothing. The churchwomen went to work and the Magic Closet came into existence. If you wonder how funds from various church rummage sales are used, ask Mrs. Tommy Darnall. Just recently she purchased several boys' jackets with money realized from just such a rummage sale.

This Christmas the Tennerton Farm Women's club and women of the First Baptist church donated to the "Closet" instead of exchanging the usual Yuletide gifts.

But, even so, good, warm clothing is still needed. We don't mean tattered rags but clothing that your own child may have outgrown but still has a lot of wear. If so, contact Mrs. Darnall or Mrs. John Weimer. They'll be listening for that phone to ring.

Other active workers in the project are Mrs. Paul Mackey, Mrs. Rex Longridge, Mrs. George Corathers, Mrs. Lamar Bond, Mrs. Merle D. Newlon, Mrs. Bernard Knotts and Mrs. Normal Westfall.

Have a heart! Fill the Magic Closet with faith, hope and charity.

Where Are The Birds?

January 29, 1960

An incensed South Florida street reader suggests we ponder why Buckhannon has so few birds in our town. She and her neighbors had a drove of cardinals, West Virginia's state bird, that came to their back porches regularly, feeding when there was little natural picking. But, they had to stop. Neighborhood children shot the birds as they landed on the bird baths and feeders! This particular irate reader burned her bird boxes and feeders because it seemed heartless to lure the birds to be killed and crippled.

To quote our reader, "the stray cats and dogs put in their two cents worth by catching the birds or scaring them so that they refused to come back where danger lurked. "Wild life is wild life and that's the way it was intended and if West Virginians don't soon get "hep" to some of the conservation know-how, we're going to be the laughing stock of our neighboring states.

"We don't have to go to school to study how to handle such situations; we can just do what comes naturally and knock the whey out of these Mama's little angels when they try to act so sophisticated. It makes my blood boil to see such dastardly tricks condoned by mothers who spend their time lying on chaise lounges and smoking cigarettes when they could so easily read their youngsters little stories and develop in their darlings a love of nature and respect for others' rights and privileges that will stand them in good stead when they are old, white-haired great-grandpas and grandmas. "Incidentally, when I tried to keep water out for thirsty animals last summer, someone stole, honestly, the roaster I was using. I foxed them by replacing it with an old beaten-up pan that was left alone." The reader concludes with "the farmers will like this idea because birds eat many pests that work on their crops and in this way the farmers not only save money that ordinarily would be spent for "dope" to kill the pests but they have the bird songs and neighborliness."

"This too will establish good examples for youngsters in how to get along with each other and with wild life, and, learn that the world isn't their oyster. Since science has prolonged life and for various reasons so many people are thrown together, it's about time we begin thinking about getting along with each other, cultivating tolerance and understanding at the same time." Strong words, Mrs. Reader, and we must agree with some of your philosophy.

Miss West Virginia

February 5, 1960

Miss West Virginia will tell you it isn't all glitter and glamour. It's hard work! Exciting, yes, but hard work.

Miss Janet Hill, of Nitro, reigning now as Miss West Virginia, spends her year traveling from town to town, making numerous personal appearances and plugging products. This week she concluded a three-day appearance in Buckhannon climaxed by a fashion show Monday night under the sponsorship of the Business and Professional Woman's club.

Appearances such as this one are a strain. It hardly could be otherwise, Miss Hill is constantly in the limelight – paraded, poised and posed. But, she says it's interesting and sometimes fun.

Her interest lies, as one would imagine, in dramatics and the theater. Experience is gained in this one year of reigning as the fairest and the best. Valuable contacts are made which she hopes will pave her way to the lights of New York. But, the price of stardom comes high. Even now it has meant that Janet has given up her job, her friends and even her family temporarily. She has a $750 scholarship good in any school or with any theater group with which she dreams may help her along the way following this year of royalty.

She has family moral support at least. Janet comes from a family of 11, six brothers and four sisters. Janet is right in the middle. Her father is a retired New York Central railroader and proud he is of lovely Janet. May her dreams come true!

Distinguished Students

February 12, 1960

Two Buckhannon young men have distinguished themselves in recent weeks in the field of education – proving that state schools can't be as bad as recent publicity would picture.

John Curry, a freshman student at West Virginia University, has made a perfect mark in his final semester chemistry examination, and Graham Carpenter has completed the requirements for a Ph.D. degree at the University of Maryland, having his dissertation microfilmed and a copy placed in the Congressional Library.

Both young men are graduates of Buckhannon-Upshur high school, a credit both to the school and to the community.

John is the son of Mr. and Mrs. Paul Curry, of Marion street, and a graduate of B-U with the class of 1959 serving his class as valedictorian.

His perfect mark in chemistry at the university is the first one in the professor's memory and following the announcement of his perfect score, John was honored by the chemistry department with the presentation of an expensive science-math textbook and citation.

The examination was a uniform test given to all freshmen and as a double check his exam was passed to various professors in the department. All were unable to find a flaw. His overall average for this first semester was 3.82 out of a possible 4.00. Quite an achievement.

Graham, research chemist employed by the American Cyanamid company at Stamford, Conn., and a son of Mr. and Mrs. Simon Carpenter of Fayette street, is expected home this weekend. Carpenter has completed the requirements for his doctor's degree at College Park, Md. and will receive his diploma next June.

Snow Storm 1960

February 26, 1960

Well, we no sooner got the snow shoveled off from one storm than the area was hit harder by a second. There's always something to laugh about even in times of trouble and last weekend's snow caught motorists in all sorts of predicament. Fred Iden will vouch for the ruggedness of the Jeep. Thursday night he and his employees attended the Monongahela Power Company's clinic for appliance dealers and advertisers in Clarksburg and started home only to find themselves hung up just outside the city limits. Fred called on his friend and Jeep dealer in Clarksburg who loaned him one of the "motorized mountain goats" and they arrived in Buckhannon – late but safe.

Leon Lantz was marooned in Richwood Thursday and with wife, Dottie, pacing the floor and telephone lines out, Lantz didn't get home until Friday night. He was snarled in a snowdrift three miles out of Richwood at Fenwick for several hours after he did start home.

With school closing on Friday, some working mothers got caught with children at home and no place to send them. "Skip" Hodgkiss solved her problem by bringing Ricky right along to work with her to the county clerk's office. So the dignified air of the courthouse was dispelled with the sight of comic books, crayons and toy cars atop law books and registers.

One bridge club disbanded hurriedly during the height of the storm Thursday night. Mrs. Joseph Pagnillo was entertaining in her home on South Kanawha street when a tree limb came crashing down taking the telephone lines with it. Members put on boots, hiked to a phone, and scampered home with cards the furtherest thought from their minds.

Harassed mothers who shoveled snow, separated kids in the dozen fights during the school holiday, and tried to plan meals without the use of electric at times found their jobs all the harder without TV to entertain the youngsters.

The busiest Buckhannon merchants have been in ten years was Friday morning when they wielded snow shovels and went to work on the sidewalks up and down Main street. But the prize picture of the year was a city policeman brushing off snow on windshields of automobiles, ticketing them for overparking, as they sat three feet from the curb.

For a time the only means of communications in and out of Buckhannon was the short-wave radios manned by State Police and the State Road Commission. WBUC operated without the use of their Associated Press wire for two days but did a great job in keeping Upshur county residents aware of developments weather-wise and informed on local events.

And we salute the power and phone linemen for a job well done in the most adverse of situations.

Bandmaster Harold Fultz

March 4, 1960

From the moment any Buckhannon youngster first placed a band instrument against his lips, he heard the name of Harold Fultz, bandmaster, conductor, composer.

A graduate of the first U. S. Naval School of Music, Fultz packed a lot of living into the past 25 years of his life – a Horatio Alger story one might say. But for his tragic death last Thursday in a mid-air collision over Rio de Janeiro, he might have become the greatest of American composer of marches.

A completely selfless person, Harold never lost sight of his hometown. Time and again he returned here to conduct clinics. Two years ago at his own suggestion the B-U band toured the Navy School of Music as his guests and just this Christmas he had mentioned to Saul Fisher that he was intending to dedicate a composition to the local school band.

Harold played trumpet as a lad back when Bartlett L. Lyons and Clyde Ervin directed the local school aggregation. His horn was his life. He played in those old pit bands when the last of the vaudeville troupes hit the stage in Clarksburg.

Dick Lawson as a lad in sixth grade came under the tutorage of Harold and from what at first was hero worship turned later into a close friendship. Dick this week paid tribute to his teacher and friend. "Harold possessed a brilliant mind, a gigantic capacity for work and amazing versatility. During our last conversation he very humbly paid tribute to his wonderful teachers of public school days.

"He took justifiable pride in his endeavors and accomplishments and encountered life's problems with the positive approach of a highly successful and confident man. He received many honors and his services were very much in demand. And yet, he remained a loyal friend and guide to all who sought his assistance.

"His quick wit, his intense love and interest in people, and his unselfish sharing of his vast store of knowledge endeared him to all."

Back in the 30's, "Stickley" Martin had a dance band, the Musical Aces. Two nights a week that group drove to Webster Springs making $5 a night – just like $50 now. They lived in tents at the Pocahontas County Fair and played in an open pavilion a couple of years.

Remember Harold, John Fitzwater and Dave Casto on trumpet – and Carl Martin, Jim Ramsey and Gillette Berry on sax, Louis Reitz on drums, Eph Berry and his guitar and "Stick" at the piano? A lot of music came out of that group and that era – good music that the present generation will never understand.

Harold was just a kid then. The first time Dave Casto ever did a dance job was as fill-in for Harold at one of those old Roosevelt Balls. Harold had a fever blister and one of the group suggested the application of melted wax – it didn't heal the blister but caused it to spread all over his mouth. So, Harold sat behind Dave singing the parts, because Dave had never played such music before.

They wrecked a couple of cars in those days. And the Musical Aces made the rafters ring in the big barn at Upco Inn when 3.2 beer first came in at the end of the prohibition days.

The other fellows thought Harold was crazy when he enlisted in the Navy School of Music. Just like they thought John Fitzwater was crazy to want to fly long before any thought of World War II.

But that summer, a couple of Navy bandmen had come to Wesleyan for a summer band clinic and Harold knew that this was what he wanted – a chance to play his horn and put down on paper the notes he heard in his mind – and Johann Harold Fultz did exactly that. Not only a fine musician, he was a fine administrator too. Many of his ideas were used in the establishment of the Navy School of Music. He was in line to succeed Commander Charles Brendler as commander of the band.

In November 1936, Harold went aboard the USS Indianapolis with Unit Band No. 1 for the trip with President Roosevelt to the Pan American Conference. He played daily concerts for the presidential party aboard the ship during the trip and concerts in Brazil, Argentina and Uruguay while in port. He transferred aboard the USS Pennsylvania, flagship of the commander in chief, Christmas Eve and remained aboard until February, 1941, as assistant conductor of the band, playing all the while in the dance orchestra and concert orchestra.

He reported for duty with the band at the Jacksonville Naval Air Station in August, 1941 where he drilled and rehearsed the Service School Drum and Bugle Corp for the National Legion convention. He attended classes at Jacksonville College of Music with private study under the president of the college. He played with the Civic Symphony and sang with the Civic Choral Society and St. John's church, continuing to write marches and started dance arranging. He served as minister of music at the Woodlawn Baptist church and joined the Masonic Lodge completing Blue Lodge, Royal Arch, Council and Commandery with degrees up to and including Knight Templar.

He transferred to the DD-DE Escort Task Group Flag Band at Bermuda and in March, 1945, was assigned as bandmaster of the band for the commander-in-chief, U. S. Atlantic Fleet, with the largest band ever to be sent afloat. Visited the islands of the Caribbean and East Coast ports and then accompanied President Truman to the Potsdam Conference in the fall of 1945. He received a presidential letter and was the only enlisted man mentioned in the Presidential letter to the Secretary of Navy concerning the Potsdam trip.

In 1945 he became chief instructor at the Navy School of Music and conducted broadcasts and television shows and appeared as guest conductor of festival bands, including our own

Strawberry Festival, and as an adjudicator of high school band festivals in the eastern states along with being director of the Virginia All State High School band.

The first publication of his own composition came in 1949, following his marriage, the "American Sailor March", published by Leeds Music, Inc.

In February 1951, Harold transferred to San Diego, as bandmaster of the newly organized Naval Training Center Band, one of three 60-piece bands set up by the Navy which became the most publicized band, playing in the Los Angeles Coliseum and Rose Bowl in Pasadena.

Other publication of compositions followed – "Navy on Parade", "A Gypsy's Fireside Dreams", "De Capo", "Mexicana", "Swingin' Along" and "American Sailor".

Like we said, Harold packed a lot of living in his past 25 years, and his music will live a long time after.

On The Bus To Bluefield

March 11, 1960

Neither snow nor sleet nor drifted roads kept me at home last weekend. I doubt though that one should consider this an attribute but rather places me in the category of a darn fool. I had planned four days off from the smears of ink, ring of telephones and clang of the typewriter and after three calls to the bus station they insisted a bus would run to the southern end of the state.

I bought a round-trip ticket with the comment that if the Reynolds line were crazy enough to run a bus, I was fool enough to climb aboard. Sot it snowed and it snowed and the wind blew and the roads drifted and I sat nonchalantly in my seat with an air of confidence in the bus driver and his driving.

At Elkins just three stupid passengers were aboard – a pilot who had been forced to land, and a trailer-truck driver who jack-knifed on a mountain and I. Around Marlinton we got through drifts up over the bus wheels just because snow plow fortunately was inching along ahead of us. At Lewisburg, two of us stupid three disembarked for Richmond, Va. and Detroit, Mich. Alone, but undaunted the bus driver and I headed for Glen Lyn, Va. and Bluefield, doubts beginning to loom in my mind – not in the ability of the driver but rather in my sanity. The phrase, "Put a little fun in your life", kept whirling through my head but I don't think Kathryn Murray meant quite this way.

Sure 'nuff, at Glen Lyn nine tractor-trailers blocked our way up Oakvale mountain. We sat and we sat and we waited and we waited and suddenly the driver discovered we didn't want to go over the mountain to Princeton anyway. Determined, he turned off on Route 12, recently plowed, and we crawled along a country road minus traffic, and inched into the Bluefield terminal – the last bus into Bluefield and the last bus to leave for the next 12 hours.

I arrived at my friend's home to find that the weather was the least of their worries. Their prime concern, "How does one housebreak a pre-Easter chick?"

Mt. State Visitors Bureau

April 8, 1960

At last West Virginia is taking a giant step toward realizing the potential of its mountain beauty and Monday will get down to the business of figuring out how to get extra business through a boost in tourist trade.

The Mountain State Visitors Bureau will convene in Charleston at the Daniel Boone Hotel at 10 a.m. with the hope of accomplishing some broad aims. A non-profit sharing corporation had been proposed with the hope of getting more people to visit West Virginia and more West Virginians to travel around their state.

They propose to go about this through advertising, participating in travel shows throughout the United States, luring conventions to various sites, printing and distributing literature about West Virginia, collecting facts that will help members expand their existing facilities or establishing new businesses and keeping members advised of developments directly or indirectly affecting their business.

The state has been divided into eight regions through work of about 40 persons in the past four months. Upshur county is in Region 5 along with Monongalia, Preston, Marion, Taylor, Barbour, Tucker, Harrison, Doddridge, Lewis, Randolph and Webster counties.

A proposed slate of directors from each region will be presented Monday morning. Named for Region 5 are Sam Kistler, recreational and tourist counselor, Monongahela Power Company, Fairmont; George Brase, Central West Virginia Auto Club AAA, Clarksburg, and Norman Laughlin, manager, Upper Monongahela Valley Association, Fairmont.

The effectiveness of the Mountain State Visitors Bureau will depend on just how much the small businessmen and communities want to increase their incomes.

The planning committee figures that by 1963 when the state celebrates its 100th birthday, tourist dollars will hit $600 million – and that, they say, will be only the beginning.

Eye Bank

April 22, 1960

One of the most unusual of civic projects is being undertaken here by members of the Junior Department of the Buckhannon Woman's club – Eye-Bank for Sight Restoration.

Modern surgical science has made it possible for us to bequeath the most precious gift of all – the gift of sight. Several hundred surgeons are now performing corneal transplants, handicapped only by the lack of eyes.

Eye pledge cards are available through the Junior Department and the chairman of the project, Mrs. Nathan Rexroad, Jr. Cards can be obtained at any of the three local drugstores or from Dr. Bernard Knotts or Dr. Ronald George.

The primary purpose of the Eye-Bank for Sight Restoration has been and will always be the procurement of eyes to be used in restoring sight which necessitates informing the public of the need and the opportunity that exists for the donation of eyes at the time of death to help those afflicted with the loss of vision regain their sight. Through the cooperation of 250 affiliated hospitals, the airlines and American Red Cross Motor Corps, it is possible to distribute the vital corneal material to surgeons within the 48-hour time limit which is the safe period between the time of removal of the eye and its actual use in the corneal grafting operation.

The question of age has no bearing on donating one's eyes; the eyes of a baby or of an elderly person can be used if the corneal tissue is healthy and the cause of death has little significance with regard to usefulness of corneal tissue. Eyes should be removed as soon as possible – preferably within several hours after death and they are good for corneal transplants for approximately 48 hours. In the case of the Buckhannon location, a Pittsburgh doctor will come here immediately to remove the eyes to be placed in the eye bank at Pittsburgh.

The gift of eyes should not be made through a will since the eyes must by used before wills can be probated. Tell your next of kin or whoever would be responsible in the event of death and it is suggested that one give his eye donor form for safekeeping. What greater gift can anyone make than to help make possible the gift of sight.

Bob Ours & Others

April 29, 1960

Bob Ours, son of Mr. and Mrs. H. M. Ours, of Buckhannon, is on the Associated Press staff in Norfolk, Va. and for part of the time, runs the AP bureau himself. Bob is to be congratulated on his recent story concerning the rescue of 23 crew members of the Lebanese freighter Ethel C, rescued 13 hours after the ship sank off the Virginia coast.

Mrs. Eve Haymond, of North Pole, Alaska, mailed us an interesting colored picture this week (sorry, it won't reproduce) of the North Pole post office building. The front of the building shows a huge picture of Santa Claus and is gaily decorated in red and white stripes and evergreen. The large sign on the front reads "Santa Claus House, 511 Santa Claus Lane, North Pole, Alaska." Mrs. Haymond tells us that North Pole is about 13 miles south of Fairbanks and is advertised as Santa Claus Land. The post office also specializes in souvenirs and groceries.

Gypsies tangled with a gubernatorial aspirant Saturday prior to the Victory Rally. Truckloads of gypsies moved through Buckhannon and their van tangled with the street banner which was promoting Harold M. Neely. Workers at the GOP headquarters rushed onto the street protesting, the gypsies retreated and the city police solved the entire problem by restringing the political banner themselves. The gypsies will probably vote Democratic. It doesn't pay to tangle with a Republican. Will West Virginians help each other? Mrs. Harry R. Hall said this week that a very great need for good used clothing and canned meats has developed in our state during the last two years and it now seems time to do something about it.

An appeal has been made to the United Church Women of West Virginia for donations of any kind of canned meats which need no refrigeration, and clean clothing with wear in it. All churches will be observing National Family Week, May 1 to May 8, and this period has been set for the churches in Buckhannon to help the less fortunate people in West Virginia. Take your contribution to the church of your choice during National Family Week.

This is a volunteer program from start to finish and must be done at the least cost. The nearest receiving station is in Morgantown. Any person who is making a trip to Morgantown after May 8, and would be willing to help transport materials collected, contact Mrs. Merle Newton, 168 South Kanawha street, phone 1303-J.

Doctors And Medicine

May 13, 1960

A native of Buckhannon, Dr. Raphael J. Condry, of Elkins, is joining the staff of the Clarksburg VA Hospital, effective May 23. He has been a consultant at the VA hospital since 1950.

Dr. Condry has been in private practice from 1929 until the present time in Elkins but along with the private practice served as a consultant in cardiology at St. Joseph's hospital in Buckhannon. He is well known throughout northern West Virginia where he has spent the greatest portion of his professional career, except for a tour of duty, 1941 to 1945 with the U. S. Navy, performing the function of chief of medicine.

Speaking of doctors and medicine, Franklin Hartman II, son of Dr. and Mrs. I. F. Hartman, of Marion street, is among 46 West Virginians who have been selected as West Virginia University's 1960 entering freshman class in medicine.

Hartman, a preparatory student of West Virginia Wesleyan College will be eligible for an M.D. degree in 1964.

Two other Wesleyan students were selected, William Jerry Echols, of Richwood, and James Eastman Wilkerson, of Whitesville.

And still more about doctors, Dr. Martha Coyner, of Harrisville, daughter of Erik Coyner of Lightburn Street, last week was one of the five new directors named to the West Virginia Academy of General Practice, the Mountain State's organization of family doctors.

Dr. Martha along with another Buckhannon native, Miss Mary Kay Moats, RN, operate a clinic and practice in the Harrisville area. Miss Moats, a graduate of Buckhannon-Upshur high school with the class of 1943 and St. Mary's School of Nursing, is the daughter of Mr. and Mrs. Edgar Moats of Harrisville. Moats at one time taught chemistry at B-U high school.

John R. Curry, son of Mr. and Mrs. Paul Curry, of Island Avenue, was among 11 freshmen men at West Virginia University cited Sunday by Sphinx, national senior men's honorary society, for outstanding grades during the first semester.

The awards were presented by President Elvis J. Stark, Jr. during the Mother's Day Sing at the University Field House, an event that climaxed Greater West Virginia Weekend. Curry's grade average was 3.812 out of a possible 4.0.

Kathy Kay, top vocalist of London, England, sister of Ken Thornhill, of Deanville, appears May 16 with Billy Cotton's band in a Royal Command Performance in the Victoria Palace in London. This is her second appearance before the royal family.

Kathy's appearance will be re-televised on May 22. Miss Kay has a weekly TV show in London and is a recording artist. Her recording of "Tammy" was one of the top ten records in England.

She is married to Archie McCulloch, journalist, has three sons and lives in Glasgow, Scotland. Her recordings are used over Buckhannon Radio Station WBUC quite frequently.

Among things I never knew 'til now – Mrs. Louisa Holt Hughes, the only native West Virginian to have two sons who were Methodist bishops, was at one time a resident of Buckhannon.

Bishops Matt S. Hughes and Edwin Holt Hughes are descendants of the famous and vigorous Holt family of Lewis county, through her father, Matthew Holt, who was considered the best informed layman of his day through his knowledge of Methodist doctrine, law, ritual and history.

For years she lived in at least 11 Methodist parsonages and for four years her husband's salary was only $100 a year. Yet, at one time three of her boys were in West Virginia University.

When she lived in Buckhannon, Mrs. Hughes lived in the parsonage without electric lights, bath or running water. Dr. Hughes traveled on horseback or by buckboard over the district as superintendent.

Bishop E. H. Hughes attended grade schools in Buckhannon. His portrait now hangs in the lobby of the new Wesleyan library.

Election Results

May 20, 1960

The election is over and the results tabulated, at least until November, and we can be civil again in this newspaper office. There's nothing like the newspaper profession during election. Even the veteran gets excited and the confusion is unbelievable. This primary probably was more confusing than usual with the lengthy ballots and at 2 a.m. Wednesday morning only eight precincts out of Upshur's 25 had been tabulated. That meant the entire day of Wednesday was spent in the courthouse office and we were trying to go to press at noon.

I explain this only as an excuse to justify my carelessness in missing names and votes in two very important local races. I completely omitted Warren Hosaflook's name in the board of education race and I probably have every Democrat in the county mad at me for omitting the three-way gubernatorial contest. Believe me, it was unintentional, and please blame it on the confusion and 11th-hour deadline.

To point out more of the confusion for the past three weeks – I had Howard Gould running for an unexpired term as county commissioner and for five whole days we had $7.92 over in the drawer and it wasn't until last Friday that we discovered Earl Sayre's account was paid out but I had never put it down on the cash book.

But, temporary peace is restored, the Value Daze supplement is printed and distributed, the kitchen shears are going well and the political cards of thanks are now a thing of history. I've even gotten around to cleaning out drawers with a year's accumulation of notes to myself and I await with bated breath the return of Mary Liz sometime this summer to her editorial duties.

Perce J. Ross, local merchant and member of the State Board of Education, last Friday made presentations to individual seniors and to the school during Class Day observances. Silver cuff link sets were presented to each senior and depicted an open book with the inscription "A Date to Remember – May 23". Newton Anderson, principal, and John Snyder, senior class president, received the presentation of a new 50-star silk flag, standard and flagpole from Mr. Ross.

Mayor Hinkle this week handed me an interesting list of per capita expenditures for West Virginia cities with populations of 5,000 to 10,000. Buckhannon with a 1960 population of 6,016 spent 15.40 per person for an estimated operating expenditure of $92,635. This is fourth from the lowest in the state. Even in the depressed areas of Welch and Logan those two cities show 40.42 and 41.82 per capita and operating expenditures of $266,893 and $212,391.

The president of the West Virginia State Bar has commended the Upshur County Bar Association on their activities in the observance of Law Day USA. Rupert A. Sinsel, of Clarksburg, said in his letter to local chairman Myron B. Hymes, "my congratulations to you and your committee upon a very well planned program. I doubt if any of our County Bar Associations will submit a better report. On behalf of the officers and governors, please accept our appreciation."

Jeff Manser, son of Mr. and Mrs. William C. Manser, formerly of Buckhannon, received his master's degree in February from Cornell University's School of Industrial and Labor Relations. In addition to his studies, Jeff served as a graduate assistant at the school.

Since February 15, he has been employed by Lukens Steel company, Coatesville, Pa. as an industrial relations trainee and is currently assigned to the employment department. Jeff was joined in Coatesville by his wife, the former Sue Garrett of Clendenin and three-month-old son, William Jefferson. Their address is C-5 Elmwood Gardens Apartment, Coatesville, Pa.

The April issue of Teen Times magazine, official publication of the Future Homemakers of America, contains a story about the annual state conservation camp at Camp Caesar, Webster county. The story was written by Jeanne Bell of Bridgeport, and Lana Tomblyn, of Buckhannon, vice president of state projects for the organization.

The dates for this year's camp will be June 6 to 11.

Oddities in the news…Last Thursday morning Keith Jones, a farmer of French Creek, upon checking his livestock, found a fox trying to get to a newborn calf. The mother was putting up a desperate fight in fending off the marauding animal, forcing the fox to retreat by knocking the animal down. Edward Warner, who was tending to the stock along with Jones, ran for his deer rifle and shot the fox in the head. The cow and calf are being confined for signs of rabies.

Polio

May 27, 1960

You can throw your calendars away because you can always tell that summer is approaching when I start preaching sermons about polio immunizations.

The control of poliomyelitis is still unfinished business. Yes, I know that in the five years since Salk polio vaccine was announced safe and effective that at least 7,500 persons in the U.S. have been saved from death and another 47,500 have been spared the crippling after-effects.

But, during 1959 more than 5,000 paralytic cases were reported – a 50% increase over 1958 and more than double 1957's record low number. Upshur county had two paralytic cases under five years of age in 1959. These two children still wear braces and will probably wear them for some time to come.

One of the leading newspapers published for physicians has taken note of the changing pattern of polio cases. Although the incidence of polio is down, the number of paralytic cases continues to climb. If the pattern of the past four years is repeated, polio will aim its most vicious blows at the 9.6 million children under five who have had fewer than three immunizations.

The American Medical Association is urging state and county medical societies to give leadership to community-wide vaccination programs. Just such a program was the polio immunization program inaugurated last year by the Junior Department of the Buckhannon Woman's club. But one can not stop there. The danger is always present and it is the hope of health officials that parents see that children are immunized immediately.

There is polio vaccine available, no longer is it scarce as in periods past, so make an appointment NOW with your local physician and be both sure and safe. Fifty-one percent of the U.S. population is still unvaccinated., this includes nearly five million children under five years of age.

Dr. Jacob C. Huffman, of Buckhannon, president of the West Virginia State Medical Association, received special honors Friday evening during a Clarksburg dinner meeting of the Captain Kem White Alumni club of the Phi Sigma Kappa social fraternity. The Delta chapter of West Virginia University, presented Dr. Huffman with the Founder's Day Alumni Award which is presented annually to a member of the alumni who has excelled in his chosen field of work. Dr. Huffman has an outstanding record of work in the State Medical Association.

Raymond Bogert, Jr., of South Florida street, received a twenty-five year silver certificate presented to those who have been members of the fraternity for 25 years or more. Jack Plunkett, of Boggess street, also an alumni, attended the meeting.

Oddities in the news…Ever see a bouquet of 175 four, five and six-leaf clovers? I did, this past weekend. Mrs. Cashus Lanham picked 50 of the multiple clovers in about 15 minutes in the backyard at her home near Hodgeville, Friday. I couldn't find a four-leaf clover if it were growing six inches above everything else in the field!!

Gary H. Athey, of Keyser, son of the former Miss Lora D. Townsend of Buckhannon, is one of two West Virginia University College of Law students, who have been elected to membership in the Order of the Coif, national law school honor society. Gary, the son of Attorney and Mrs. H. R. Athey of Keyser, will receive his law degree with the May 30 graduating class. He is the grandson of Mrs. Katie Townsend, who resides with the Angelo Pappas' at Buckhannon Route 3, and the late W. W. Townsend.

Recipients of this honor are selected by the College of Law faculty from the 10 percent of seniors ranking highest scholastically. Only a highly-select group of the nation's leading law schools have chapters of the Order of the Coif. The WVU chapter was instituted in 1925.

There may be an explanation for this…Mrs. Dane E. DeBarr, of Ten Mile, writes that Sunday morning an unusual phenomenon occurred in what is called the "Blue Hole" in the Buckhannon river. There was a low rumbling sound and when observers looked bubbles began to form and roll out in a circle of about 30 feet or more in diameter. In the center of the circle a spout of water arose over six feet, bringing with it what looked like pieces of wood and mud and leaves. For the remainder of the day there was a huge circle, some bubbles and the pieces of debris floating around.

Of course there is some explanation but we don't know what it was. Perhaps gas, for it lies underground in Ten Mile. Anyway I'm told it was interesting to see.

Mr. and Mrs. Matthew Edmiston, Jr. and four daughters of South Florida street, will leave Sunday morning for St. Petersburg, Fla. to visit her parents, Mr. and Mrs. George Wharton, and his brother and sister-in-law Dr. and Mrs. John Edmiston, of Plant City, Fla.

Strawberry Festival – 1960

June 3, 1960

The flags are waving, banners flying, music blaring, traffic tied up in knots, restaurants crowded, and Buckhannon is bursting at the seams with both delegates to the Methodist Conference and visitors to the Strawberry Festival in town at the same time for the first time in the town's history.

Red of the strawberry is the color this week...as displayed in the windows of the H-P store and Sexton's Gift Shoppe. And if one really wants to go all the way, quickly stitch a dress using strawberry cotton print from Strader's.

Fraises des Bois – the color picked just for your lips – or for that wild strawberry taste, eye Thompson's Pharmacy window. And right next door, Miller's Pharmacy has displayed pictures of each of the princesses from the participating Strawberry counties.

But the busiest center is Strawberry Headquarters where commercial exhibits jam floor space and WBUC has set up operation, broadcasting direct from a corner niche, making personal interviews and displaying the Associated Press wire service teletype in operation.

Petunias are growing in every shop window through the efforts of the Fred Brooks Garden club, a clever promotion adding to that "scrubbed" look this week.

Unger's Shoe store has displayed samplings of previous Festival programs and the children are taken care of by Gottfried's with knitwear, socks and caps topped with Mr. Red Strawberry.

The Home Hardware has devoted the entire window space to a picture display from counties of Central West Virginia in the Tygart Valley Soil Conservation owned by Clark Lane; to a unique button display by Mrs. Nola Lane, which looks like a mosaic pattern, and to paintings by Isobell Ward.

Have fun – it's only once a year!

June Potpourri

June 10, 1960

June is traditionally the month of graduation for colleges and universities throughout the United States. Delores E. McCollum, of Buckhannon, graduated June 2 with a bachelor of science degree in nursing at the University of Colorado, and on the same day was among eight nurses commissioned in the U. S. Navy.

Hallie Lu Hallam, daughter of Mr. and Mrs. William A. Hallam, of Meade street, received her masters degree last Saturday from Florida State University at Tallahassee.

Charles Shaffer, of Shaffers' Appliance, Inc., enjoyed Florida sunshine this week at the Fountainbleau Hotel at Miami Beach. Shaffer was one of 20 salesmen in the state winning an expense-paid trip for sales of Admiral appliances. He left Sunday morning by plane from Charleston and returned home yesterday (Thursday).

Miss Evelyn Ours, daughter of Mr. and Mrs. H. M. Ours, of Camden avenue, was responsible for bringing the Pykesville, Md. Prancerettes here for the Strawberry Festival parade Saturday. Miss Ours is director and accompanied the following, Doris Bernscala, Judy Alt, Wadaline Rehmert, Terry Ann Crane, Diane Andrews and Gary Smith.

C. G. White of Buckhannon, has been selected as the 4th District national committee alternate following the three-day state convention of the Disabled American Veterans which ended Sunday at Parkersburg.

Steve Lesondak, of the Handy Camp Pheasant Farm at Hall, stopped in the office one day this week enroute to Fairmont with 150 day-old pheasants. The consignment was being delivered to Dr. Joseph B. Romino, who raises several pheasants each year, then turns them out on his private preserve for some fine hunting. Steve has 500 chicks that hatch out every Wednesday in the incubator at the farm – which eventually leads to some mighty fine eatin'.

Newsmen

June 17, 1960

What would you expect newpapermen to discuss at an annual press outing – why, newspapers, of course. Cost of production and newsprint, hiring and firing, dealin' and wheelin' – all through the blue haze of cigarette smoke and the shouting to out-shout the couple crowded next to you.

Newsmen sit through innumerable banquets throughout the year and what do they do at the annual outing – sit through another banquet, of course. We need feeding just like the other animals in this world although it's claimed we have ink for blood and zinc for bone.

We do have a heart though and a fierce love for a line of type that compensates for the brusque manner in which we're often rebuffed or worse yet – ignored. We have sensitivity – we may look calm and methodical as we go about writing our stories of lust and greed, crime and passion, but we cry inside just like ordinary people.

Our sense of sight though often insight is more often hindsight. We see too much at times – the disappointments and the unscrupulous.

We hear too much – things that mortal men can repeat but we cannot in fairness record as history.

Our sense of smell – smell of the evil is too often acrid but more often sweet because of our genuine love of mankind and its contribution to the comfort and ease of humanity.

And the taste in our mouth can be sour, salty, bitter or pleasurable depending on whether we're proud of our accomplishments, disappointed in the results or weary with the inner workings of the fickle human mind.

So why do we enter this jungle of machines and deadlines, tensions and frustrations – who knows? Maybe its for that once a year when newsmen can congregate and vent their fury – knowing they are understood, their problems similar, their compensations little but rewards great.

Treat us kindly – we too have a sense of taste, feel, smell, sight and hearing.

Our Children

June 24, 1960

David Lynn McCartney, 7-year-old son of Mr. and Mrs. Charles O. McCartney, of Hinkleville, partly blind and deaf since birth, is a patient in the Children's Hospital of Pittsburgh, Pa. for observation and evaluation.

The hospital, one of the finest in the United States, is part of the Medical Health Center and is a teaching hospital for students of the schools of the health professions and related fields of the University of Pittsburgh. It began its service in 1883 and has developed rapidly over the years. Several times the hospital has been enlarged and at the present time is undergoing remodeling and expansion.

The construction is part of an $8,000,000 modernization program to make this hospital second to none in the country.

Each small patient has his own nurse at all times. David will be a patient for the next six weeks.

Carolyn Griffin, 14-year-old daughter of Mr. and Mrs. A. E. Griffin, of Meade street, has won $10 with a first place photography award. Her picture of the family cat poised back of a chair watching the pet parakeet will be pictured in the July issue of American Girl magazine, sponsors of the contest.

James G. Wilfong, son of Mrs. Martha Wilfong, of Fayette street, compiled a mark of 3.3 to 3.59 in forestry school at West Virginia University, according to Dean A. H. VanLandingham. Fifty-five students in the college of agriculture, forestry and home economics earned scholastic averages of 3.3 or higher during the semester to win places on the college honor roll.

Another Buckhannon boy, John Crites, son of Mr. and Mrs. Freal Crites, of Marion street, will enroll this fall in the School of Forestry at WVU, after two years of pre-forestry work at Wesleyan. John is working this summer at Crescent, Oregon, with the Department of Agriculture forest service.

In a brief session last Thursday members of the Buckhannon Sanitary Board divided $992,216.21 from the sale of bonds and deposited the money in the two local banks. Work is progressing rapidly on sewerage lines and the sewage treatment plant.

Mr. and Mrs. Jerrold Haddix, of Boggess street, will leave July 6 for their new home in Peoria, Ill. They have been residents of Buckhannon for 18 years. Their home has been purchased by Dr. and Mrs. J. M. Helm, of Wheeling, minister of the First Methodist church at Wheeling, who will move here upon his retirement.

Miss Bonita Lea Huffman, French Creek Route 2, is attending the Union College Institute in American Studies, June 13 through July 22, at Barbourville, Ky.

Miss Huffman's graduate scholarship is provided through a special grant of the Coe Foundation, which includes board, room and tuition for a term of six weeks. A graduate of West Virginia Wesleyan with the degree of bachelor-of-arts, Miss Huffman teaches at Red Bird Mission, Beverly, Ky.

The graduate program of the Union College Institute in American Studies is designed for the purpose of aiding colleges in offering refresher courses to high school teachers in the social sciences.

Political Slogans

July 8, 1960

As early as 1840, when a political party promised the voter "Two Dollars a Day and Roast Beef", the slogan was as much a part of presidential election campaigns as the handshake and the stump.

It's a fitting arena for the slogan, which was once the battle cry of the Scots. According to World Book Encyclopedia , the word comes from "sluagh", meaning "army" and "gairm" or "call". The voters of 1840 took up the battle for two dollars, conceding that "Van, Van (Martin Van Buren) is a Used-up Man". They gave their votes to "Tippecanoe and Tyler Too" – William Henry Harrison, the hero of the Indian battle of Tippecanoe, and his running mate John Tyler. In 1864, when Lincoln was running for a second term, the Union was warned: "Don't Swap Horses in the Middle of the Stream". The cry was to echo 80 years later, when Franklin D. Roosevelt won a fourth term in the dark years of World War II. Horace Greeley thundered "Turn the Rascals Out" in 1872, but Grant held the presidency for another term. The country wasn't ready for "The Plumed Knight" as James G. Blaine was called in 1876, and the election went to Rutherford B. Hayes.

Blaine was back in 1884. But he had the misfortune of being labeled an opponent of "Rum, Romanism and Rebellion". The Catholics turned against him and helped elect Grover Cleveland. William McKinley promised "The Full Dinner Pail" in 1900, setting a precedent for Hoover's later pledge of "A Chicken in Every Pot, a Car in Every Garage".

In 1916 the country re-elected Woodrow Wilson with the explanation "He Kept Us Out of War". Five months later the U.S. was in the war. When the next election rolled around, the voter wanted "Normalcy" and Warren G. Harding. In 1924 the electorate decided to "Keep Cool with Coolidge". By 1932 they were ready for a "New Deal" and the "Forgotten Man" gave his vote to FDR. More recently some people thought "We Need Adlai Badly", but the voters of 1952 and 1956 proved that more people like Ike. What will the slogans be this year?

Maybe we'll hear "I'll Stick With Dick"…or "My Cup of Tea is Kennedy"…it doesn't appear that "What's Good for the Country is Hubert Humphrey".

Boy Scout National Jamboree – Colorado

July 15, 1960

Five Upshur county boys leave this Sunday afternoon by train to join 55,600 youths and leaders at the fifth national Boy Scout Jamboree at Colorado Springs, near the new Air Force Academy.

Boarding special train No. 401 which consists of 10 air-conditioned coaches and two baggage cars are Gary Evans, son of Mr. and Mrs. R. T. Evans, Jr., of Hodgeville, Neal Zinn, sone of Mr. and Mrs. Harry J. Zinn; David Waggy, son of Mr. and Mrs. Robert C. Combs, Eddie Canfield, son of Mr. and Mrs. LeRoy Canfield, and Randy Tucker, son of Mr. and Mrs. Randall Tucker, all of Buckhannon. The local boys will aid in building Colorado's Fourth Largest City, "Jamboree City" which will arise overnight with 30,000 tents – a real city – fire department, water mains, garbage and sewage disposal, hospital, telephone, radio and television studios and a daily newspaper.

The two-week stay includes some interesting facts on food – facts that Dad can appreciate after buying groceries for one growing boy. Read these figures in the feeding of 53,000 growing boys – 9,000,000 pieces of paper dishes will be used.

The preparation of one meal will require as many as 16,000 charcoal cooking fires going at one time. Over 283 tons of charcoal briquettes, or 20 freight car loads, will be used.

It will take 1,330 head of steers to supply the needed cuts of top sirloin for the final dinner on July 28th. The daily fresh milk requirements of the Jamboree is 74,480 quarts of milk. An equal portion of chicken legs and thighs for every boy will come from 27,800 chickens.

If laid end to end, the frankfurters consumed by the boys extend over 17 miles. Over 752 tons of nonperishable foods will be used (52,920 cases).

The commissary department will spend the following for things boys like, such as $11,690 for jam and jelly; $19,700 for cake, pie and doughnuts and $12,000 for ice cream.

All this at a total cost, including travel, of $230 per boy!

Janet Cosgrove With The Queen Mother

July 22, 1960

Be sure your TV set is in good working order next week and plan a party – a Nixon Volunteers Television Party, that is. According to an action memo distributed from Washington, D. C. party members can capitalize on the interest and excitement of the Republican National Convention and officially launch the Nixon for President campaign in every community of the nation.

Wednesday and Thursday seem to be high points of action when nominating speeches and voting on presidential and vice-presidential candidates are scheduled and acceptance speeches by both nominees on Thursday evening.

Speaking of excitement, Janet M. Cosgrove, daughter of Mr. and Mrs. O. O. Roby, of French Creek, is one hillbilly that has "rubbed elbows" with royalty.

Mrs. Cosgrove, who lives in London, England, where her Air Force husband, M/Sgt, Roy T. Cosgrove is stationed, was honored at the yearly Royal Agriculture Show on July 7. Mrs. Cosgrove, who has made a big effort in becoming acquainted with the English people and their customs, was invited by the British Women's Institute to attend the Royal Agriculture Show held at Cambridge, England, home of the famous Cambridge University.

Mrs. Cosgrove got a real surprise when she was given a medal and ribbon which permitted her free admission to the fairgrounds, flower show and to the Royal Box in the grand ring.

The biggest surprise was when all overseas visitors were invited to the Royal Pavilion to hear the Queen Mother give a welcoming speech and to have a "spot of tea" with her.

It's not every day that a West Virginia hillbilly has tea with royalty.

Republican National Convention

July 29, 1960

The bleary eyes of Mountain State hillbillies had just returned to normal, sans water and redness, after the donkey antics of the Democrats two weeks ago in Los Angeles, when more than the usual amount of recognition in West Virginia sparked renewed interest in TV viewing this week with the opening of the GOP national convention.

With Governor Cecil Underwood honored in the role of temporary chairman and even mentioned by some commentators and press representatives as a likely nominee for the vice-presidency – Upshur countians gloried in the long overdue political acknowledgement of a governor – that like Eisenhower has had to push through programs without help from either Congress or the legislature.

The GOP convention seemed like old home week for some Upshur countians with the "red eye" of the TV camera focused not only on Underwood but Dorsey Joe Bartlett whom we like to think as belonging to Buckhannon, and Senator William S. Colwes, of New Mexico, a real true-blue native son of Upshur. Senator Colwes, of Albuquerque, who was introduced Monday night, was born in Buckhannon. His father, of the same name, grew up here and operated a grocery store and later a gent's store where the Perce Ross retail store is now located. His mother, also born in Buckhannon, is now Mrs. Walter Goodnow, of Topeka, Kansas. His aunt was the late Mrs. Kitty Stockert, of Florida street.

Bartlett, a native son of Clarksburg and former Wesleyan student, was the unanimous selection of the Republican national committee to serve in Chicago – calling the roll of delegates for nomination of the president. Bartlett serves regularly with the U. S. House of Representatives as its reading clerk.

Dampening the spirits of the West Virginia delegates was the illness of Walter Hallanan, national committeeman since 1928, who this year bowed out of the national spotlight to push Governor Underwood in his bid for prestige.

Hallanan, who served as temporary chairman of the 1952 convention, was stricken with a cardiac condition at his Chicago hotel Monday and is now a patient in the Presbyterian St. Luke's hospital. Hallanan told associates that he became fatigued Sunday when he stood for more than two hours trying to get across Michigan Boulevard during a huge political parade.

A sidelight to the convention – Croner Brown, of Lincoln street, chairman of the Upshur County Republican executive committee this week received a souvenir gavel from Governor Underwood and a letter expressing the governor's appreciation for Brown's personal friendship and his loyal service to the Republican party. Engraved on the gavel are the words "To My Loyal Friend" – Cecil Underwood, Governor 1960.

An added note – the Underwoods celebrated their 12th wedding anniversary in Chicago Monday and on Wednesday, Hovah Underwood was one of several governor's wives modeling gowns worn by previous First Ladies of the White House.

Hay Fever

August 12, 1960

This is the time of sneezing and reddened, runny noses and brimming eyes or what the unafflicted call "Hay Fever Month". The afflicted have better names – unprintable – but satisfaction in knowing that August 15 to September 15 is dedicated not merely to sympathy for all sufferers but to practical assistance.

It's little consolation to me to know that I am one of 17 million Americans afflicted with hay fever that cost the national economy some 25 million man-days a year and spreads misery over many times that number of man-woman-child days.

It helps even less to know that the sale of tissues jump, cost of prescriptions rise and the number of patients in the doctor's offices increases. It doesn't even help my mental attitude to know that I have a less severe case than millions of others – I am infuriated by the fact that I am a so-called "sufferer" at all.

It's not an easy task to interrupt telephone conversation to quickly grab a Kleenex and sneeze, not once but 12 times within a short span of a call, it's embarrassing to turn aside from a customer to avoid sneezing in his face and the swollen, reddened eyes are certainly not conducive to good salesmanship in this profession.

Several thousand Americans, including me, have dug down into their pants pockets and handbags and under the loose brick in the hearth and broken a few piggy banks each year and come up with loot to buy nasal sprays and tablets and shots – with and without prescriptions – which have helped stem the running rivers from both eyes and nose – at least temporarily.

As yet, there is no cure for allergy and there are doubtless many allergies yet to be discovered, so pardon – while I SNEEZE.

David Plate

October 21, 1960

Some college boys wait tables, some work as stock boys in local stores, other do janitor work or direct campus traffic, but a recent graduate of West Virginia Wesleyan – David Plate bought and sold wrecked or used cars to parlay a talent into big business – the business of getting through college.

A native of Erie, Pa., married and the father of one infant daughter, David graduated after two years and eight months of study and in addition to his car enterprise, waited tables at 49 South Florida street dorm.

At the age of seven, Plate operated farm machinery at the family home in Pennsylvania where his father is an attorney. At the age of nine he bought a 1930 Model A Ford for 50 cents, towing it home on the roof of the family car. At 12, he bought a '49 Chevrolet cab for $20 selling it later for $250.

As an example of his tenacity, David, at the age of 17 bought a two-year-old wrecked car for $250, invested $700 in the repairs and was given a $1,700 trade-in on a new Chevrolet.

All in all, since the age of nine he has repaired and traded 57 cars. In fact, just before he left for Boston Theology School this fall, David in one weekend bought and sold three cars.

As a freshman student here he lived in the men's dormitory using the backyard for a garage. Later, living with the Thomas Weavers or College avenue, he again worked in the backyard repairing automobiles that others had wrecked or discarded.

But his days as a mechanic may be at an end – David is the recipient of a three-quarter scholarship to the Boston School of Theology and knowing how much work will be involved in receiving his degree as a ministerial student, he doesn't feel that he'll have the time for the used car business.

Somehow, his story has left me with a warm feeling – proof again that if one wants something bad enough, say a college degree, one can find a way.

Homelife With Teenagers

November 10, 1960

I'm a stranger in my own home! I've been dispossessed of my favorite lounge chair and my pattern of living these past 16 years has been changed.

As a mother of two teenage sons, I no longer can don the comfortable old robe over pj's and wallow in the luxury of my evening TV programs. Nor can I pincurl my hair while watching Johnny Ringo outshoot the bad men.

Now I'm supposed to be the glamorous mother, charming hostess and lenient chaperone to a variable sea of strange faces who come and go between living room and refrigerator. Subsequently the food bills are rising – not because of an enriched diet of fare – but rather due to an influx of pizzas, popcorn, apples and doughnuts into the bottomless pits of teenage stomachs. No longer can I prepare a salad, a casserole, cake or pie for tomorrow's dinner. I'm forced to hide my favorite cheese or a banana for my morning cereal.

I've been reading more these past few weeks, hidden away in the bedroom – ejected from the living room and rejected by my guests. I can take leisurely, luxurious bubble baths to pass the time away as the giggling goes on in the front of the house accompanied by outrageous music and outlandish guffaws that even invade the privacy of my bath.

My kitchen is remarkably clean since I spend the better part of my evenings now wondering what I can be doing while at the same time keeping the right eye and left ear tuned to the living room. I've shined the silver, scrubbed the refrigerator and taken a blowtorch to the kitchen range. It's fantastic the number of small jobs one can do in the course of an evening if forced. I probably could win a position as tackle for the Houston Oilers for I've had lots of practice – becoming most proficient in the shoestring tackle on small sister who is enthralled by the antics of the teenage guests and who is so disdained by same!

As a linguist my skill is reaching profundity – I, at least, can interpret what my ears hear with only an occasional asking of a translation. They tell me I have several years left whereby I'll have no home and many years of serene and quiet afterwards. Wouldn't it be wonderful if the teenage invasion could last forever – or would it?

Funds For Athletic Programs

November 23, 1960

I'm angry – not so much at anyone else but rather at myself because until last week I was unaware of several problems that confront state coaches, either junior high or senior high.

I'm mad too at the apathy shown when only six parents turn out for a booster's club meeting from a possible 100 to remedy a situation that exists in both basketball and football for junior and senior high. Up until last week I was unaware that no board of education in the state can budget so much as even a shoelace for football shoes – that junior high boys wore hand-me-down helmets, minus the foam rubber padding, this season and a similar situation exists in the high school. Don't misunderstand me – I am not blaming the board of education – they are governed by a state law in regard to athletic equipment – but I am blaming myself along with other parents for not doing something to see that athletes are well-equipped when they go on the football field or a basketball court. Through the generosity of Wesleyan College and even the high school, the junior high boys have uniforms, but even hand-me-downs wear out in time and unless the parents band together and provide some much-needed new equipment I doubt that the junior high coaches can carry on either basketball or football in a year or two.

It costs roughly $100 to equip a boy for football. Only through an organization – call it parents' club or a boosters' club can money be raised for athletes. Buckhannon does have a high school organization which has raised approximately $900 during the past year but even that is little enough when it is spread among 60 team members in both football and basketball, and, it surely is not enough to budget anything for the junior high. Of that $900 enough must be laid aside for the annual athletic banquet and must pay insurance premiums for every football squad member.

The junior high is fortunate in that the regular school insurance takes care of injuries sustained on the playing field or court.

So – let's try it again. Next Tuesday night at 7:30 p.m. will parents of team members please meet in the junior high gym and this time let's really make some plans whereby the needed football and basketball equipment can be purchased.

Athletic Funds – Follow-Up

December 9, 1960

Two weeks ago I was furious – today my faith in people has been restored. Two weeks ago I lashed out at the apparent apathy shown when only six parents turned out for a booster's club meeting for junior high athletics – today the youngsters are richer by $355.42.

Actually, I've known for a good many years that the only way in which one attains a goal is to help one's self – and that is exactly what these junior high football and basketball boys did last Saturday.

They sold tags – and tags and tags – in fact, so many tags that the DELTA plant was called on early Saturday morning to print more tags. The boys hit every nook and cranny of this city – they caught the B&O conductors and engineers as they stopped their runs at the local depot. They stationed themselves at the banks and caught customers coming and going. They told one bank cashier that the competing bank had contributed so much – which resulted in a contribution doubling the original amount. One Main Street merchant gave them a $15 check.

Dressed in worn, dirty football jerseys with the biggest rips and tears and torn seams, the boys were pathetic to see – which is exactly why the tags were being sold, and sure enough, the public responded with pennies, nickels, dimes, quarters, half dollars and the crisp, green stuff.

With gate receipts from basketball and football games and with a couple of other projects this winter that some parents have in mind, these young men won't look quite so much like stepchildren another season.

We thank you, the public, for responding to their plea, and thanks to the 43 young men – Dusty Williams, the top salesman, Dale Darnall, James Beer, Ed Teets, Jim Whitehair, David Slaughter, Gary Casto, Stan Stewart, Dick Smith, Mike Cutright, David Feola, Steve Brown, Gail Plum, Mike Whitehair, Jim Lofton, Ken Cutright, Larry Frisby, David Hornbeck, Drew Boni, Joe Shaw, Bob Kiser, Paul Harper, Larry Able, Jery Able, John Dean, Donald Hutchinson, Pat Pagnello, Butch Shreves. Jim Curry, Stan Boyer, Jake Huffman, Jr., Bill Hornbeck, Stanley Boyles, Larry Lantz, Roger Riffle, John Casto, Tim Bacorn, Brent Phillips and Danny Smith.

New Year's Resolutions

December 30, 1960

I like to think I'm a cock-eyed optimist and like the proverbial columnist at year's end I'm looking to the bright side of 1961. I may not be the first to list my New Year's resolutions but then, since I like to live dangerously, I at least am publicly announcing previous faults with an aim toward remedying the same.

Actually, if psychoanalyzed, I'd probably be classified as Janus-faced – Janus, an ancient Roman deity, to whom the month of January was sacred, and who is represented with two opposite faces. I see myself as an optimist and yet I'm contrary and willful – so, because I'm pertinacious, I firmly resolve to have fewer deadline jitters and tension tantrums. (At least in the Delta office.)

I resolve here and now to stick to a rigid schedule, both at home and at work. (This is a downright lie – I shan't do anything of the sort.)

I promise to read one good book a week and spend less time lying on the couch watching the big eye of television. (Truthfully, I plan to read only if the following programs aren't scheduled – Peter Gunn, Hawaiian Eye and Surfside 6.)

For the sake of a happy household, I promise dessert every other meal. (The teenagers have threatened to leave home otherwise.)

My friends, after January 1, can expect prompt answers to all letters. (If I don't start writing soon I'll have no friends.)

To say nice things about other people. (Or if I can't say anything nice – forget it.)

Save some money. (That is, if the gas, water and telephone companies will cooperate.)

Stop arguing with the boss. (He owns the joint, so why should I worry.)

And, if I follow through on all these resolutions you'll know I'm an optimist – and cock-eyed.

City-County Progress

January 6, 1961

About this time last year I was writing of the fabulous 50's and optimistically forecasting an era called the Golden Sixties. I'm not one to say "I told you so" but Upshur county in the past year has chalked up gains that would have been beyond the comprehension of our grandfathers.

Things look right rosy around the county – on one side of the ledger Wesleyan College is expanding, Corhart Refractories plant has located here, new National Guard facilities are being constructed, improvements are in sight at the French Creek Game Farm, road improvement is at an all-time high, bank deposits are rising and the Central National Bank is planning to expand. Yet, in red ink, we must note that coal production in the county is slightly down over 1959, Reidbord Brothers garment plant has had seasonal layoffs, 791 families are existing on DPA allowances and building permits are far down over the preceding year.

Buckhannon is a good town in which to live! Real estate increased $110,136 this year with total valuations standing at $11,708,599. True, not as much home building is going on but remodeling indicates a sign of progress and improvement on the part of the homeowner. Approximately $300,000 was spent in '60 according to building permits issued at City Hall. The new sewerage project and treatment plan has put men back to work and at an estimated cost of $428,581 it will serve a population of 20,000. It is hard to believe that in the future Buckhannon might grow to such proportions. To provide housing for those persons over 65 years of age – the city is working now on plans for a public low rent housing project – a healthy indication that officials are looking ahead.

Probably the brightest sign of a stable economy for the city was the location here of the Corhart plant which will open this spring employing at least 60 persons but geared to provide employment for hundreds in the future. The new men's dormitory at Wesleyan is almost complete (again providing employment) and better still – there are innumerable plans for expansion. Within the next few months a new girl's dorm should be rising on the campus grounds and a student union building. Wesleyan continues to hire new faculty members as the enrollment swells – this year's freshman class broke records, more students than were enrolled in the entire college 15 years ago. On the outskirts of town $138,169 is being spent on office facilities for the National Guard and $49,906 for a maintenance shop. With the transfer of personnel from Pt. Pleasant at least 20 new families are expected to call "The Strawberry Capital" their home. Churches and schools have not been neglected. A beautiful new Catholic church is open to worshippers on East Main street, fulfilling a need in a two-county area. Academy school construction provided nine new classrooms for elementary students this fall, another indication that officials are looking ahead to an increased enrollment.

Central National Bank, with bank deposits at $6,760,000 and resource at $7,495,000 is so confident of a prosperous future that the officials have purchased valuable Main street property for a modern institution complete with drive-in banking facilities. The Knabenshue property on North Locust street, the Farnsworth property on Main street at $16,000 and the Harvey property at $30,000 will be razed to make room for the bank's "home". County road improvements totaled 76.9 miles in 1960 – greater in miles than all work in past years combined. Land has been leased by the county court for an additional 1,000 feet of runway – another progressive step – looking to the future of quick, efficient transportation for both industry and individuals.

At French Creek engineers have been busy the past few weeks laying off contour maps and planning landscaping for a $75,000 rustic-type lodge which will be built where the present concession building now stands. Already an additional $38,000 has been received for remodeling and improvements at the state-maintained park. At nearby Audra State Park $20,000 out of an appropriation of $27,600 has been expended for park and building improvement. If this progress report isn't convincing then I'm surely a cock-eyed optimist. But, just so we won't become so complacent or feel that we've accomplished enough, remember – we can do better. Miners are out of work, coal production is down slightly and 791 families are supported through county, state and federal funds.

In November of '60, the local DPA office distributed checks ranging from $5 to $60 to 791 families, 345 of whom are old-age pensioners. Every month around $43,736 of state and federal money is dispatched and 42,602 in county and state aid. This is in addition to medical assistance. So – we can do better. Reidbord Factory has 99 persons working right now – a decline from the 140 employment this summer. Rather than lay off even more, Reidbord employed many at less working hours, thus providing some monthly income rather than none at all. The Elkins plant is now working at capacity and new contracts are expected locally which will see employment stabilized. With the banks indicating an upward surge in business, I'd say it's been a very good year!

Civil War & Stonewall Jackson

January 27, 1961

With the commemoration of the one hundredth anniversary of the division of the nation during the 1860's, readers will probably live and relive the historic days of the Civil War through printed material released by newspapers, magazines and textbooks.

Because the study of history requires the separation of fact from legend, historians will rely heavily upon those relatives and friends who perhaps grew up hearing the stories of their fathers and grandfathers and from those stories find out that out of this great struggle emerged facts little known and unpublished. Two of the relatives who have grown up with the history of the war forever etched in their hearts are grandnieces of General Thomas J. "Stonewall" Jackson, Miss Grace Arnold and Mrs. Marie Jackson Arnold Pifer, of South Kanawha street.

Last Saturday marked the 137th birthday of General Jackson, native West Virginian and hero of the Confederate forces, who during the Shenandoah Valley campaign of 1862, marched his force of 16,000 men over 600 miles in 39 days, fighting five major battles and defeating four separate armies totaling 63,000.

Little known to Upshur countians is the fact that "Stonewall's" sister and brother are both buried here. Laura Jackson Arnold, grandmother of Miss Arnold and Mrs. Pifer, rests in Heavner cemetery, and Warren Jackson is buried in the Brake private cemetery two miles outside of Buckhannon on the Clarksburg road. Another sister died in infancy.

Laura, who died in 1911, differed with her brother, Thomas, on only one issue during her lifetime – sympathizing with the Union forces, but, she opened her home at Beverly as a hospital for soldiers of both the North and the South during the War Between the States.

For many, many years Laura's grave has been decorated each year along with that of the soldiers. One of two women honored by the Grand Army of the Republic at the close of the war, Laura was also honored with membership in the Virginia Militia. Mrs. Rutherford B. Hayes shared honors with Mrs. Arnold as a member of the GAR.

Warren, who died at the age of 20 of tuberculosis is 1841 while teaching school in the Hodgesville area, lies in an unmarked grave – the tombstone erected and paid for by General Jackson in 1856 has long since disappeared – having been crushed and used for mortar for a neighboring farmer's basement. The residents of the Hodgesville area apparently held the young man in high esteem for when Upshur county was redistricted the area was named Warren District in honor of the young schoolteacher.

It is my hope that throughout the next four years Upshur countians will aid me in the search for little known facts concerning local residents and their roles in the war that we may preserve for our children the finest traditions of our American heritage.

Civil War – 100th Anniversary

February 3, 1961

For good or evil the nation is observing the 100th anniversary of the War Between the States. I say, for good, if the commemoration preserves the finest traditions of our heritage – or evil, if old wounds are reopened or definite sectionalism rears its ugly head.

It is my purpose in publishing any material dealing with local events during those war years to record, if at all possible, the poignant and the chaotic feelings of the era. No war in history has gripped the imagination as has the Civil War nor are there more students of that period of history either by hobby or profession.

This week I read a letter written April 5th, 1862, from a southern sympathizer to his wife and children from a Union prison camp. My first instinct was also of sympathy – the Randolph county man was being held hostage, he was separated from family, he was worried about the health of his family and concerned with the spring crops.

On closer investigation it has developed that William Apperson, as a prisoner at Camp Chase, Ohio was enjoying life in a prison camp known for its luxury and lax restriction of prisoners. Camp Chase, in the heart of Columbus, Ohio, was established for southern Army enlisted men and officers and for the men who had merely spoken aloud of their sympathy for the southern cause. Here Rebel officers were allowed to live in hotels with their wives and families, if financially able. Passes were issued to those who just wished to spend a weekend with wives. Perhaps, the enlisted man did not fare well.

Claude Phillips, a retired carpenter, who now resides with his son and family, Mr. and Mrs. Ernest Phillips, on West Lincoln street, has the letter penned by his grandfather, William Apperson. The letter was found among papers belonging to Mr. Phillips' mother, Mary W. Phillips, who died in 1915. Apperson, a farmer of Kingsville, Randolph county, was one of those unfortunates who was taken from home and family for voicing southern sentiments.

The letter follows:

April 5th, 1862 Camp Chase Ohio

"Dear Wife, I now seat my selfp (sic) to wright (sic) a few lines to inform you that I am very well at present hoping these few lines may find you and the children enjoying the same blessing. I received…?..and was very thankful to you my friend, for your kindness but it would not do. At present I presume we are held as hostage. We are well treated.

"We have plenty of flower, corn meal, bacon and pickles and fresh beans, pork, coffee and tea and a nice stove to cook it in. So we have a race to see who can keep the nicest house and the best table. I have ten boarders and could have 40 more if I would.

"Dear wife, I am afraid that is not so with you. I spend a many our when I ought to be asleep thinking how can make out and how you have made out but trust to God and keep trying I think.

"There is some prospect for the better at present. Do not know how things may turn out even if I should be released in a few weeks. I cannot get home time to plant a crop so I am thinking about the year that is to come then the present. But be of good chere my dear the lord noes best all way, where there will there children. Give them my best love.

"Dear children as if I was with you now. Do think of me and do the very best you can to try and make something for another year. I love you Dearley but I can not help you now. I may be at home sooner then I suspect but no certainty. Things are uncertain in this troblesom world but try and prepair for the hereafter.

"If you wright me direct your letters to Camp Chase, Ohio. Fair well my dere."

To Elizabeth Apperson and children

William T. Apperson

William evidently returned to his normal farm life and raised a family for nine of his grandchildren at one time or another lived in this area. Still residing here are Claude and Dennis Phillips, Mrs. Jessie Rusmisell, Maude Phillips and Bertha Stalnaker. Deceased are Margaret, Cecil, Walter and Warwick Phillips.

Winter Is Wonderful

February 10, 1961

Who says winter isn't the most wonderful season of the year! I see no reason why mothers and housewives should complain. After all, what in the world would you do with all the time on your hands if it weren't for this wonderful white stuff?

Just think – no drying mittens and long underwear after the sleigh rides, no muddy, dripping boot tracks across the kitchen floor, no hunting for lost parkas and scarfs, no fixing of the broken steering apparatus on the Christmas sled.

And what right have the men to complain! I know they look forward to putting on and taking off chains, peering dismally into the snowstorms on hazardous roads, the back-breaking work of shoveling sidewalks and driveways and the dusting of store merchandise for lack of customers.

Snow can be such a wonderful excuse for skipping the club meeting, forgetting church, PTA meetings and that drive to Aunt Sarah's. It's so much more fun to be lazy in front of the fireplace, sipping hot chocolate and quarreling with the youngsters who have missed another day of school. Haven't you noticed that families show more of that "togetherness" these days – marooned in that tight little castle called home.

And, according to some clipping or other I read some time or other we have 300,000 years in which to look for colder weather gradually working toward another ice age. Then the Arctic will end up in the Antarctic or Alaska will rest in West Virginia, if we aren't submerged altogether, that is. Somehow or other my day hasn't been in the least brightened by the thought that I must look forward to winters "just like granddad's".

Right now affairs of the state and international affairs are far from my thoughts – I'm concerned with the immediate problem of snow-free sidewalks and an electric blanket on the blink.

Executives Can't Write

February 17, 1961

It has been proved to me in the past two weeks that top executives can't write. I've suspected much for many years believing that all correspondence, especially those answers to the lower caste of working people, like me, were nonchalantly scribbled by high paid secretaries.

Don't ever expect a prompt reply to any inquiry sent to a corporation department head despite the new metropolitan plan inaugurated by the post office – that of one day delivery. Evidently, a letter received by a corporation within a 24-hour period takes two weeks to wend its way to the proper desk. It was two weeks ago that I mailed a routine letter of little importance to a company but of major importance to me. A week later – no answer. I called the local district manager and enlisted his aid. The department head might be on vacation, etc., etc., etc. What were the secretaries doing in the meantime, I queried, "painting their toenails in addition to caring for their well-groomed cuticles on both left and right hand".

The district manager, who probably thinks I'm a smart-aleck kid right now, dutifully got off the hook by promising to make a memo of the matter and even went so far as to offer to call the department head himself. Fearing I might get the D.M. fired and in the federal bread lines sooner than he had calculated – I thanked him and wrote another letter to the department head. This letter touched a little on the side of sarcasm. It contained that touch of apology – "you're busy but would appreciate an answer from someone in the office"…surely they don't just close up shop – but evidently they do…

Then, just to let the D.M. know that we're on the ball in this office I informed him later in the week that there still had been no answer to the second letter. At this phone call he went a little off his rocker, laughing hysterically and slapping his knee at the same time. O boy, o boy, he used to work in that general office and it gave him a great deal of pleasure to ride those boys…he sure was enjoying my dilemma, I'll say that for him!

Yesterday, I finally got the order that had taken two weeks of letter writing and phone calls, but to my delight and disgust – no letter. I tell you – those executives can't write.

Executive Writes Reply

February 24, 1961

LARGE CORPORATION, INC.

Dere 'Lizabeth:

Yore colym of last week was looked at with intrist. Im now takin my pin in hand to thank you for all them kind wurds. You jist dont no how much there liked!

Now bleeve me, 'Lizabeth, we got reesons fer holdin off frum anserin letters. Iffen you wood tak a littel time fer the ritin of your letters so's you cood use littel bitty words it wooden tak us so durn long to figger out what you ar wantin.

An dont you think for a minit that yore letters aint important to we top executioners. Why we jist purely love to here frum you!! But great balls o' fire, 'Liz, ther aint no sich all-fired hurry. You kin surely wate til we kin figger out what you sed in your butiful letter.

I jist took anuther look at that their columm. I see wher you accuse me uf thinking you ar a "smart-aleck" kid. Now really, wher wood I ever git the idée that you ar a kid? Im sort uf hurt deep insid!

An I'll jist haf to tak you to task for talking about me goin off of my rocker. Now dont you get yore back in the air caus I aint goin to say it aint so. Im just gonna say that their aint a rocker aroun this here place. Never use em so how coud I.

Im sure glad you got that there order you were ritin about. I sure wood hait to hav you down on us cause we jist purely like to do busness with you fellers. Nex time you rite us a letter I shore hope them eity fellers anser you quik like. Iffen they dont you jist let yer old frend the district manager no about it.

yours friendly like

   X (his mark)

District manger

Coffee Breaks

March 17, 1961

I don't suppose there is another employee in town who takes more coffee breaks than I – although the coffee pot bubbles merrily most of the day right in this office.

But, this week my conscience went "zing" when I read an item concerning just how expensive time can be. For instance, if you have 10 employees and you are paying them an average of $1.25 per hour, five minutes wasted per day will cost you $531.20. With a much larger plant, with 500 employees, and the same time wasted, there'll be a whopping $26,560 down the drain in a year.

Suppose your wage rate is higher at $2.50 per hour. Those five minutes per day will cost you $1,062.60 with 10 employees, $5,313 with 50 and a fantastic $53,130 with 500 employees.

All these figures are based on an eight-hour day, five-day week, and 255 working days per year, overhead cost taken equal to hourly rate. They do not include Saturdays, Sundays and holidays.

But, like the boss said – you can't lose something you never had – like $531.20 a day because of coffee breaks around this office.

I'm A Giggler!

March 24, 1961

I'm a giggler! Well, anyway I giggle at the wrong times and usually all alone. It's embarrassing to my friends – they aren't mind readers and they can't understand why I giggle at such inopportune times. I giggle in the midst of solemn ceremonies like weddings and christenings, I giggle in the middle of speeches (especially political speeches) and I giggle reading the daily newspaper.

Now, for instance, just this week Mrs. Clark Gable gave birth to a son – a birth that had been long-awaited by the world for millions remember Gable as their favorite movie hero. There wasn't really anything unusual about Gable's looks – rather an ordinary guy – but who can forget those roles with Jean Harlow in the '30's? And what male didn't secretly envy Gable's latest role with the sexiest sexpot of the century, Marilyn Monroe.

Any darn fool man of 59 who insisted on roping horses and playing the role of a cowboy and all the while resisting the charms of Marilyn should have known he'd suffer a heart attack sometime during the shooting of this latest production. Sure enough, Clark Gable died and I, like millions of others mourned his death, remembered Carole Lombard and even Marilyn flipped a little and entered a private sanitarium for a brief respite.

So the world waited – Gable's wife, Kay Spreckels, was expecting his child and as the days moved along at a snail's pace, newspaper reporters and gossip columnist shadowed the house, wrote reams of copy and Las Vegas gamblers took odds on whether Pa's child would be a boy or girl. And, Kay brought forth a son.

And right here is where my giggles started – on this most solemn occasion, the world rejoicing, reporters dashing for telephones – and then the doctor (hero of the hour) made this most profound statement – the baby looks like the late Clark Gable. My God! Thought I – it can't be, you mean this child is destined to have ears like his father!

And so the world turns.

History Notes

April 21, 1961

Newspaper people are notorious for their cluttered desks and usually, though not always, we wade through the notes on the spindles and the desk drawers in one grand sweep of spring housecleaning.

This I attempted to do this week and came up with a few interesting notes that seemed worthy enough to pass on to those readers who may be interested in past history.

For instance, W. S. Crawford of Frenchton walked in here recently to re-subscribe to the Delta, bless him, and in the course of conversation mentioned that he is now the only living county veteran of the Spanish- American War of 1898. Benton C. Radabaugh, of the Kesling Mill road, who died this winter, was next to the last survivor from Upshur county.

Crawford told of volunteering at the age of 21 at Fort Monroe, Va. for a three-year enlistment serving with the coast artillery. He was one of the crew that set the gun that won marksmanship honors and still has a letter that can prove his statement.

Crawford's father, a Civil War veteran, was a little unhappy about his enlistment pointing out that more men would die from disease than bullets.

Then W. E. Smith, of South Florida street, walked in one day with a scrap of newspaper dated 1882 that he had found wadded up in a Civil War pistol holster. Sulphur-dipped matches were wrapped in the newspaper and stuck in an old belt that had held caps and balls. News items that were still readable included an announcement that S. L. Loudin had opened a new saddlery shop on Locust street. The hack service from Buckhannon to Weston and back was "right speedy" according to one item. The hack left daily every morning at 7 o'clock making connections with trains at Weston, arriving at Weston at 11 a.m. and leaving at 1 p.m. for the return trip to Buckhannon.

Then in the past week Mrs. Quay Koon brought in an old deed that has been in the family for some years and still in remarkable condition considering that it is dated December 4, 1866, and signed by Arthur Boreman, first governor of the state of West Virginia.

The deed shows that in consideration of two dollars paid by Daniel W. Simmons, he acquired 100 acres of land lying in the county of Randolph on the waters of Cascadies Fork, a branch of the Middle Fork river.

Remarkable, but not in such good condition, are 13 deeds now at the courthouse, rolled up in a 1935 calendar and fast deteriorating, dating from 1795 to 1864. It seems downright criminal to me that these rare documents have not been microfilmed or any effort made to preserve them. Most are legible but a few cannot be read. For instance, Thomas M. Randolph, governor of the Commonwealth of Virginia, conforming with a survey made 20th of September, 1798, granted to Henry Banks a certain tract of 600 acres in the county of Monongalia adjoining John Judy's settlement. The deed is dated July 2, 1822.

And to prove that farmers were great landholders in those days, compared to present day standards, John B. Floyd, then governor of Virginia, granted to James H. Logan and William S. Ward, a tract of 980 acres in Randolph county on the dividing ridge between Mill Creek, of the Middle Fork waters – this one dated June 2, 1851.

Barely legible is a deed dated 1795 in May to Robert P. Means and another deed, this one on heavy parchment paper, grants several Hickmans, 1,000 acres in Randolph county, dated April 18, 1789.

Another deed to Robert Means shows 500 acres in Harrison county on Stewart's Run, dated May 8th, 1795 and still another, dated April 18, 1789 – and remember Virginia had been a commonwealth for only 19 years at the time.

In 1854, so one deed shows, 2,640 acres in Randolph county on top of Rich Mountain, on waters of Currence Mill Creek, Middle Fork of Buckhannon waters, was granted to William L. Ward. And for those historically minded or readers of Civil War action – in less than 10 years that ground was bloody from one of the early conflicts between Yankee and Rebel forces. The extent of large holdings is shown in one lengthy chancery suit involving 30,000 acres in Mason county between Henry Middleton versus John B. Shreves, dated March 10, 1837.

As I said, it seems criminal to me that these valuable documents should be left to the ravages of time but other than framing them as wall decorations I don't know what the county court could do about it. These documents are court records and as such can not be moved from the courthouse but still, without some care they will fade away along with some memories of when this country was young and untamed.

City Image

May 26, 1961

The local merchant who neglects his advertising should not be surprised when potential customers look to outside firms which do provide essential shopping information.

The same holds true for cities that neglect courtesy and appearance – tourists and industry will look elsewhere for pleasure and surroundings.

Buckhannon is fortunate to have West Virginia Wesleyan College and to have acquired Corhart Refractories as its newest industry. With this thought in mind, the local Chamber of Commerce at last week's meeting called on townspeople to put on their "best front" when delegates to the West Virginia Methodist Conference begin arriving in town the first week of June. A pleasant smile and a neat appearance should do much toward keeping the conference here although there is always talk of moving the annual session to Charleston. No one in Buckhannon, least of all the merchants, care to see this happen.

But, as C. of C. officials have pointed out, we can't take the conference, or industry for granted. We must not assume that everyone loves our town and will rush pell-mell to the Strawberry Capitol of West Virginia for the sheer pleasure of visiting. Every Buckhannonite must welcome conference delegates, or for that matter, every stranger. Who knows, they may be representatives of potential industry.

To further the welcome of conference delegates, the C. of C. has ordered placards for individual store fronts, written a formal letter to Bishop Halloway extending an invitation to the 1962 conference, suggested courtesy cards for automobiles of visiting delegates and perhaps, best of all, have recommended a general cleanup of Buckhannon.

Let's join the business and professional men of Buckhannon in seeing that our visitors' stay is most pleasant and that they will be receptive to a return trip.

Introduction To Civil War Feature

June 16, 1961

Beginning the week in which we celebrate July Fourth, I will be starting a rather lengthy series of articles dealing with Upshur county's role in the Civil War.

It has been a winter of research and reading, tedious hours of deciphering old letters and debating conflicting reports. It has meant hours at home at the typewriter until late at night and the wee hours of the morning.

To students of the Civil War it will be, perhaps, a repeat of stories but to a generation that knows little of this county's history the story may be a revelation.

I do not claim to have read everything there was to be read on the subject – I do claim that I have read everything that was available in both the city and college library and in private libraries where reference books were loaned. I do claim that to the best of my knowledge what I have written is correct – as correct as 100 years will allow.

I have tried to record Upshur's conflicts in chronological order and must give credit to W. B. Cutright for his history of the county published in 1907 and to Major T. F. Lang, of Clarksburg, who in 1895 published a history that has been important to me as a guide. I relied heavily upon these early works.

For those who will doubt certain versions, I can only show them what I found already in print – to believe or dispute as they see fit.

But I am most grateful to those individuals, who like I, love history and who were so helpful in guiding me to sources of reference.

To French Morgan who has already made a study of one of the particular skirmishes in Buckhannon – bless him, he turned the complete material over to my care.

To Robert G. Smith, Jr. of French Creek, who allowed me to use his story verbatim on the 1863 raid on Centerville (Rock Cave).

To Mrs. Mabel Gilmore, who supplied me with coffee and cookies, as I copied priceless letters in her possession.

To Virginia Bly Hoover who steered me to various pamphlets published earlier on the history of French Creek and vicinity.

To Dr. George Glauner who tipped me off to a booklet published in 1879 by an Ohio citizen soldier who camped in Buckhannon.

To Fred Schroeder, editor of the Monongahela News, published for the Monongahela Power company, who loaned maps in relation to the Imboden raids of '62 and '63.

To Mrs. Marie Pifer, grandniece of Gen. Stonewall Jackson, who spent hours on the telephone encouraging me in my story.

To Matthew Edmiston, Jr., who loaned books inherited through his relationship with the Farnsworth family.

To C. A. Jones, of Columbus, Ohio, past president general of the Sons of the American Revolution, who 50 years later knew the month, year and in what column of the Buckhannon Delta and Knight Errant a story appeared for my use.

And to Mrs. Quay Koon, L.A Newcome and Croner Brown, all of whom related incidents pertinent to my story.

All in all, over 19 references were used for the series. I have found over 12 instances in which Buckhannon was occupied either by Rebel or Union forces and five instances when skirmishes were fought, counting among the 6,000 engagements, battles and skirmishes of the Civil War – over 300 of which were in what is now West Virginia.

West Virginia's Birthday

June 23, 1961

West Virginia this week celebrated its 98th birthday. There wasn't much fanfare – not even a picture of an oldster born on June 20. The banking institutions, city and state offices closed their doors for the day.

All in all, no one had much comment except one party who remarked that we should give the whole shebang back to Ole Virginny. This same idea came up in the state legislature two or three years back and Virginia didn't want us. Some constitutional lawyers argue to this day that legally West Virginia isn't a state. And, we probably would never have been granted statehood if it hadn't been for the Civil War and the resistance to the Ordinance of Secession.

But, be that as it may, we are a state and now, three years later, I just wonder if Virginia wouldn't like to have us back. Economically the state is a powerful sight better. Within the past two weeks an aircraft manufacturer has announced a plant site in Mercer county, Eastern Gas and Fuel Associates soon will start a multimillion dollar coal cleaning and preparation plant in Wyoming county, and the old ordinance plant in Kanawha county has been purchased. But, if West Virginians never landed an industrialist in the entire area we could still become the playground of America if, like Florida, we spent millions advertising our lakes, the mountains, the dams and the streams.

I had the opportunity Sunday to spend the day at the new Sutton Dam which will be formally dedicated sometime in July. There were several hundred people taking advantage of the boating, swimming and picnicking area but I wondered, too, how many thousand might be in attendance if the area had been highly publicized.

The picnic tables were adequate, the area clean, the roads nicely blacktopped and the dock area even paved for the convenience of the boat owner.

West Virginians should well be proud of this newest addition to the playground of the state.

The problem now is to get that dollar from tourists of surrounding states. The Poconos don't have a thing we can't match – except publicity and advertising.

Feeding The Boys

July 14, 1961

The government these days seems pretty well to take care of the aged, the insecure, the veterans, the lame and the halt and after buying groceries last week it occurred to me that with all the money being thrown around why couldn't the government subsidize the feeding of all teenage sons.

It doesn't show up on any X-rays but I have no doubt that every boy between the age of 12 and 18 has two hollow legs and a tapeworm. It is impossible to think that one stomach could hold the pop, the cake, the potatoes and gravy and the vegetable dish full of cereal consumed in the space of one and one-half hours.

I'm absent from home during the day so I have no way of accurately itemizing the food eaten between the hours of 8 a.m. and 5 p.m. but, I do know that not even the heart or the gizzard is left from a full grown frying chicken, not a pinch of potatoes for potato cakes the next day, a scrap of salad or a dab of vegetable from the dinner meal. I must hide a banana or two and a few pieces of fruit for a gelatin salad.

And, before I can get the dishes washed by 7 o'clock, Son No. 1 has had a ham sandwich, one orange, a dish of cereal and a washtub of popcorn before bedtime. A nice-sized cake lasts one dinner and lunch the next day, maybe. Kiss a pie goodbye in one meal. Son No. 2 has inquired what's for breakfast on his way upstairs to bed.

It has come to the place where I am embarrassed to attend covered-dish affairs, as my offspring are usually first in line and back for thirds before I've buttered my first dinner roll.

At cafeterias, Son No. 1 carries two plates – one for the meats and the other for the vegetables and salads.

Growing boys, yep, and hardly a doctor bill either, but if the government really wants to help us mothers who need help – either deduct food from my income tax or pass a few of those food stamps my way.

PRICES IN EFFECT APRIL 15, 16, 17, 1965   QUANTITY RIGHTS RESERVED

A MOST BLESSED AND HAPPY EASTER TO YOU AND YOURS.

SPECIALS for your EASTER FEAST

Your KEY to GOOD EATING — KEY MARKETS

KEY KWICKIE
"A GOOD TURN IS ONE THAT GETS THE BLANKETS BACK ON YOUR SIDE OF THE BED..."

SWIFT'S PREMIUM SMOKED HAMS — SHANK PORTION — LB. 39¢

Swift's Premium

SWIFT'S **Cubed Steak** BONELESS NO WASTE LB. 89¢

SWIFT'S **Standing Rib Roast** LB. 69¢

Item	Size	Price
Swift's Premium Smoked Ham	BUTT HALF LB.	49¢
Swift's Premium Smoked Ham	WHOLE 14 to 16 LB.	45¢
Swift's Premium Ham Slices	CENTER CUTS LB.	89¢
Swift's Premium Canned Ham	5-LB. CAN	$2.79
BROAD BREASTED TURKEYS	ALL SIZES LB.	35¢
GRADE A EGGS	Large White For Coloring	2 DOZ. 89¢ med. ... 2 doz. 75¢

DOLE **PINEAPPLE**	BELLVIEW **PICKLES**
CHUNK 2 NO. 2 CANS 75¢	Process Kosher Dill / Process Dill — MIX OR MATCH 3 QT. JARS $1.00
SLICED 2 NO. 2 CANS 79¢	LUSCO

PILLSBURY **CAKE MIXES** *WHITE *YELLOW *CHOCOLATE — 3 Boxes 79¢

MUSSELMAN **CHERRY PIE FILLER** — 4 No. 2 Cans $1.00

MUSSELMAN **APPLE SAUCE** — 8 303 $1.00

3 CANS $1.00	2 JARS 89¢

STOKELY **BEETS** *SLICED *CUT — MIX OR MATCH 4 303 Cans 49¢

KRAFT PHILADELPHIA **Cream Cheese** 3 8-OZ. PKGS. $1.00
OCEAN SPRAY **Cranberry Sauce** WHOLE/JELLIED 3 300 CANS 79¢
LITTLE DARLING **Sweet Potatoes** 3 NO. 3 CANS 89¢
PILLSBURY **Frostings** CREAMY VANILLA/CREAMY FUDGE 2 PKGS. 79¢
DEL MONTE **Fruit Cocktail** 3 303 CANS 69¢
KRAFT MACARONI & CHEESE **Dinner** 3 7¼-OZ. PKGS. 59¢

"DESSERT SPECIALS"
SPICE BAR **CAKE** WITH CARAMEL ICING REG. 49¢ SPECIAL 39¢
JELL-O GELATIN ALL FLAVORS 6 3-OZ. PKGS. 63¢
LUCKY WHIP TOPPING 2 7-OZ. PKGS. 89¢

Fairmont Dairy Fair **ICE MILK** Half Gallon 49¢

Miracle Margarine 2 1-LB. PKGS. 69¢
Toilet Tissue SOFTWAY 8 ROLLS $1.00
Facial Tissue SCOTTIES 4 BOXES $1.00
Musselman Vinegar QUART JAR 25¢
Cottage Cheese FAIRMONT FAMILY SIZE 59¢
Disinfectant Spray LYSOL 6-OZ. CAN 89¢
Hi-Ho Crackers SUNSHINE 16-OZ. PKG. 39¢

--- **FANCY FRESH PRODUCE** ---

GRAPES LB. 19¢
VALENCIA ORANGES 5 LB. Bag 39¢
GREEN ONIONS 2 Bunches 19¢
FROZEN STRAWBERRIES SLICED SUGAR ADDED 20 oz. PKG. 19¢

Also A Complete Line of Fresh Produce such as: New Cabbage, Carrots, Celery, New Potatoes, Bananas, Lettuce, Radishes, Lemons, Fresh Peas, Tomatoes, Grape Fruit, and Apples.

SHOP **HILL BILLIE** KEY MARKET — OWNED AND OPERATED BY YOUR FRIENDS AND NEIGHBORS — PLENTY of FREE PARKING — SUPER MARKET

FLUFFO Shortening 3-LB. CAN 79¢

DOLE **PINEAPPLE JUICE** or **PINEAPPLE GRAPEFRUIT DRINK** — Your Choice 2 46-oz. CANS 79¢

Man Will Conquer

July 21, 1961

I suppose since time began man has attempted to conquer the unconquerable. He looked at the horizon, wondered what was on the other side and walked until he had solved this mystery.

He came to a stream, followed it, coming eventually to a wide, deep river and slept nary a night until he had invented a boat that could carry him to the other side.

Then came the ocean, bigger and better boats, and finally man's greatest desire was to cross the ocean to see what was on the other side.

When the ocean was conquered, man desired eventually to travel underwater. He watched the birds fly and schemed and dreamed until he had attained even greater heights than the birds. If there was a mountain unclimbed, he schemed and dreamed until it too was conquered.

Now man reaches into space – to the moon and to other planets. I admire Astronauts Sheppard and Grissom, or should I say their courage.

But, even as the hair stands up on the back of my neck, and the lump comes to my throat and my stomach flip-flops, my only thought is, why, why, why? What is there in space that man believes he must go. Felipe probably stood on the shore of Spain and wondered why Columbus wanted to cross the ocean to the other side. Hiram on the east coast of America probably wondered why his neighbor wanted to risk certain death in the West. Stanley probably scoffed at Hillary's climb to conquer Mt. Everest.

But, then, thought I, it's like the river, the ocean, the mountain – a challenge, space must be conquered – simply because it is there.

So I sneer at something I don't understand. Why does man risk life and limb to settle on a planet where nothing grows, where even the air is unfit for use and where eventually my grandchildren will walk in fashionable space helmets and suits.

Simply because he can boast that man again has conquered the unconquerable.

Pearl Nutter and Civil Defense

July 28, 1961

Right about now I'd say Pearl Nutter is the woman of the hour! She and her co-workers this week ably proved their ability to meet a disaster and an emergency with the gathering and distribution of supplies for victims of the Kanawha flash flood.

Upshur county was the only county outside the immediate disaster area that promptly carried aid to the stricken. And, that I'd say, is a feather in the cap of the county Civil Defense unit.

Already a lesson has been learned too in this hour of state tragedy. Another room is being readied for the stockpiling of emergency supplies including first aid equipment at the State Road Commission headquarters which also houses the CD offices.

I'd say Pearl is way ahead of President Kennedy, no thanks to Buckhannon residents, Pearl and the county workers have borne the brunt of the workload when it comes to any interest in the work of the CD. In fact a good many have made light of this work or fussed at the cost to the city and county. Well, right now, Pearl and her workers can have a good long laugh.

The president Tuesday night very clearly demanded some sober responsibility from the citizenry of the United States, something new to us Americans – bombs just might begin to fall. Those of us who have learned little of the Civil Defense work just might possibly be the first to claw and fight our way to protection – protection established through the work of CD.

Kennedy is requesting of Congress new funds to identify and mark space in existing structures that could be used for fall-out shelters; to stock those shelters with food, water, first-aid kits, tools, sanitation facilities and minimum essentials for survival; to increase their capacity; to improve our air-raid warning and fall-out detection systems and to take other measures that will be effective at an early date to save millions of lives if needed.

All of us had better do a little more thinking on the subject of Civil Defense work and most of all, thank our lucky stars, that there are pearls like Pearl who have had the foresight to do some preliminary work in readying this nation for possible attack. This gem of a gal has my pledge from this moment on – you call me, I'll help – I want to see a long, long life.

Please Buy My Book #1

August 18, 1961

One of the mysteries in the life of a columnist (I'm using columnist in a broad sense in my case) is the fact that the 100 or so lines whipped out during the week in the course of five minutes time as a usual rule brings some sort of comment.

But, a column or series of columns that has meant months of time, research, sweat, blood and tears lays a big, round, fat egg – or so, it would seem to me at this stage.

To be explicit, this week you'll notice an ad, my ad, elsewhere in this issue, pleading for advance orders for a book dealing with Upshur county's role in the Civil War.

Let's be truthful about this whole thing – outside of six people and my family there's been little comment and I guess one could classify today's column as plain, downright begging – begging for comment (pro or con), begging for advance orders and begging for $2.50 for BFFCE – Betty's Fund for Children's Education!

The DELTA is hardly set up as a book publishing house and just this one time I'm asking a big, big favor – we must know whether to invest time and money and paper in this project – that's the reason for begging for comment or orders.

My story will continue to run for at least 20 more weeks. I believe in its truthfulness and its record as a written history of Upshur county. I'm also disappointed from the apparent lack of interest in this series – so, if you're reading it, if you think it will be interesting to your children or grandchildren, won't you let me know?

"The Girls" – After 20 Years

August 25, 1961

Summer is the season of reunions, the reacquaintances with old friends, the visits with classmates home on their annual trek to scenes of childhood and perhaps happier memories.

"Never look back" one is told, but twice this summer I've been subjected to all-girl parties and why we call ourselves girls is beyond me.

Pity the poor guest of honor – she's scrutinized the most severely for a sign of age – more gray hair than her friends, that added weight or the extra lines in the face.

There's a sense of embarrassment when the "girls" meet. Each scanning the other's face for some sign that even yet we look as we did 20 years ago. We lie – all have changed but no one has the grit to say it aloud. We laugh, we talk, we reminisce, there are lulls when somehow the conversation has switched to local events that the guest of honor cannot fathom. The old school papers are unearthed from the foot of the closet, the yearbooks opened, the photographs – we giggle – time has stood still we all tell ourselves.

And finally at a very late hour, the party breaks up. The "girls" leave one by one, a little ill from too much smoking, sleepless from over-coffeed, a digestive upset from too much food – now the "girls" realize their age. Late hours are gone for us. "Does she, doesn't she – we know! All are ten pounds heavier and most, like Panama Hattie, at this age cannot stand another sun wrinkle. We have sons and daughters taller than we, less disciplined we are certain and problems we feel that the still older generation has never faced.

Ah, yes, only the brave look back!

The Salesman

September 8, 1961

Tucked away among the debris in the middle drawer of my desk, I found a tribute to The Salesman. Don't ask me where the clipping came from, but as the daughter of a traveling salesman, thought there would be wives among our readers who would enjoy the definition of her better-half. Besides, I'm a salesman, too.

Nobody ever says a kind word about the salesman, except maybe another salesman. But can you think of another single segment of our work force more vital to the national economy? People stop selling, people stop buying. Simple as that.

We've heard the remark. "Aw, anyone can sell." But the speaker is talking about an order-taker, not a fellow who artfully demonstrates an unwanted product, creates a consuming need. He's a fellow who deals in ideas, not things, and he probably knows more about basic psychology than most of the deep-domes in plush offices.

You see him every day in plush hotel lobbies, in good restaurants, at innumerable airports and railroad stations, you might take him for a bank official or a young professor, except there's an engaging friendliness about him, you know what he is by his well-cut suit and well-worn briefcase, his armor and shield in the modern crusade of selling.

He's a guy who pounds the pavement, hits the road, beats the bushes, snares the orders with a smile and an order-blank. He's the advance patrol in the battle of marketing. He and his female counterpart suffer the slings and arrows of irritated customers numerable times daily with remarkable restraint.

He's a veritable fountainhead of facts and figures and data and design who sits strangely silent when a buyer wants to talk. He's uncommonly patient and polite and persistent, money is his motivation, but the best ones are instilled with a burning desire to help, to serve, to sell.

He'll follow a lead to the end of the earth if he really believes there's a need for his line, he modestly tells the manufacturer that the product "sells itself", but secretly believes that without him the company would fold overnight, he loves his work and is fiercely proud of it, but dreams of the day when he can settle down and get to know his wife and kids again.

He's a guy who's an expert at figuring job estimates and expense accounts, but can't seem to keep his family budget straight.

He's a salesman, a guy who is worldly but warmly human, easy going, but always alert, tactful but tenacious manners, tired feet and a fresh outlook.

He may be a vendor, a drummer, a peddler, a pusher, a conniver, a promoter, a pest depending on how you look at it, but he's been with us for a long, long time, since people first started wanting things. And ever will be.

Cleanup Campaign

September 15, 1961

I've said it before and I'll say it again, I don't care what your politics are, I still like the idea behind the current state cleanup campaign. Most of all, I hope the promotion of West Virginia doesn't end with the exit of the present administration.

Governor Barron and members of his official party toured Upshur county Wednesday and they liked what they saw.

But, as the governor said during brief remarks at the luncheon, the best can be better and by 1963, when West Virginia celebrates its Centennial, he intends that this state be spick and span, the cleanest state in the entire Union.

His question to county residents is "How much are you willing to do yourself?" Just give Barron or federal officials a plan, a plan of what must be done or could be done in Upshur. They have the money, the means, the labor to provide, if the county court will set up a planning commission and submit a format.

So, some of you will say, we don't like federal aid, we don't believe in federal aid, we don't want federal aid, okay, but nevertheless federal aid is here. You're paying for it with those tax dollars and why pay for projects to go into some other county when this county has the potential to attract tourists through development of its historic sites and recreational areas.

All it takes is a little initiative. Members of the Upshur County Historical Society have started the ball rolling, now, it's up to you the residents of Upshur county to petition the court for a planning commission, and within a very few months, we may have a program of development, the like of which has yet to be seen in West Virginia. I hope so!!

Career Diplomat

October 6, 1961

Fifteen years and three months ago my eldest son was born. Approximately two hours later on that June day, a daughter of college friends was ushered into the world resulting in us mothers sharing a semi-private hospital room which leaned more toward an atmosphere of college dorm life than a maternity ward.

In 14 years our paths had not crossed until about a month ago when I was surprised with a visit from mother, father and daughter. In those intervening years we found that we certainly lived in separate worlds. The mother, a native of Costa Rica, and the father, from West Virginia, had long ago entered the diplomatic service of the United States, residing for the past six years in Sao Paulo, Brazil.

The daughter, two hours older than my son, attended school populated with students of 25 nationalities. She speaks five languages, her mother's native Spanish, and Portuguese, French, Italian and, of course, English.

But, nevertheless, we found much in common and have been visiting quite frequently prior to their departure soon for one of the many trouble spots in this limping world, the Dominican Republic. Much of my misconception concerning life in South America and the Latin American attitude toward America has been a little cleared through long talks with this consulate, his wife and daughter.

But as in every profession, there is amusement even in the hectic life of a career diplomat. Multiply misunderstanding in the social life of Ambassadors and staff and one, perhaps, can better understand the grievous misunderstandings among nations.

For instance, these friends must be prepared at any hour of the day or night to receive diplomatic visitors, adjusting to their habits and prepared for any eventuality, however unusual.

Imagine their consternation, entertaining 150 at dinner, honoring a guest from Thailand, when their guest of honor began eating, petal by petal, the orchids, which had been tastefully placed at each individual table setting.

Not to be outdone, my friends also began eating the orchid petals and at the same time rang for the majordomo, whispering in his ear, to find out if the diet of orchid petals would be poisonous. At the close of the meal every guest had risen to the occasion – eating the orchid decorations.

And, still another time, they were summoned from their beds at 7:30 a.m. to welcome Kentucky and Tennessee representatives to find them drinking their favorite brand of bourbon. This call was far beyond duty to imbibe before breakfast.

But these instances are really only minor inconveniences as far as I'm concerned compared to the killing of five tarantulas in one day and the purchase of numerous electric irons, simply because the servants did not know how to operate electrical appliances.

But perhaps most interesting to West Virginians is the fact that of all 48 state flowers flown to Brazil for cultivation only the rhododendron brought personally by former Gov. Cecil Underwood flourishes at Sao Paulo, a source of pride, of course, to this native hillbilly and his foreign born wife.

And, to prove that one learns by doing, the couple told of wiring $15 worth of flowers to her mother in Costa Rica as a tribute to the Americanized Mother's Day, only to receive a frantic letter to cease and desist – flowers were overflowing the house. Upon investigation of the rate of exchange it was learned that for $15 they could have bought the entire flower shop. For days, bouquets had been arriving – the florist had stripped his entire stock and ordered more when matters were finally brought to a halt.

Ah, yes, we live in separate worlds and what an interesting world!

Sunday at Home

October 27, 1961

It seems just yesterday that the picnic table and the lawn chairs were washed and repainted and placed on the patio, the garage cleaned out, debris tossed away, the garden plowed and seeded and the flower beds a-bloom.

Here it is fall housecleaning time, the picnic table and the lawn chairs to be placed back in the now unclean garage, more debris to be tossed away, the garden to be cleaned and raked and the flower stalks to be cut back for another season. This season I find myself more disinclined to do any of the above named programs. In fact I'm trying to promote the art of doing nothing, a complete day-off at least once every two weeks and hopefully once a week. It would seem that when one has two teenage sons, one could sit back in the comfortable easy chair with a bull-whip occasionally and disperse orders, such as, rake those leaves, carry those chairs, scrub that porch.

But I have a surprise for those mothers of small sons who look forward to the day when they will be of some help around the house. Forget it!

By the time they are able to be of some help they have a program of their own. If they participate in football or basketball just figure on doing some extra maid service, warmed over meals, (they won't get home until dark), extra washing of ball uniforms, an even bigger meal, extra dose of vitamin pills, cool nerves for all the ups and downs depending on the win or loss of a game in addition to the one night out a week (on Saturday), a hayride or two, car wash at the church, Scouts, 4-H, Brownies, birthday parties, excursions and hikes, meeting, dates and telephone answering service. (Don't figure on any personal calls, the phone is invariably tied up by one of the three in my family.)

Sunday afternoon all was quiet in my house. The eldest was watching a pro game on TV at granddad's, the second was in Philippi with a church group and the youngest was at the skating rink. Hot dog, thought I, to heck with the ironing, to heck with the flower beds! I'll throw some potatoes and carrots and onion on top of the roast, stretch out on the couch and watch that pro game in peace.

Alas, before the half time ceremonies I had long before fallen asleep to be awakened by the telephone. Not for me, of course, I took the message. Back on the couch, once again to be lulled to dreamland by the voice of the announcer, only to be awakened by the phone. A repeat performance. Back on the couch, dozing, again, the telephone.

The front door banged, once, twice, three times, the mob is home, they're hungry. "When do we eat," open and shut the refrigerator door, raise the lid on the saucepan, open the oven door, bang, bang, bang, has long ago replaced the sound of the pitty-patty of baby feet.

But, I still have an ace in my hand, I'm going to forget to give them their vitamins and double my dose, then maybe I'll have strength enough to lift that bull-whip and the garden will be raked, the flowers cut, and the porches scrubbed.

Main Street

November 10, 1961

Buckhannon's Main Street is having its face lifted. The shift in store locations, the building and tearing down of store sites is keeping the sidewalk superintendents well occupied, somewhat curious and a little nostalgic.

One of the major attractions these days is the destruction of the old Heavner Tavern House which will make room for the erection of a modern bank building housing Central National Bank personnel.

The destruction of the 100-year old hotel meant the shifting of three businesses. Mrs. Florence Johnson, proprietor of Sexton's Gift Shop, occupied the building on the corner of Main and South Florida and went so far as to change the name of her attractive new home to "Florence's Gift Shop". It wasn't long before the sound of hammering was heard as Perry "Pug" Lewis moved his jewelry business just next door where the Firestone store was once located. But the peal of those hammers was crowded out as Kenneth Phillips and Allen Hamner started construction of a whole new building to house the Style Shop at the corner of Spring and Main streets.

When everyone was moved it gave the "relocation itch" to some other concerns, Bob Tetrick decided he was getting too old perhaps to climb the steps in the Central Bank building so he moved bag and baggage into the storeroom once occupied by Bill Whiffen's shoe shop next door to the Colonial Theater, adding another attractive store front to Main street. But, Earl Young really started it all when he and his son, Dick, moved their office location from over Koon's Restaurant to the ground floor next door to Shannon's Hardware.

Another major relocation for a local business will culminate by next spring but we've had definite instructions not to give the secret away. We can say this much, the former location of Palace Furniture store is being remodeled inside and out and will soon brighten up the street across from the courthouse. And, not to be outdone, Smitty is even adding a new chair to his barber shop next door.

It seems when the snowball starts rolling there's just no stopping it.

Howard Hiner Collection

On down West Main street, C. A. and C. B. recently opened a new service department in a new building at Curry Chevrolet company, that added 5,000 square feet of working space. The body and painting shop for customers was moved from the used car lot on South Kanawha street to the rear of the showroom on West Main street.

Probably the entire "new look" started when C. Fred Iden, over a year ago, opened Central West Virginia's most modern furniture center on Spring street. The wide use of glass and modern lighting more than beautifies the Appliance Furniture Mart in its transfer of location from the Weston road.

Even the gentlemen of the town have pleasant surroundings during an hour or two of relaxation. Virgil Rinard had been doing business now for several weeks in his new location across the street from where he operated the Old Town Tavern for so many, many years.

Ed Baxa is adding a two-level unit to his motel court on North Kanawha street, an indication that tourists and guests are prevalent to Buckhannon.

On North Locust street, Quay Koon has purchased two homes from Mrs. J. C. McCoy and the demolition of one home is now in progress to make way for another new business enterprise.

In other words, residents of long ago just may not recognize this fair city on their trips home.

As I said before, nothing though is arousing more interest than the destruction of the old Heavner Tavern House. That old building saw history made. The lot was purchased by Elias Heavner in 1861 from Daniel Carper, Andrew Poundstone and David S. Pinnell and the hotel was furnished in time to house the officers of both the Rebel and Northern armies that occupied Buckhannon during the Civil War.

The Tavern House was sold in 1875 to Mrs. Jacob Reger who changed the name to Heavner House. Then in 1879 N. M. Ferrell bought the property and renamed it Valley Hotel, Adams Hotel and Parsons Hotel and finally housed business establishments.

Progress, ain't it wonderful!!

Football Season's Over

November 17, 1961

Football season is over! I don't know about the team but the parents are glad. I for one, am exhausted. I've felt every tackle, every disappointment, every loss.

But the best thing about the end of the season is that the family is intact and still on speaking terms. Now that statement may sound a little strange, but it's true. At the beginning of the season I was beginning to doubt that granddad and grandmother would be speaking or that my younguns' would even love me come November. Granddad likes to coach from the bleachers and I do mean coach. I'm sure every fan in the stadium had heard his familiar "O my goodness" when anything went wrong.

It embarrasses grandmother. She'd shush granddad and threaten to never sit next to him again.

At the Weston game early in the season grandmother even threatened to move to the other end of the field. About that time my son completed one of those quick passes over the middle and I raised up out of my seat with a great, big "Wow-e" and my little Ann, seated next to me, said, "Well, mother! Everyone is looking at you."

Not thinking, I turned and told her she could go sit with her grandmother at the other end of the field. That did it! Eight-year-old Ann refused thereafter to even go to a game. She couldn't talk, she couldn't interrupt and she always ended up getting a scolding, in fact, her whole evenings were just one big flop, so she much preferred the movies on Friday night. In fact, I figure she has felt much like an orphan these past 10 weeks.

But I will miss these post-mortems at home after the game on Friday night. Granddad would sit and grumble about this and that, and why they didn't do this and that, and how everything would have worked out right if they would have just done this and that. So, old Dave would walk in the door and we'd play the whole game over again,, this way and that.

Course, maybe granddad has a right to coach. He was reminiscing enroute to Shinnston last Friday night about the time he played in the rain on the Shinnston field down near the river and an apple tree stood on the 10-yard line. We met Newt Anderson on our way through the gate and he swears it was fact, one guard closed his eyes and ran 'til he hit something, the apple tree and was out for two hours! Those were the good old days they talk about. I suppose.

I will say this for granddad. He believes in the written record. Not just any written record either. We have an old family Bible at home published in 1895 with a section in the back for births, deaths, marriages, etc. and on the miscellaneous page is the following, written in a schoolboy' scrawl:

Glenn Dutton made 7 field goals for J. H. School in 1921.

Glenn Dutton made 6 field goals and two fouls for J. H. School in 1921.

It goes on and on like this through 1922. Now that's what I call a written record and maybe it gives him the right to coach.

You lookin' forward to next year, Dad?

Welfare Letters

November 22, 1961

We've had a barrel of laughs around the office these past few days, all because of a certain George Lawless in Charleston who wrote a gem of a daily column for the Gazette.

The Delta Staff has unanimously voted George's column of last Friday the "Best of Year". With hope that our readers will get the same 'belly yaks' as we did, here goes:

A great gap in communications presents one of today's dangers to society. People don't always say what they mean.

In written communications, complex sentence structure often times causes misinterpretation. It can lead to embarrassing, even dangerous, results.

Here are a few examples of what we mean. They are excerpts from actual letters received by a Department of Public Assistance office in one of our southern counties:

"I am forwarding my marriage certificate and six children. I had a seventh, but one died which was baptized on a half sheet of paper…"

"I am writing to the welfare department to say that my baby was born two years ago. When do I get my money?"

"Mrs. (Jones) has not had any clothes for a year and has been visited by the clergy."

"I cannot get sick pay, I have six children, can you tell me why?"

"I am glad to report that my husband who was reported missing is dead."

"This is my eight child. What are we going to do about it?"

"Please find out for certain if my husband is dead, as the man I am now living with can't eat or do anything until he finds out."

"I am very much annoyed to find that you have branded my boy as illegitimate, as it is a dam lie. I was married to his father a week before he was born."

"In answer to your letter, I have given birth to a boy weighing 10 lbs. I hope this is satisfactory."

"I am forwarding my marriage certificate and my three children, one of which is a mistake as you can see."

"Unless I get my husband's money pretty soon, I will be forced to lead an immoral life."

"My husband got laid off from work two weeks ago and I haven't had any relief since."

"In accordance with your instructions, I have given birth to twins, in the enclosed envelope,"

"You have changed my little boy to a girl. Will this make any difference?"

"I have no children as yet as my husband is a bus driver and worked day and night."

"I want money as quick as possible. I have been in bed with a doctor for two week, and he hasn't done any good. If things don't improve, I will have to send for another doctor…"

Births and Deaths

December 1, 1961

In this world of automation, surveys, statistical inquiries, etc., it's interesting to note that no matter how small a pebble on the beach, no matter how much or how little one has contributed to society or no matter how good or how bad one's existence on earth, the rich and the poor all end up as a numerical statistic on a plain white sheet of paper for preservation. I suppose, for other statisticians 100, 200 or even 1,000 years hence.

At least this all came to mind this week while thumbing through a vital statistics booklet distributed through the public health service of West Virginia. For what it is worth Upshur countians are no different than the rest of the country, less of us dying, all are living to an older age and we're having more babies. In West Virginia 39,696 live births were recorded and only 18,040 deaths.

The causes of death in the state and in the county are the same Big Three tabulated throughout the United States, heart disease, cancer and vascular lesions affecting the central nervous system. The only deviation is the fact that suicide is now the eighth leading cause of death in West Virginia while it is not represented in the top 10 causes in the nation.

And the fact still remains that the most unsafe place is home where in 1960 there were 230 fatal accidents. It's just a wee bit safer to work in a coal mine or quarry where 111 deaths occurred last year.

Upshur county recorded 367 births, 362 by physicians in hospitals but five spankin' new infants were delivered by midwives. Four stillbirths were tabulated.

Total deaths from all causes stood at 240, deaths under one year of age 10 deaths, and those under one month, 5.

For those readers who lean toward figures and statistical data, Upshur county recorded 34 deaths by cancer, 3 by diabetes mellitus, 21 by vascular lesions affecting the central nervous system, 111 through diseases of the heart, 7 by pneumonia and infection, 3 by cirrhosis of the liver, 3 congenital malformations, 13 premature birth and three deaths by suicide.

How To Raise Delinquents

December 8, 1961

Now that it's getting to look a little like Christmas, it brings to mind that the Buckhannon Jaycees are due their annual pat on the back for their work with county youth.

Plans have been moving for sometime toward their third annual shopping trip for underprivileged children, a time when the young grasp some greenbacks in their hand and learn the pleasure of giving to someone they love.

But sort of a year-round gift to the young people of Buckhannon is the Youth Center. (I can detect some mutterings in the background from the oldsters as soon as that sentence is digested.) The fact remains that whether you approve or disapprove of the youth center, young people are going to congregate some place, somewhere, and it might as well be at a chaperoned, non-alcoholic, non-cigarette-smoking establishment. Otherwise, will you as parents know exactly in what direction of the four winds your offspring have sprung?

Saddest of all though is the fact that very, very few of the participating parents have bothered to enter the doors of the center to judge or criticize the good or evil. And it must also be pointed out here that the burden of the chaperoning has fallen on a handful of the Jaycees themselves, although the local chapter as a whole received statewide recognition last year for their effort in supporting a youth program.

I was amazed to learn also this week from one of the chaperoning Jaycee members that in the rare cases where there is petty thievery (like the acquisition of ping-pong balls), or smoking or an attempt at just plain roughhousing that a telephone call is always made to the culprit's parents. But in many instances the parents refuse to take the matter seriously or laugh it all off as "sowing some wild oats".

Because I have teenagers, and because none of us is infallible and for the edification of those who call it "sowing some wild oats", the following is a sermon that just might lift a few eyebrows.

HOW TO RAISE DELINQUENTS:

(The following "Twelve Rules for Raising Delinquent Children" were issued by the Houston, Texas Police Department.)

1. Begin with infancy to give the child everything he wants. In this way he will grow up to believe the world owes him a living.

2. When he picks up bad words, laugh at him. This will make him think he's cute. It will also encourage him to pick up "cuter" phrases that will blow off the top of your head later.

3. Never give him any spiritual training. Wait until he is 21 and then let him decide for himself.

4. Avoid the use of the word "wrong". It may develop a guilt complex. This will condition him to believe later, when he is arrested for stealing a car, that society is against him and he is being persecuted.

5. Pick up everything he leaves lying around, books, shoes and clothing. Do everything for him, so that he will become experienced in throwing all responsibility on others.

6. Let him read any printed matter he can get his hands on. Be sure silverware and drinking glasses are carefully sterilized, but let your child's mind feast on garbage.

7. Quarrel frequently in the presence of your children. It will keep them from being too shocked when the home breaks up.

8. Give the child all the spending money he wants. Never let him earn his own. Why should he have things as tough as you had them?

9. Satisfy his every craving for food, drink and comfort. See that every sensual desire is gratified. Denial may lead to harmful frustration.

10. Take his part against neighbors, teachers and policemen. They are all prejudiced against your child.

11. When he gets into real trouble, apologize for yourself by saying "I never could do anything with him".

12. Prepare for a lifetime of grief. You'll probably have it.

So says Philip B. Gillam, juvenile court judge of Denver, Colo.:

"Always we hear the plaintive cry of the teenager: what can we do? Where can we go? The answer is: go home!!

"Hang the storm windows, paint the woodwork, rake the leaves, mow the lawn, shovel the walk, wash the car, learn to cook, scrub some floors, repair the sink, build a boat, get a job. Help the minister or priest or rabbi, the Red Cross, the Salvation Army; visit the sick; assist the poor, study your lessons. And when you are through, and not tired, read a book.

"Your parents do not owe you entertainment. Your city or village does not owe you recreational facilities. The world does not owe you a living. You owe the world something. You owe it your time and energy and your talents so that no one will be at war, in poverty, or sick, or lonely again.

"In plain, simple words: grow up! Quit being a cry-baby. Get out of your dream world and develop a backbone, not a wishbone, and start acting like a man or lady.

"You're supposed to be mature enough to accept some of the responsibilities your parents have carried for years. They have nursed, protected, helped, appealed, begged, excused, tolerated, and denied themselves needed comforts so that you could have every benefit. You have no right to expect them to bow to every whim and fancy…

"In Heaven's name, GROW UP AND GO HOME!"

Bowling

December 15, 1961

Limpin' Liz has had it! I mean these new fads are OK for the younger generation --but me, the un-athletic type, I've got to have some tune-up exercises before I do any more bowling.

Let's face it -- the closest I've come to exercise in the last 10 years is stretching to the clothes line and back down to the basket. Course I do have a mean right arm, one that can reach from the couch to the pretzels on the coffee table.

To explain what's happened, I bowled one night this week. The truth is I rolled one ball. With that one ball, I thought someone had turned out the lights. I pulled a muscle in my right leg. Well, I didn't exactly pull a muscle, I tore it. Actually I didn't exactly tear it either, I think I ripped it and left some jagged edges, something like the torn edges one would get when he catches his big toe in the bedsheet.

That halted my bowling career for the next four or five weeks. I won't have sense to quit. Anyway, while I'm crouched in the corner doing calisthenics and trying to work out the "charlie horse", here's the golden opportunity to observe the sport from the posterior angle.

There's more to bowling you know than picking up a ball and throwing it down the alley. You've first got to find a ball that will release your thumb -- that usually takes 20 minutes at the rack. Then there are the shoes and I will say this, those shoes are the most comfortable I've had on my feet in many a year. Rather then call my evening of sport a complete loss, I got my fifteen cents worth of wear. But even more than the comfortable shoes, one must have the proper attire. This week I saw women with curve, no curves and too much curve in thigh slacks, loose slacks and baggy in the seat slacks. Remember, I can talk because I wasn't bowling --and watching all this from a good angle.

Now we come to the delivery of the ball, this can be jet-propelled or the powder-puff type. Also there's the push and groan ball, the player groans while the ball rolls all the way down the gutter. Or the spread eagle type, deliver the ball and flap your arms like an eagle. One can also roll and kick -- the kick gives that extra "oomph" or one can flick the wrist and twist the hips. The little "pinkie" on the right hand may also be left dangling but it really doesn't add a thing to the velocity of the ball.

Keep in mind, too, that one can balance on his left foot, right foot or on the right hand or left hand or one's nose just so you don't pass that foul line.

That's the story of my night of bowling except for one minor detail. I went home and never wanted to lie down so badly in my entire life. That too, was easier said than done. Just one minor inconvenience kept me from "hitting the sack" ten minutes sooner. I couldn't step out of my slacks. Well, you just try it sometime -- your right leg hurts so you can't stand on it to lift the left leg or vice versa. Just about the time I thought I would have to wake up one of the kids, I maneuvered my toes and the slacks sort of fell to the floor.

For those who are planning on taking up any new sport, I have just one word of advice -- beware the new dance craze -- The Twist! I hear it's every bit as dangerous.

Just What Me Wanted

December 29, 1961

Here again is that time when one looks forward to the new year and promises of this and that. The resolutions are well-meant if only for a day or until the shine has become dulled on the new toy known as 1962.

But somehow it seems this, too, is a time for retrospect, to look back on 1961, to learn from one's mistakes and to appreciate the small things in life that make up our everyday experience. Perhaps we are so overwhelmed by the big things, fear of atomic warfare, bomb shelters, the Berlin Wall, the Congo situation, space flights, politics and Cuba, that we have become quite blasé with ordinary, common, day-by-day affairs.

My smallest nephew Bart Short said it rather aptly Christmas morning as he unwrapped gift after gift with this comment "Just what me wanted, just what me wanted".

Of course we want peace and security but the little things count too, like healthy sons and daughters. "Me just wanted" a roof over my head and food on the table, a warm coat, a comfortable home and some good books, a clean bed and a soft pillow, many friends and no enemies, a secure job and a dollar or two. These I've had along with lots of laughter, a few arguments and some tears.

So, for my readers, for my family and for myself, it's these simple things I wish - happiness and health in the days to come.

Merchant Sales Up

January 12, 1962

Santa was unusually good to Buckhannon merchants this year. In fact, Santa was good to Buckhannon all last year it would seem.

From all I can gather, business was tremendous for most of the local stores this past holiday season. Furniture sales were good, jewelry sales were up, toy sales boomed and clothing merchants and department stores report the best business in history of their operations.

County-wise in the past year, a gain of 3.6 percent was noted in the volume of business. Local retail merchants showed progress totaling sales of $14,891,000 compared to the previous $14,368,000.

The 3.6 percent gain compares favorably with the rest of the nation which noted a 1.4 percent gain. In the South Atlantic states there was a 1.9 percent increase.

Reports indicate that county residents had a net spendable income of $33,393,000 in the year, after deducting for personal taxes. It was $32,404,000 in the previous year. On the average there was $6,509 in disposable income per local household compared to $5,589 in the state.

So it would seem that business indicators are moving upward in Upshur county and in most parts of the nation and the consumer is beginning to spend more freely.

As I've pointed out previously in this column, Main Street has taken on a new look with remodeling and redecorating – once again, indicating confidence in the economy of Buckhannon and its future.

Innocence of Childhood

January 19, 1962

It has often been said that if one cares to know the truth just ask a child. Ah, yes, the innocence of childhood – is it innocence really or sometimes the inner workings of the devil himself!

One of my friends, a new mother this week, arrived home with an infant son in arms. Her 11-month-old daughter took one look and said "Git!".

Another friend and her 3-year-old son were in a local drugstore recently when the fellow said "You want a cigarette?" Mother, "No, I don't want a cigarette". "You want a cigar?" "No, I don't want a cigar". "Bet, daddy would like a cigar!" "O, I don't think he does" the mother said, whereupon the little fellow blurted, "Guess you're just too damn tight!".

David, told to take his nap, vigorously protested with this statement "Me no want to go to sleep. Me too damn ornery to go to sleep." Tsk! Tsk! I don't know what they're teaching in the local institutions, but one young man we know quite well is showing extreme confidence in his own ability – just about as egotistical as one can get. He bet 35 cents he would make one hundred percent on an exam, did just that and collected.

But, in one class a student teacher asked his pupils to write a 250-word dissertation on the why or why not for like or dislike of his teaching method, what the pupils expected of him and vice versa. This same enterprising pupil wrote 250 words, "I hate Mr. Smith, I hate Mr. Smith, I hate…et cetera, et cetera."

These incidences though are only rarities, I hope in the life of a child. There is wonderment too. Mrs. Grace Stewart tells this story on her next door neighbor little Colleen Murray, who when told of the bird's bath in the backyard asked "Do you think the birds would mind if I watch them take a bath?"

My own Ann has a way of mixing up her words. In fact, for a time I was beginning to worry about her hearing for she spent 15 evenings talking about a big bloop in the sky before I found out she meant a blimp. We all about choked up on dinner one evening with Ann, who likes the crunchy crust of chicken and fish, asked her brother for his "covers" – the fish skins he had neatly stowed away on the edge of his plate.

But, if I live to be a hundred I'll never forget last winter when I waltzed merrily into a bath to be greeted with a picture of a nude figure, taken no doubt from Playboy magazine, taped to the mirror and scribbled beneath in lipstick "Our Dear Mom".

John Scott

January 26, 1962

Former DELTA Sports Editor Johnnie Scott has not forsaken the Fourth Estate but is training for the job of sports editor with the Armored Sentinel, the post newspaper at Fort Hood, Texas, a weekly publication boasting a circulation of 18,000. John, grandson of John B. Scott, of Smithfield street, recently finished U.S. Army Information School at Fort Slocum, N.Y. and in addition to sports, last week in Texas found himself covering a change-of-command ceremony, a memorial service for five soldiers killed in a recent tank-truck collision and a luncheon for a major general.

But anywhere in this United States it seems it's not uncommon to meet with someone who can reminisce about football and the feats of Wesleyan's Clifford "Gip" Battles. One such individual, interviewed by Johnnie, is Lieutenant Colonel Harry Babcock, assistant commandant of Fort Slocum, who played for the New York Giants of the National Football League as a lineman in the early "30's". He stands six feet, three inches and weighs over 250 pounds. The affable Army colonel recalls playing against Battles when the "Gipper" was in the backfield of George Preston Marshall's Washington Redskins along with "Slingin" Sammy Baugh, the duke of professional quarterbacks. Those were the days when the Redskins were battling with the Chicago Bears for the championship. Colonel Babcock recalls that Battles was a "hard hitting" back and that it was "no easy task" to bring him down. He calls Battles one of the best in the league.

Battles, of course, was one of the many Bobcat heroes of the early years. He starred with Little Wesleyan and then rose to great heights in the NFL, playing on a championship Redskin team. The "Gipper" was named to the National Football Hall of Fame a few years back. One of Colonel Babcock's teammates on the Giant team was another Wesleyan great, "Feets" Barnum, who earned the name not only for the size of his feet, but the talents of his "puppies". Barnum was one of the great kicking specialists in college and pro football of that era. With the recent resurgence of Wesleyan's football team into a state championship, it seems that many old-timers are reliving nostalgic moments of days long past when small college teams reigned supreme as giants of football. Such a man is Colonel Babcock, one of the giants of the era.

Free Groceries

February 9, 1962

Recently a stock exchange member expressed concern over the fact that to a constantly increasing degree, people are being led to believe that "a strong central government can provide them a maximum standard of living with a minimum of personal sacrifice and effort". A refreshing and surprising note in President Kennedy's special welfare message to Congress was his call to "find ways of returning far more of our dependent people to independence….of returning them to a participating and productive role in the community…"

To this end the president is asking legislation to permit states to conduct (with federal aid) work and training projects for unemployed on relief. But, may I ask that Congress take a hard look at these proposals for further spending. The pilot project in the government's depressed area retraining program in Cabell and Wayne counties of West Virginia has proved sad. Ten percent of the unemployed of that area asked to be put on the retraining payroll. The other 90 percent explained to interviewers that they were not interested or expected to be called back to their regular jobs or were too old to learn new tricks! Along this same line, a Life magazine editorial has discussed what it terms the "ultimate absurdity of the billions we spend on farm surpluses". Commenting on the results of Grocery Day (the government's current plan to distribute to reduce these farm surpluses), Life magazine reported: "For the 1,401 U. S. Counties now receiving free groceries, the $116.2 million cost in 1961's first half is nearly quadruple the $29.2 million in the same period a year ago. It has also vastly increased the popularity of free groceries.

Since January the number of people getting free groceries has risen from 4.1 to 6.2 million, even as unemployment was sharply dropping. Because each state determines its own standard of eligibility, and these vary even from county to county, recipients have included a New York City man who carried his bags away in a taxicab and some folks in Jefferson county, Texas, who took their groceries away in an air-conditioned Cadillac."

Life concluded its editorial with the following admonition to tax payers: "Groceries Day bears out the sapience of that wise man of old who when asked to compress all his wisdom into a single word, cried "TANSTAFL". When asked to explain the mystic word, the wise old man said, "There Ain't No Such Thing As Free Lunch".

Bottle Caps For Education

February 16, 1962

Dr. Clark Sleeth, dean of West Virginia University's Medical Center, has a particular love for the soft drink – not because it is nourishing or even good for one's health, he doesn't even recommend that you drink the "pop" – all he asks of West Virginians is that they buy a bottle and remove the cap. For the multi-million dollar Medical Center has been created from pennies – pennies from every bottle of soft drink sold in the state. Son of a Methodist minister who attended West Virginia Wesleyan college, Dr. Sleeth spoke last Thursday night to a combined audience of Rotarians, Kiwanians, Jaycees and Lions at the 95th West Virginia University Day Dinner where he outlined the state college's history of educational needs in medicine. He didn't even have to apologize to Dr. Stanley Martin for speaking out for the university in a Methodist college town for as both educators admitted, the schools definitely are not competing for students – their problem is to find means in which to educate all the students who are clamoring for a place in college life.

It is interesting to note that in the University's 95th year, and a student enrollment of 7,500, personnel is planning for the accommodation of 10,000 students in the next five years and by 1965, Wesleyan's 75th anniversary, five new buildings are expected to be completed with a projected 10 year program calling for more than 100 acres of Wesleyan campus and a financial goal of 22 million dollars. Does this sound like the West Virginia that Rapul Tunley so flagrantly belittled in his well-known Saturday Evening Post article of not so many months past? Dr. Sleeth in his address to Buckhannonites traced the history of medicine from the 15th century to the present day and in particular outlined medical history in West Virginia when the Virginia Legislature of 1837 first granted a charter to Wheeling University which included the granting of MD degrees. No students were ever enrolled, no degrees were granted and no funds were made available but at least someone was thinking of a proper place for the education of respectable physicians. Fifty years ago, in 1912, a School of Medicine was established at WVU. But, the first MD degrees will be granted in the spring of 1962 – again marking 50 years and this time from the state's William Canterbury, editor of the Wesleyan Pharos and Mr. and Mrs. Willard Phillips, of Elkins. Telegrams were received from former Governor and Mrs. Cecil H. Underwood Cooper Benedict, a candidate for Congress and John W. Cremeans, vice president of the Young Republican League of West Virginia.

Youth Center / Forbisider

February 23, 1962

We hear that the Youth Center may be closed up by April 1 unless some financial and moral help is fast coming.

According to a spokesman from the Buckhannon Jaycees, the organization is short of funds as memberships have dropped from the usual 250 members to around 55 or 60 kids. In other words there isn't money to buy a ping pong ball or a new cue stick let alone dance records.

The Jaycees opened the Center in 1959 and just last year received a state award for this outstanding project. It seems that there is enough manpower to chaperone the center but apparently there is a lack of interest on the part of the parents, lack of members and too much competition on the nights the center is open - Tuesday, Friday and Saturday nights.

Somewhere this week I read where Robert and Ethel are in the Far East. Ted is touring Israel and Egypt, Jackie has her bags packed for India…Jack is back from Palm Beach. That leaves Caroline…where's Caroline…Has anyone seen Caroline?

A Charleston columnist has been having lots of fun with Herb Welch's classified ad on the forbisider. Remember, "MUST SELL" brand new forbisider with built in Hemingway. Can be used left or right handed. Cost over $200. Need money so badly will sell for $25. Call 801. Well, Lawless in the Gazette ran the ad and last week got a response from a Sutton reader with an explanation of the true origin of the much discussed word "forbisider".

Several years ago, in a small town in Canada, a baby girl was crying lustily with colic pains. The nurse walked into the living room and called, "Mr. Dionne, if you would only come and take this one for a stroll in her carriage, I think I can manage the others."

Later, as he strolled his little daughter along the street, a woman stopped, peeped into the carriage, and said, "What a lovely little girls – have you got any others?"

To which the proud papa answered, "Forbisider".

Now if you aren't confused enough, here's a problem. A carpenter owed a tailor $40 for a suit of clothes. As the bill had been unpaid for some time the tailor asked the carpenter to do some cabinet work to clear the account, which the carpenter did.

When the work was completed, the tailor said, "How much do I owe you for your job?"

The carpenter replied, "Here's a $50 bill give me $35 in change and we'll be even."

How much did the carpenter charge for his cabinet work?

Have you figured it out? Okay, here's the answer. The answer is $25. When the carpenter gave the tailor $50, the paid the $40 debt and had $10 in change. Therefore, $25 over the $10 was the charge for the work.

Ken Phillips – Strawberries

March 2, 1962

I was most impressed Saturday by certain remarks made by Kenny Phillips at the annual Goodwill Dinner held for the Strawberry growers and leading up to Buckhannon's yearly event – the Strawberry Festival, June 1 and 2.

Acting as toastmaster, Phillips made the statement that there is an unlimited market for strawberries. If one mulls that statement for a moment it doesn't seem such a powerful one. But, then, when one thinks a little about it where in this whole wide country of ours, is there another product that hasn't saturated the market and where consequently, there must be heavy competition?

In other words, if state farmers cultivate, grow and harvest strawberries they can see every basket put on the market today. I would think that would be Farmer's Paradise. Wouldn't our local businessmen love to have a product to see, where the demand and need is greater than they can fulfill.

A businessman operates on two premises – hard work and profit by volume. A good businessman cannot expect a product to sell itself but Upshur county has such a product – the kingly strawberry. It has been King in Upshur county for the past 21 years and advertised through the annual festival, exhibit and auction, but this berry has yet to saturate the market.

It is my feeling that the time has now come to capitalize on King Strawberry. The farmer knows it takes more than the normal amount of hard labor to raise berries, but the good businessman also knows that it takes overtime and hard work to realize a profit in his store.

Now is the time for every individual Upshur country resident, every businessman, every salesman who travels the length and breadth of this state, to talk strawberry. Don't misunderstand me – I think local businessmen have done a tremendous job in promoting the berry crop – this was indicated last Saturday by the largest representation of growers ever in the history of a Goodwill Dinner.

Now is the time to push for more production, the establishment of a frozen processing plant, the marketing, the promotion and maximum effort to make Buckhannon really the Strawberry Capital of the United States instead of an idle boast.

Wouldn't this be following the line that both administrations in the past few years have advocated – to help oneself. We certainly don't want to be known as a pauper county. Can't we as proud farmers bend to the will of a new king, King Strawberry, to replace the aging, limping, King Coal, King Timber or King Corn or Oats.

It has already been done in one section of this state. Moorefield, after finding itself going downhill, promoted and raised chickens and turkeys by the thousands. County farmers tied in with just one chain store for the sale of poultry and processing has grown to tie in with many store outlets all because of the Poultry Festival.

Call me a cockeyed optimistic and idealist, but King Strawberry can rule the roost!

Little Mother Ann

March 9, 1962

She is a study in contrast. She's happier in one of her brother's sweat shirts and a pair of clamdiggers than in crinolines. But, she loves Barbie, Shirley, Nancy, Betsy, Queenie (all dolls) and to scrub, sweep, mop, dust and rearrange furniture in the playhouse.

She can climb a tree higher and faster and hang by her heels longer than any kid in the neighborhood but she insists on a frilly nightgown and hair in curlers every night.

She tolerates showers but hates baths, has holes in her socks, runs in her leotards, buttons off her coat and soles off her shoes but insists that a pearly necklace must be worn with sweaters.

She talks all of the time, when she isn't reading or fighting, and uses the best head-lock in the entire third grade class to subdue her victims.

"Little Mother" will scold her brothers but cries if they reciprocate. She'll track across the new carpet with muddy shoes but makes up her bed in fine fashion and is a terror at dishwashing.

She worries about her weight and talks about her diet but at the same time shovels in the starches – strictly, a meat and potato gal, is she.

She has four close friends with whom she spends hours on the telephone. The conversation usually runs from the color of the sweater for school next day to what's for cold lunch and if it's peanut butter sandwiches, what kind of jelly!

She dawdles, doodles and dangles the minutes away when it comes to bedtime and exasperates me beyond description, but for a nine year old she can be the most womanly, babyish, overbearing, cooperative, unreasonable, strong-minded, generous, selfish, lovable child I know – that's my Ann.

Grade School Basketball

March 16, 1962

Well, well! After viewing last Thursday night's final of the elementary school basketball tournament I'd say this is a sensible program without sensible parents.

The schools, teachers, officials, and particularly, the young college men who serve as coaches for the six participating teams are to be commended for the time and effort that goes into this first class athletic program for approximately 125 boys of the fifth and sixth grades. But, I can't say the same for the aunts, uncles, granddads, moms or pops.

Where do we get the idea that our 11 or 12 year olds must play like Jerry West or Hot-Rod Hundley? Last Thursday's final games reminded me of Roman gladiators being fed to the lions!

When the final whistle blew I had seen some pretty remarkable ball-handling out of these boys. I had seen some teamwork, too, and I say some tears, laughs, frayed nerves and tagged out boys. But, suddenly the games had turned into more than a grade school contest – the junior high gym was Madison Square Garden and the players were all pros! Mom and Dad had made this so!

It's certainly expected that the cheering sections with their colorful cheerleaders would lift the rafters but it's inexcusable that the parents would swarm onto the floor like so many locusts and berate the officials, the coaches and even take a swing at one of the players. Incidentally, the officials, Larry West and 'Coke' Gould, accredited officials, had given three nights of their time for free, not to speak of the hours and hours given by the program director, Richard Young.

Now that the third annual elementary tournament is over, let's all do a little searching of the soul and see that we don't over-emphasize this game of basketball. Better yet, how about allowing the fathers of the players to play in the finals! Sure, everyone loves a winner, me most of all! You can recently accuse me of jumping from my seat many times and letting loose with an Indian war-cry, but God forbid I ever blame the loss of a game on the coach or the official or worse yet, the poor individual player.

Let's be sensible. As far as my duty is concerned, my only responsibility is to provide food and insist on proper rest. From there on out, my responsibility ends – the school and coaches don't need my services as another sideline coach.

I realize these boys must be taught fight and spirit and deserve to win, but they also must learn sportsmanship, courtesy and teamwork, and in my own mind I have no doubt that this was done as far as the "college boy" coaches were concerned. My hat is off to those coaches, Bob Reger, Charles Emery, Dave Brown, the Rev. Mr. Sam Starling, Jack Wilfong, Gene Rall, Slats Laramore, and Bill Wood. I just hope they'll forgive the parents for undoing a semester's work.

The Coming Centennial

March 30, 1962

Carl R. Sullivan, executive director of the West Virginia Centennial Commission, spoke Wednesday night before a group of interested persons concerning the upcoming state observance and, believing you me, the year of 1963 will be much more than just a birthday party.

Much will depend upon individual counties to observe and plan for a gigantic centennial program, but much help will come from the state according to all the plans Sullivan outlined at the local meeting.

It is the hope of state officials that 1963 will mark the growth and progress of West Virginia. We must note increased pride in our mountainous state, talk about its traditions, heritage, increased industrial and commercial development, natural resources – in other words, sell ourselves to attract capital and most of all, change the national image that Americans have concerning hillbillies and dirty coal camps.

Sullivan estimated Wednesday night that $300,000,000 is spent by tourists within this state each year or $3 million an hour – during 1963 it is expected that this money will increase at least three-fold. State residents are being asked to invest just 50 cents each to promote the 1963 Centennial financially and to insure that Americans everywhere know that West Virginians have a progressive attitude toward the future.

Among some of the programs and plans displayed by Sullivan is a historical spectacular show which will appear in several towns within the state. Built on gigantic plans, the show must appear in adequate space such as a football stadium. Dealing with the birth of this state, elaborate costuming, staging and lighting will highlight the show.

A special exhibits train will definitely be in Buckhannon during the Strawberry Festival and the eight cars will designate industrial participation, federal and state government, labor, history, arts and crafts.

A theater in the round will be made available to groups to stage their own shows, this aimed at maximum participation by state residents.

Of course, there will be a queen, selected from 55 princesses representing the 55 counties of the state. An Ambassador of goodwill, the Centennial Queen will appear on network television and radio and make countless personal appearances.

Seven or eight major parades are planned during the year each one with a separate theme, space, agriculture, natural resources, tourism, military, youth, pioneer, etc. here again achieving maximum participation.

Dr. Kermit Cook of West Virginia University is chairman of a committee to select 50 native West Virginians, 50 non-residents as Honorary Mountaineers, chosen for their outstanding service to the state.

Prizes totaling $1,963 will be offered in the field of art, best in sculpture, best in painting, best in writing of a folk opera.

A commemorative stamp will be issued by the post office on June 20, 1963 and the U. S. Mint will strike a medallion.

The world's largest display of iris, 650 species, is already planned by the Iris Society – a tremendous undertaking for flower lovers.

Clarksburg will host the world championship. Babe Ruth League games and Huntington will host the Miss Universe contest.

So you see, state committees have been hard at work for the past three years. More than 5,000 persons are now planning the observance. But, the true test of the effectiveness of the Centennial will be the participation on the county level.

Sullivan suggested Wednesday night that Upshur county chairman, Hill Stump, start immediately to select his county historian, county tourist chairman, county program chairman, plan a temporary or permanent museum, stress Centennial exhibits by individual merchants, select a county headquarters to operate as a focal point of activity, plan county homecomings such as our annual French Creek Pioneers, plan Centennial Sings such as our annual Upshur County Sing. There are just a few of the many ideas.

In other words, this 100 year observance is a once-in-a-lifetime, one-in-a-100-year event and if we pass up this opportunity to point with pride to West Virginia's possibilities, to attract industry and capital, then the chance will never come again!

The Birth of WV Wesleyan

April 6, 1962

In the first half of the 19th century a Methodist school was operating in Clarksburg. In 1880 the Methodist Conference began shopping around for a new location for a Methodist institution: in 1883 the conference board recommended that a committee choose a site and in 1884 the trustees selected Buckhannon calling attention to the fact that the town was centrally located. Inhabited by 4,000 intelligent and moral individuals and no saloons had ever been allowed.

So it was that with the purchase of 43 acres of land at a cost of $5,551.87, the construction of an administration building and woman's hall, West Virginia Wesleyan college came into being.

Tuition for the first term was the magnanimous sum of $12 with an added cost of one dollar for laboratory fees.

These facts were called to the attention of Buckhannon residents last Friday night when Dr. Stanley Martin explained hopes, goals and purposes for a current $22 million financial development program during the school's 75th Diamond Jubilee.

Coining a phrase used by the late Dr. A. A. Schoolcraft, the competent, cultured, Christian Institution expects an enrollment of 1250 next fall with a faculty of 72. By 1963, a faculty of 90 is expected with the enrollment stabilized at the 1250 figure with emphasis on quality, student and personnel-wise, and distribution in education, religion, art, music, drama, science, etc.

Wesleyan with a $2 million endowment should have an endowment of $12 million or one million for every 100 students, falling far short of the usual plans for like institutions.

The school's budget at the present time stands at $1,800,000 and by 1963 is expected to reach $2 million, realizing an income of 72 percent from tuition. 13 percent special gifts and grants and the balance from endowments and auxiliary enterprises.

As one can see, the building program beginning in 1890 has grown beyond, perhaps, everyone's expectations even though for a period of 30 years there was no new construction. But, in 1950, things began to happen at Wesleyan. Fleming Hall was built, the new library, the fine arts building, McCuskey Hall, housing 150 mean, Jenkins Hall, housing 150 girls, Doney Hall for men, an extension to Fleming Hall has been completed. The student center nears completion and a new residence for women will start this spring.

This summer, work will start to grade a new athletic field and soon, there is hope for a new gymnasium, Alumni Hall and the No. 1 priority, a science hall including an observatory. The ultimate goal of college officials is a campus enclosing the bend from Meade street to the river, from College avenue to the river.

As one can see this all takes money. Faculty members, personnel and students have pledged their support. Now is the time for Upshur County residents to show their appreciation to an industry that has never asked help of us before. In fact, the college has been more than liberal in extending the use of its facilities for civic, social and religious projects. There has never been any conflict between "town and gown" as Dr. Martin proudly pointed out Friday night.

H. H. Thompson, local druggist, and general campaign chairman for the county, also stressed the benefits witnessed by Upshur countians when he pointed to the sports participation and use of the college field for high school games, the numerous plays and speakers available for the enlightenment and enrichment of local culture, and the visits for the past two summers of the Wheeling Symphony orchestra in open air concerts.

These are just a few of the many benefits realized by local people. I haven't touched on the economic aspects provided through the establishment and growth of the institution. The fact that this, an industry, and we must call it our greatest industry with an employment of 171, touches on the well-being of every resident is gratitude enough.

So now, with a county and city campaign underway, with the hope that it will be completed by Easter, Buckhannon needs to demonstrate its solidarity behind the school. We want school officials to say "See what the hometown has done", when they approach groups throughout the state and nation in the next few years.

Spring Cleaning

April 13, 1962

If I seem to be walking at a slower pace this week, with less than my usual vim and vigor, it's because it's spring. It isn't that I haven't been looking forward to spring – no more muddy boots, no more cooped up, bored children, no more high gas bills – but it's housecleaning time.

Now any working mother knows that spring means weekends of down-on-the-knees, stretch-and-bend, grunt-and-groan manual labor. Without any time off to sleep I can figure on 24 hours of work time, including Sunday, if the sun shines. Well, this past weekend the sun didn't shine and the weatherman predicts the sun won't shine this weekend and I'll wager the sun won't shine any weekend this month, because I had my house cleaning all mapped for completion by the end of April.

I should know better! A working mother never plans ahead especially if she's raising three children and a female dog – not when it comes to spring cleaning.

This past weekend was a case in point and a typical upsetting schedule. First off, I figure the kids would stay out of my hair with television to entertain them while I finished off the downstairs bedroom. I was wrong – the picture tube blew its top on Friday. The sun didn't shine so there wasn't any point of washing bedding, drapes, etc.

Secondly, there wasn't any point in washing any time Saturday afternoon, while tossing in the third load of laundry in the automatic, the washer decided it'd had it and stripped its gears!

Thirdly, I decided there was still a few hours of daylight left and never wasting a single minute, started cleaning kitchen cabinets – all the time looking forward to this weekend when I can wash down the kitchen walls – I mean, I think I can wash down kitchen walls. (Fate no doubt, will have something in store to upset the schedule.) But, ho-ho-ho and ha-ha-ha, while industriously scouring and scrubbing cabinets what do I find but evidence that a mouse or maybe mice have invaded the warmth of my kitchen! Undaunted, Son No. 1 is sent for DeCon and I begin waging war.

Fourthly, all at once it dawns on me that there is a suspicious number of callers for pet, female dog. That's right – we don't discuss the birds and bees around my house, no sir-ree, we jump right to the basic facts. (I forgot to mention that granddad was there for dinner and he thinks this latest crisis is funny and I sent him home with the admonition that if he can explain things better to the eight year old, then do it.)

Come bedtime, I lay my weary body on the clean bed when sniff, sniff – that's a peculiar odor! Peculiar, alright, the odor of a dead mouse or mice, wafting from the basement or under the house or in the furnace pipes. That DeCon works fast! At this point, I'm too tired to care, drag my weary body upstairs and pile in with Ann – maybe it will all be better in the morning. It was!

Self Image

April 20, 1962

I've been more than a little amused this past week at comments tossed my way in regard to the new picture that accompanies this so-called column. You have no idea the amount of teasing I've taken in the past three years concerning the cut that we in the newspaper trade call a thumbnail.

In three years this makes the fourth picture – none of which has ever pleased anyone but me. I just didn't worry about what I looked like, regarding the entire picture-taking situation as hopeless. And more hopeless, when one local photographer informed me it was impossible to get my big nose and big, loud mouth in thumbnail size!

To my friends, they see me as a career woman, escaping household drudgery, constantly ringing telephone, door-to-door salesmen, and children's quarrels. I meet such interesting people, they say, I know all the inside gossip that can't be printed. 'Tain't so, say I. The household drudgery, the ringing telephone, the salesmen and the children's quarrels are still there when I get home. And I'm far from a career woman – for, at the end of nine or ten-hour day, the makeup is smeared, the hair uncombed, there are runners in my hose and mud on the feet.

To my children, I'm that woman who bursts through the front door, unkempt and disheveled with a voice like a fishwife that demands clothes be picked up, toys be put away and breakfast dishes washed in preparation for a haphazard, hurried evening meal.

To my parent, I suppose I'm still a child, much to learn, inadequate patience, a haphazard housekeeper, part-time cook, laundress and chauffeur.

To my boss and co-workers, I'm a necessary evil at least necessary until something better comes along. I'm demanding in that everything must go my way, I'm selfish in that no one becomes harried or tired but me, a whiz one day and a dolt the next, amiable one day, a tyrant the next, cooperative one day and critical the next.

To myself, well, I'm none of these things – you really wouldn't expect me to admit it if I were!

I Am West Virginia

April 27, 1962

I have long been disgusted with the cry-baby attitude of many native West Virginians, long been dismayed by the Tunley-like and Murray-like articles describing the misery and woe of West Virginians and still more concerned because so few "hillbillies" refuse to acknowledge a situation and then do something about it.

So you can imagine I was quite delighted Tuesday night to hear a public relations man from one of the state's largest corporations stand on his own two feet and with courage deliver a thought-provoking masterpiece that promoted a deeper appreciation of being a citizen of West Virginia – a subject near and dear to my heart.

George E. O'Connor, of Charleston, PR man for C & P Telephone company, addressed members and guests of Buckhannon BPW at the annual employee-employer dinner and ended his program with the following essay written by Ted Ferrell, editor of the C & P company publication, and worthy enough to have been reprinted this past January in the Employment and Industrial Review.

I am West Virginia. I was born nearly 100 years ago when the fierce pride of my people counseled them to defend the freedom of all men. Since that time freedom and individual initiative have been the badge of my people.

I am proud of my people: From my rugged mountains and my fertile valleys they learned to be independent in thought and action. They learned to be proud of me, their homeland, and they looked up to my hills and received strength when they were troubled. They grew wise to my ways and coped with the life I offered them.

Over the years they have learned some of my secrets, and they have used my many natural resources to start an empire. They have tapped my strength to find coal, oil, natural gas, salt, fine glass sands, and other resources with which to build industry. They have relied on my soil, my timber, my rivers, and my other wilderness assets for many years.

I have neither starved them nor pampered them. When they treated me with respect and cared for me, I yielded my bounty to them. But, I have made them earn what they received, and they have been stronger people. They have absorbed the spirit of the West from my name, and they accept life with a challenge. In the early days my mountains formed a barrier and isolated my people from the rest of the country. At first progress came slowly to my land, and my people learned little from the outside world.

Then, my rivers were improved and railroads and highways were built over my stubborn soil. Great quantities of my wealth began to flow out of West Virginia. Coal became a king industry and some of my natives joined immigrant workers to remove it from this hiding place. My long established lumbering industry boomed, and much of my walnut, oak, maple, poplar, and other hardwoods were shipped away to be made into homes, ships, and fine furniture.

West Virginia glass became familiar in fine homes across the nation and in the market places of the world. My high quality sands had made the grade. Based on my salt deposits, a new chemical industry was born, and one found a haven along my Ohio and Kanawha rivers. My people prospered, and as my raw materials were shipped away my people bought automobiles, appliances, clothing, and many other products to make living easier and more enjoyable in West Virginia. They were happy, and I was happy for them.

Some say that I have been exploited, that outsiders have taken my wealth and that my people haven't enjoyed full benefits. They are partly right; some of my wealth has been exploited. In places it has been stripped bare, and West Virginians are left with the poor remains.

But, my wealth hasn't really been tapped yet and my barren lands can be restored. My people have learned new skills and new ways to conserve my wealth. They still have their birthright, and I depend on them for the future of my mountain empire. Machines began coming to my mountains at the very beginning.

After the end of W. W. II, a new word, automation, began to scare some of my people, and they began to fear that the machines would drive them from my land. This has happened in some of my industries and many of my people have been dismayed.

But the change was good; for my people have rallied. They have learned or are learning that they can no longer rely on strong backs alone – they have learned that they must learn new skills for their hands and minds. In the future they will make the machines their servants, and as they become wiser I will again pour out my bounty to them.

Yes, I am West Virginia. I'll soon be 100 years old. Their first 100 years have carried me through a revolution from mountain wilderness to the brink of an industrial empire. My progress hasn't been easy, but my people have been strong.

Now I am approaching the golden years, when I may become a jewel among the 50 states of this great country. The sounds of the future are already stirring. West Virginia, industrial empire. West Virginia, mountain vacation wonderland. West Virginia, a proud state, filled with proud, self-sufficient people. West Virginia, a model for troubled states that want to solve their problems.

Perhaps I sound boastful and overly optimistic, but my people don't think so. They know that the great majority of my resources are untapped. They know that the potential of my undeveloped assets is almost unlimited. And finally, they love my ruggedness and the challenge I offer them. They are my salvation.

Letter From Mary Harman Carl

May 4, 1962

One of the nice things about this job is the fine people one meets. The new friends one learns to know and the interesting and, oftentimes, amusing letters that one receives.

But, it is also a little terrifying to know that a column such as this one is read enough to have a little influence on the thinking of its readers – good or evil – or at least, becomes at times a conversation piece. This week I received a letter from a B-U graduate of 1940. Mary Harman Carl, who enclosed a clipping of a column from Baltimore Sun. The column also used a picture of its writer, Eleanor Arnett Nash, sister of the famous Ogden Nash, and at the head of the column Mary had penciled "your photo is much better than this one" – referring of course, to a column of mine several weeks ago in which I made light of the trials and tribulations concerning my posing for a new picture. Mary's letter was so interesting and so flattering concerning this so-called column that I'm printing it here:

"Dear Betty Hornbeck (or the Eleanor Arnett Nash of Buckhannon)

Some weeks ago you wrote about your daughter, Ann. I was fascinated! I'm a former Buckhannon girl, I have a daughter, Ann, age 12. She does all those mixed up things too. You put me in an envious mood.

When I was in high school in Buckhannon I used to dream of being a writer. I didn't pursue my dreams too far but became satisfied with a career of homemaking. It is fun, but then I thought, Betty is a housewife and mother, has her writing too. Isn't she lucky! This week you compensated by writing of the problems of a career woman and housewife. Now I'm down to earth again. Incidentally, even though I don't write too well, I can bake a good cake or pie. Wish you could join me for a cup of coffee and some hometown gossip."

Well, Mary, I don't know you but you certainly sound like someone I'd like to know! And, I wager that your cake or pie goes down a lot easier sometimes than this column. Which proves we all have a niche to fill someplace, somehow, somewhere in this complicated world of ours!

W. W. Wimer Roadside Stop

May 18, 1962

It gives one a warm feeling to know that some people don't consider the government the "given-ment" but show some initiative in providing a service that most times is left to the state or nation. Wonderful people – the W. W. Wimers of Rock Cave – are providing a service that has too long been overlooked and which deserves credit. On their bus highway near junction of Routes 4 and 20 they maintain picnic and recreational grounds for the passing tourists; the community in general and the county at large. A project that was started a few short years ago, instigated by an idea from members of the Happy Hustlers 4-H Club, continues to grow and grow with each passing season. The Wimers own and operate a grocery store, but in the meantime have built 10 picnic tables and placed them in three areas, provided playground equipment for children such as a slide, swings and merry-go-round and installed a horseshoe pit along with a croquet court. It would be impossible to tally the monetary value, but several hundreds of dollars have been spent on this "Operation Bootstrap". Just this past fall, Mr. Wimer even built a storage shed which in the summer is used as a refuge against sudden showers. Along with the ordinary accessories provided, the Wimers have also piped water from a well and lighted certain areas for additional convenience. A job in itself is the maintenance of the grounds, the mowing, the trash collection and plain litter. Mrs. Wimer has commented that as a general rule the public is more than careful with litter especially when it finds the grounds clean in the first place. Two prominent signs direct the passing motorist to the area behind the store but the grounds can be easily seen from the busy highway.

Hundreds of tourists use the area, the most prominent perhaps was Stuart Symington's visit last year – he's a senator from Missouri. In fact, Symington was so impressed he wrote his appreciation of the facilities in a letter to the Wimers. Clubs and organizations are welcome to use the area although Mrs. Wimer does suggest that someone telephone just in case the grounds are packed. Credit, too, should be given Wimer's son and daughter. Miss Imagene is an Upshur county schoolteacher and the son, Jim, who was instrumental in starting the project, now lives in Bridgeport where he is an accountant for National Carbide. Jim is serving now with the local unit of the National Guard at Fort Meade, Md. So, it seems the Wimer family personifies something that President Kennedy has stated. "Ask not what your country can do for you, but what you can do for your country."

Spring in The Yard

May 25, 1962

To most people the sound of spring usually means bees, birds and blossoms. But on my busy residential street the sound of spring means power mowers, power tractors, bicycles and wiffle ball.

What a wonderful time of year! The major housecleaning is completed, the yard is trimmed, the geraniums are blooming and the boys are even cooperating in the home paint-up, clean-up, fix-up campaign.

I've even noticed that Son No. 1 and Son No. 2 are so anxious for dismissal of school that even the challenge of housecleaning is something to be conquered. Of course, last Saturday Son No. 1 was threatening "to turn me in" to proper authorities on a charge of misuse of child labor – that was after we had spent the afternoon cleaning the garage.

Anyone interested in a broken baseball bat or bicycle wheels, deflated football, empty paint cans, doll dishes or pop bottles? Yep, we've taken the governor's clean-up campaign to heart!

But the nicest time of all is that quiet hour – early Sunday morning, sitting on the screened-in back porch watching Papa and Mama Robin teaching Junior to spread his wings and fly.

Or, the evenings with a baseball game in the backyard, a basketball game in the driveway and a football game on the front lawn. Yes, sons are a paying investment -- free manual labor with a touch of entertainment thrown in for fun! Ain't life grand!

Strawberry – Vegetable or Fruit

June 1, 1962

A Hodgesville couple, Mr. and Mrs. H. A. Casto, has given us something to ponder about during this 21st annual Strawberry Festival. Is this Strawberry a vegetable or a fruit? I can tell you this – it just depends upon where you are.

According to an AP release they found in the Miami, Florida Herald while vacationing this past February, even the experts at the Food and Agriculture Organization wish they knew. Sometimes, it seems King Strawberry can be both either fruit or vegetable.

Denmark and Yugoslavia, for example, count strawberries as vegetables, because they don't grow on trees and bushes. In England and most European countries, they are classed as fruit.

But in West Germany the strawberry wanders from one classification to another. While it's on the ground, growing, it is classed with vegetables. When it's picked and in the basket, ready to eat, it is considered a fruit.

It may make little difference to those who eat them – unless one is subject to "hives". But it has proved a headache for statisticians who have to include them in crop surveys. Experts are trying to sort it out in sections of a study group on problems and definitions in agricultural statistics. These specialists, from FAO and the U.N. Economic Commission for Europe, say the problem extends even beyond the puzzling strawberry.

Melons, for example, are vegetables to the French, Italians, Greeks and Yugoslavs. But they are fruit in the rest of Europe.

Potatoes are vegetables in Greece, Italy, the Netherlands and Yugoslavia. In Germany, they are considered field crops. In Turkey they are classed as an industrial crop.

The Turks also list green onions and garlic as an industrial crop, while other countries say they're just vegetables.

But getting back to the Strawberry – we don't care whether they're vegetable or fruit, just as long as they are produced in Upshur county, and responsible for this festive time of the year.

The Flag – The Trees

June 15, 1962

This is a gloomy, rainy Monday morning as I write this – perhaps, a reason for the dark mood I'm in and the urge to do some preaching.

I'm upset on two accounts, namely, No. 1 – people just don't respect the flag, nowhere, nohow, no more and No. 2 – why is everyone so hell-bent on cutting down the beautiful maple trees that line our residential streets? Concerning the flag situation, I really hadn't noticed until the Strawberry Festival grand feature parade. I watch the parade year in and year out on the steps of Whitescarver-Rundio funeral home. The flag came by, I think, this year, four times, I'd say 10 people stood up the first time and the 50 others sitting looked at us like we had holes in our head. The second time the flag came by I don't think another soul stood outside of the original ten. What's wrong with the American people? I imagine the ones who remained sitting comfortably on their well-padded rears sometime, somehow have had someone in their immediate family serve in the armed forces. In this day and age, I just don't see how they can escape the fact that our young men must serve some months of duty and been affected by the loss.

So, I presume from the lack of respect that we are willing for others to serve and die for this country as long as we are not disturbed in our way of life or made to serve any inconvenience. Now I know why Khrushchev is so confident that he "will bury us". We won't lift a finger to defend this country, our rights, or our way of life (outside of total war) but allow him and his Commies to worm their way through church, school and government. We just won't be bothered or can't be bothered outside of our own little, narrow world of make-believe that we have created for ourselves. Maybe, if we stick our heads in the sand, the "boogie-man" will go away. Secondly, I thought it was only my odd way of thinking that I shudder each time I see our beautiful trees lying stripped and naked along what-used-to-be tree-lined streets. But, this morning one of our civic-minded fathers called to me from his car bellyaching about "our town losing its personality". He's right! When the trees all go in Buckhannon, the town won't be the same. It will be just like any other town in any other state – sterile concrete. O, well, I can't change the world, just shout to high heaven! I'm getting to the age where it just wears me out to preach sermons!

Fractured Nursery Rhymes

August 17, 1962

When football practice starts you can just about 'figger' it's that time again – school days! For some parents it will be a big relief to get back on schedule, regular meals, regular bedtime, and regular risings! But I don't know that I'm so anxious for the school bells to ring.

Since I'm gone from home at least eight hours a day I've rather enjoyed Son No. 1 and Son No. 2 dropping into the office now and then – even if it is just to borrow money! Then, too, it isn't every mother who can iron in the evening and still be entertained with nursery rhymes – fractured nursery rhymes, that is.

For you "old fogies" that don't know what the term 'fractured' means in teenage language, it's simple, stupid, idiotic, cool or crazy. And for your enlightenment, these are the nursery rhymes. Keep in mind that Son No. 2 recites these with a deadpan expression and stupid smirk.

"I walked into a restaurant, Myself and Mary Drew. Mary had a little lamb, and I had Irish stew."

"Little Jack Horner, Sat in the corner, Eating his Christmas pie. He stuck in his thumb and pulled out a plum and said, "I ordered cranberry!"

"Starlight, star bright, First star I see tonight. Wish I may, Wish I might, O, shucks it's only a satellite."

"Spider, Spider on the wall, Spider, Spider, big and tall, Don't you know that wall's just been plastered. Get off that wall! You dirty spider."

"Little Miss Muffet, Sat on a tuffet, Eating her curds and whey, Along came a spider and sat down beside her and said, "What you got in the bowl, Huh!"

"Baa, baa, Black Sheep. Have you any wool? What do you think this is, Bud, nylon?"

"Mary, Mary. Quite contrary. How does your garden grow? With silver bells and cockle shells and one damn Petunia!" And finally, if you've read this far, the finale…."Mary had a little lamb. A little bread. A little jam. Some pickles and a great big roast. Some chicken and some buttered toast. She topped it off with soda fizz and Boy! How sick our Mary is!"

This one is way out…."Thirty days hath September, April, June and November. All the rest eat peanut butter. Except my grandmother and she drives a 1961 brown Chevy!"

O well, maybe an institution is where Son No. 2 belongs, after all.

Upshur County Forgotten

August 24, 1962

La te da! And whoop-te-do! Little old Republican Upshur county has been missed again.

With plans for the state's observance of its 100 birthday swingin' into high gear and with state officials swearin' that politics are not involved in the distribution of exhibits and etc., a nicely printed little old pink brochure has been published and mailed listing various Centennial Events – and guess what, Buckhannon's Strawberry Festival isn't there!

I may be wrong but it was my understanding that the Festival would open up the summer-long events with debut of the Centennial Exhibits Train – the reason for moving the Festival dates to June 13, 14 and 15.

So what happens? The state lists Centennial events starting June 17-23 in Charleston with a Civil War Exhibit and on through summer and fall to October, when Elkins will tout its you-know-what, the Forest Festival.

I don't intend to imply that Elkins should not be favored with a historic spectacle show and Centennial Parade. Of course, it should. But is not Buckhannon's Strawberry Festival also a crowd-pleaser?

The Strawberry and Upshur County have become somewhat synonymous after 21 years and, though I admit there is room for improvement, Festival events have long brought thousands to this fast-growing Central West Virginia community.

It's also an early event in the month of the state's birthday that should be a natural when it comes to lighting candles on a birthday cake.

Since we are a small county, in size, that is, but big on ideas, please, state Centennial officials, give us a break. We don't ask for money, although that would help, but we could use some of that free publicity that is pouring out of headquarters.

We don't like it when we're treated like step-children.

Ban The Bikini

September 7, 1962

Last week The Ravenswood News reprinted an editorial from the Pompano Beach, Fla. Town News that we enjoyed immensely.

Early this summer the ruling fathers of Pompano Beach were beset with a most serious problem which Editor Ed Seney discussed with tongue in cheek.

The problem in Pompano Beach –

It would have been a rough fight. We can envision mobs of angry men storming city hall in Pompano Beach, armed with clubs and stones, lighting their way with smoking torches, illuminated by eerie light. We could see our commissioners pleading vainly as the tar was heated and the pillows were torn apart for the feathers.

But all this didn't happen. It is well. The subject under consideration was the banning of the Bikini bathing suits.

At the last minute, Pompano commissioners fortunately chickened out and decided they wouldn't bare the details of their plan.

We are not sure how it all started. If the city fathers had decided to fire an official, or rezone a residential area to commercial, they could always expect a fight. They might even expect to face a recall.

But banning Bikinis is a far more serious matter, getting down to the basic fundamentals of our way of life – more or less – and in a manner of speaking.

Banning Bikinis is a terribly important decision on a terribly important matter. To fully get down to the rather, to probe beneath this – or, better, to bring out the bare facts – well, it's best not to start the sentence this way.

It's best to take this problem and approach it from the male standpoint. The problem, not the Bikini, that is. A man feels about a Bikini much the same as he feels about sin.

He doesn't want to see it run rampant and he doesn't believe in it, but he's not quite sure he wants to get rid of it. He likes it around in an abstract way because it (1) Reminds him of his own virtue, (2) Gives release to his imagination, (3) Gives him something to cluck his tongue about, or (4) Reminds him of his weaknesses.

The moral right or wrong about Bikinis is something that could probably be argued very strongly by any two given sides. Those who would oppose the wearing of Bikinis on our beaches would no doubt have good points to make about how they expose too much skin, how they cause temptation, how they suggest immorality.

Those who would argue for the Bikinis could counter by saying that nature is wonderful, anyway, so why hide it? They could also say that to imply that skin is immoral is an immoral viewpoint to start with. After all, they could say, don't nudists gather without shame and without making an orgy of their cult?

Having superficially examined the moral aspects of Bikinis, which are also superficial, the problem – also superficial – seems as exposed as ever.

Perhaps we should not take Bikinis too lightly, figuratively or literally.

Perhaps tomorrow we can take up less serious problems, such as beach erosion, outfall sewer systems, left and right wing extremists, or the trouble in Laos. We understand that the female natives there, too, are rather scantily clad.

And beach erosion, too – might apply to bathing suits as well as sand.

Entering The First Grade

September 21, 1962

Despite the fact that I may soon gain a reputation for "treading where angels fear to tread", I must raise my voice in protest against a recent ruling of the State Board of Education.

The ruling concerns children entering first grade, even though they may not be six years of age before November 1, if the child passes certain psychological tests. This in itself does not seem too much of a problem. If a child is mentally advanced for his age, it is well and good that he should start school early. But, at the same time, is it not well and good to also retard a child of less mental ability even though the child may meet the required age standards?

This particular ruling was sprung on parents and teachers less than a month prior to school opening and one can only guess at the stress and strain put on the few qualified people in this state to give the Stanford-Binet Intelligence test. Fortunately, for Upshur county, one person was qualified to give the test and she was suddenly deluged by applicants, not only from this county, but surrounding counties. Just for the record, five such students were accepted in Upshur county schools.

The unfairness of the ruling is what I must protest. Psychological tests cost money. The tests are not part of the free school system. In other words, the ruling applies only to the "rich". If by chance, I, a member of the low-income class, happen to believe my child is eligible to enter school early, I must also be willing to fork over $15 to $25 for the required test. This is unfair. No child, regardless of economic status, should be held back because his or her parents are unable to meet the cost of testing.

If the State Board of Education is going to continue to enroll children under this new ruling, then the board should also make some allowance for testing funds. And, the test should not only concern the intelligent child but the less-bright child as well.

Surely, funds for a testing program can only be a pipe dream. As it is, we doubt finds will be available. We're having trouble finding teachers and classroom space, but then, that's another column another time.

Watching "Lunch Eaters"

October 12, 1962

I eat lunch in a restaurant everyday – five days a week, 52 weeks a year for a total of 260 lunches at a cost of approximately $195. Why do I bring this up? No particular reason – just doodling while eating lunch one day this week.

Elaborating somewhat on this subject of "eatin' out", I've begun to watch "lunch eaters". Have you ever seen anyone eat a hot dog delicately or gracefully? It can't be done! And when it comes to "sandwich eaters", everyone has a style of his own. Do you bite into each corner first? Maybe you're a circular eater, by that I mean a healthy bite right "smack dab" in the middle of the sandwich. Of course, the bite all depends on the shape of the sandwich. Most persons prefer the triangle-cut, but then there are those who cut on the square or rectangle.

How does your taste in sandwiches run concerning soft, fresh bread or day-old? Thin-sliced or thick? Do you prefer the crust trimmed and what about a smatterin' of mayonnaise as well as a dab of butter? What about the pickle? No restaurant serves a sandwich without a lonely pickle slice on the side. I figure I'm paying for it, so I eat the pickle. I've even been known to get my money's worth by eating the parsley that decorates the side dish of potato salad.

Then I have a pet hate which concerns all sandwiches. Never allow a slice of tomato on a sandwich – at least not while eating out, save it for the privacy of home. Invariably one bites down on one side of the sandwich and the tomato slitters and springs from its trap, bouncing arrogantly onto the sandwich plate.

Another thing, do you use the lemon slice that rides along on the rim of the iced tea glass? I like lemon in my tea but I don't like the juice running to my elbow so in public I forget about my taste for lemon. Do you drink your tea with the available straw or are you a "sipper"? How many spoonfuls of sugar do you dispense (here's where the restaurant loses money) and how many stirs to a glass? The "stirrers" can be broken down into three classes – vigorous, half-hearted and low-gear.

So, on and on, every taste, every kind of "biter" and every sort of "sipper". Look for the types the next time you eat out!

Folks At The Delta

October 19, 1962

Since this is National Newspaper Week, I would assume that readers of this newspaper are waiting with bated breath for my annual sermon concerning good and bad newspapers, why The Delta is better than any other newspaper, why one should buy The Delta and, most importantly, why one should buy advertising space in The Delta.

As continuous readers of this newspaper by now realize the staff of this concern does not wait until National Newspaper Week to publicize the merits of The Delta. We preach our quality every week of the year.

Publishing a newspaper, even a weekly edition, is a tremendous job. Contrary to the belief of some subscribers, we don't wave a magic wand in the composing room, with a perfect printed page suddenly appearing on demand. Publishing a newspaper involves mechanics plus a fair degree of intelligence on the part of every staff member.

A tour of this building would show you, the reader, the many operations involved, beginning with the rolls of newsprint. The editor, Mrs. Mary Liz Herndon must go over reporter's stories, rural correspondence, she must write headlines and stories for government, births, celebrations, nature, crime, sports, weddings, deaths, and legal proceedings.

If her job sounds demanding, if she looks harassed, remember this quaint piece of literature:

An editor knocked at the Pearly Gate.
Her face was scarred and cold.
She stood before the man of fate for admission to the fold.
"What have you done," St. Peter asked "to gain admission here?"
"I've been an editor, sir," she said "for many and many years."
The pearly gates swung open wide. St. Peter touched the bell.
"Come in," he said, "and choose your harp. You've had your share of hell."

Dana Deane – Howard Hiner Collection

In the shop, these news stories are set in type on a linotype by either Blonda Dawson or Mary Ellen Howes and sometimes, on the automatic teletype setter, by Mrs. Densel Crouso.

Meanwhile, ads are being prepared by me while the news flows in. Businessmen and women in Buckhannon after almost four years have become somewhat used to seeing me "pop my head" in the front door with a message that may seem stale after hundreds of weeks – why it is important to advertise in The Delta.

In my job, I hear a lot, see a lot, not all that can be printed. I take a lot of kidding, some teasing, along with some rudeness and unkindness, for like every other job I meet the good and the bad. Happily, my clients are mostly thoughtful. I haven't stepped on too many toes to my knowledge and my advertising lineage continues to grow.

If our jobs seem demanding and some days tempers flare, we also have our laughs. I'm teased once in awhile about my reputation – am I selling or soliciting ads. Yes, I'm getting quite a reputation about this soliciting. During one community progress days sales event, the composing room was becoming more and more jammed with advertising copy until Dana Deane, the best darn composing room foreman I've run into anytime, anywhere, demanded that I not schedule another ad. It finally got to the place where I was sneaking into the back shop but Dana caught me and again told me not to schedule another ad. I retorted that the ads were coming in unsolicited, whereupon Dana said, "Then stop peckin' on the windows."

But getting back to the mechanics of this operation, as I schedule ads, Alfred Walton, Earl Dee Edgell and Stuart Smith, are casting mats, putting type into galleys and setting page forms which will be placed on the press. E. Q. Miles, job work foreman, in the meantime has spent his eight or so hours a day with an operation, completely separate from the newspaper operation. His work concerns the thousands of forms pages of booklets, tickets, tags, envelops and letterheads turned out every week and classified as "job work".

With the newspaper operation, growing each month, even now another operation is taking place in the front office, bookkeeping, billing, circulation; all handled by Mrs. Rita Deane and "Bertie" Crouso.

So, perhaps, from just this short resume, the Delta's readers can understand that time and effort are put into this newspaper operation – an operation that puts information in your hands in a form to be read and digested when you need it and have time for it.

Cuban Missile Crisis

October 26, 1962

The world can only guess what is going to happen in the Havana poker game with its flesh and blood stakes but one thing is sure – too many of us have brushed off Khrushchev's words "We'll bury you!".

Too many of us have been sure it can't happen. Too many of us still think of Castro as the mangy master of Cuba when he is, in fact, but another slave of the Communist conspiracy – the tool that has opened the way for the first mass penetration of the Western Hemisphere by Red arms and troops.

The Cuban pot appears about ready to boil over. A missionary for 20 years in China until expelled by the Chinese Reds, recently wrote in an article "The first essential to combating communism is to realize that communism is a conspiracy of criminals who are waging war on the whole fabric of Western civilization. Communism is primarily a conspiracy – an internal criminal conspiracy dedicated to the use of all illegal and immoral means to achieve its goal of world conquest."

According to Ralph de Toledano, writing recently in National Review, the President told a press conference in September that 61 ships have carried Red troops and arms to Cuba. That 59 MIG-17's, armed with tactical nuclear weapons have been added to Fidel's air force. Nine launching pads for 1,700 mile Intermediate Range Ballistic Missiles (not 25-mile rockets) are now operational with 15 more under construction.

So now we wait. God grant that Russia will back down. If not, God grant the American people have the courage to stand up to the suffering and the heartbreak.

History of Voting

November 2, 1962

A Greek citizen in the 5th century B.C. would certainly be awed by the array of levers on today's voting machines. His archaic way of voting – with balls of white or black to indicate a yes or no vote – would look more like sport than politics to a modern American voter.

In ancient Greece, a voter dropped a white ball into an urn to express his preference for a candidate for office. Defeated candidates were literally "blackballed". According to Collier's Encyclopedia, our present word "ballot" is derived from the Italian ballotta, meaning "little ball" and denoting the way in which these first secret votes were cast.

Centuries later, Indian corn and beans were used in voting in the early American colonies by the settlers. "Papers", the colonial name for paper ballots, first appeared in the United States in a secret vote in the Salem, Mass. church in 1629.

Out of these rudimentary forms has come the Australian ballot, so called because it was introduced in Australia in 1856. With the increase in the number of voters in many countries in the 19th century and the consequent possibility of vote manipulation for corrupt purpose, there was a need of a voting procedure that would protect the individual in the exercise of his suffrage and at the same time guarantee to the public that the results of the election would be accurate. The Australian ballot met these qualifications by assuring uniformity and secrecy in balloting and providing for the printing of ballots at government expense. Originally a simple ballot listing one office for which a few candidates were entered, the Australian ballot has been given several complex patterns by its American adapters.

The advent of the voting machine in the last half of the 19th century has automated voting to a considerable degree, but has preserved the essential format of the Australian ballot, still the most satisfactory balloting method to be used by democratic countries.

But, whether beans or balls, this next Tuesday – VOTE!

Election Notes

November 9, 1962

It's all over but the shouting – the election, that is, and Wednesday morning there were the usual smiles and frowns, post-election summaries, and the "wait 'til next year" prediction.

For the third time in the history of Upshur county a Democrat was elected to the House of Delegates which should lift some eyebrows in Charleston where year in and year out the county is written off as a bulwark of Republicanism. But, there again, just think a little on Nixon's defeat. They all fall and just as hard – little or big.

One Democrat to serve Upshur in the House of Representatives was David Poe from 1882 to 1883 and to top it all off he was a darn Rebel having served as a colonel in the Confederate Army. An earlier Democrat was William C. Carper serving in the House from 1855 to 1856 and another was T. J. Farnsworth who served two terms from 1874-76 and 1876-78. He also ran unopposed in the state Senate, was elected and served as president of that body. The circuit clerk's office, always the focal point on election night, was quiet due to a couple of issues of more than usual interest to the voter – the alcoholic liquor control amendment, and the levy for the swimming pool at the 4-H camp – all of which went down to oblivion.

Someone mentioned Tuesday night that he had just about decided after looking at the results that democracy is a place you can vote for the Kennedy of your choice. Then someone else began selling shares in a new club organization on Election Night – shares sold for a dime and the certificates read "a share in the Democrat's donkey. Now don't just sit down and make an ass of yourself – Go get your dime the way I got mine."

Of course, there are always laughs, with radio, TV and newspapers fighting the Moore-Bailey congressional battle, one confused voter called the newspaper and accused the staff of running the wrong ballot – Bailey's name wasn't anywhere on the ticket!

Earlier in the week, one voter called the circuit court clerk trying to find out where she should vote. Told to vote at the Academy School, where there are two precincts, 8 and 14, the caller asked which one was for the Democrats. And, to prove that five amendments are four too many on any ballot, just think how those voters must feel who defeated the fair representation amendment and have now voted away their only delegate due to a decrease in population.

Weekday Holiday

November 16, 1962

Even at the risk of bringing down the wrath of all housewives, I must ask – what do you do with your time? Whether for good or bad, I had a holiday Monday. The holiday was good in that I spent a day at home and leisurely cleaned house instead of the usual hit and miss on Saturday afternoon. The holiday was bad in that by 3:30 in the afternoon I was bored. Here it was I asked myself the question – what do you housewives do with your time? For the first time in many a month I was home at lunchtime when Son No. 2 and Sis came breezing in. They didn't care for my lunch and informed me they'd just as soon go back to the routine of lunch at Grandmother's. In fact, Son No. 2 also informed me that Grandmother had his meal ready, waiting on the table when he made his entrance.

I've always had visions, misguided visions I'm afraid, that one's youngsters came bouncing in at noon full of bright sayings and bubbling over with stories saved for the lunch hour. It t'aint so – they come in for lunch only because they're hungry. But, getting back to my holiday. Up at 7:30 a.m. and for a big change, a hot breakfast for Son No. 1, Son No. 2 and Sis. At 8:15 a.m. the house was strangely quiet. By 9 a.m. I had sipped three cups of coffee while listening to the news. I still hadn't decided whether the day would be fit for drying clothes outdoors, so I hung a load of towels in the basement. I changed linens on four beds, cleaned the house from top to bottom, washed two more loads of clothes and these I hung outdoors. Came noon, Son No. 2 and Sis bolted in and bolted back out again, so I proceeded to clean shelves under the sink and the work counter. Now, looking for something to do, I baked a pan of gingerbread. Still looking for something to do, I remembered the storm door needed repairing. Went next door to the neighbors to borrow a hammer after looking high and low in vain for my hammer in the dirty garage – took a broom to the garage.

Had two cigarettes and a cup of coffee with my neighbor and on the way home noticed my leaf rake in their garage. Helped myself to my rake and worked 25 minutes in the backyard. Fixed storm door. Prepared meat loaf.

At 3:15 I was sitting in front of the picture window in the living room wondering what time the kids got out of school. At 3:45 I had my answer. And, it was now my usual evening routine, dinner, dishes. Holidays are nice. I'm just glad I don't have two a week.

Housewife Reply

November 30, 1962

I surrender, help! Don't send me anymore letters, don't stop me on the street, don't call me on the phone. I'm sorry, I'm sorry, I wondered what housewives did six days a week.

If my faithful readers recall, two weeks ago I told about the Veteran's Day holiday I spent at home, how much work I accomplished and then remarked "If all this work can be accomplished in one day, what do housewives do the other six days of the week."

Well, I tell you I found out – by letter, and by phone, I was accused of probably having the dirtiest home in the county (sorry, it's only the third or fourth dirtiest), a traitor to the female race and a fascist, because as one wife told me, the housewives do loaf, but one never allows one's husband to discover this fact.

One of the most interesting of the letters I received was this one from Mrs. Richard Kitzmiller on Pocahontas street, who signed her letter, "Not from a bored housewife, just a Busy Homemaker."

"On behalf of the housewife I'd like to answer your article as to what we do with our time. I'll use the week of November 12 as an example.

"Monday, 12th – A holiday (for whom?), not the housewife! I got our son off to school, dressed beds and washed, picked up the usual weekend litter, straightened (not cleaned) the house and got lunch. In the afternoon, ironed, started dinner, washed dishes and by 7 was at a special meeting for homeroom mothers. At 7:30 attended PTA. Got home, wrote a few letters and watched "Ben Casey" before retiring long after the rest of the family was in bed.

"Tuesday, 13th – Regular rush of getting the family off to work and school, with one exception besides making the beds I had to be ready to deliver flowers to teachers at four schools and the superintendent of schools office for American Education Week. I might say, I was only on the committee, not the chairman, another housewife had that responsibility. After we got home, made cookies, straightened the house and cooked dinner. Dishes done, I dressed to attend a board meeting for a civic club, by 12 I was in bed.

"Wednesday, 14th – Everyone off to work and school, beds made and I'm ready to go shopping, not for myself but for Thanksgiving party the homeroom mothers are giving the 21st. Barely managed to get home and start lunches, one to be served at 11 and one at 12. After my son had left for school, dishes to be done and floor scrubbed while washing machine is doing its share of housework. Then, I ironed, got dinner, more dishes and off to choir rehearsal. Had an extra lot of leisure time from 8:30 till 11 – really lived it up by watching TV.

"Thursday, 15th – Finally got the house cleaned, in between cooking and doing dishes for three meals besides breakfast. At 7 attended an executive meeting of the WSCS and 7:30 the meeting - bedtime as usual.

"Friday, 16th – Everyone up and ready to go, beds made and I'm casually dressing to visit the school (American Educational Week) in between phone calls and a neighbor stopping by to say Hi. Back home for a quick lunch to all and at 1 out again – to decorate and set up tables for a special dinner the gas company is having on Saturday evening. Home by the time school was out and fixed dinner – at last I really relaxed in the evening.

"Saturday, 17th – Straightened the house, baked extra for the weekend at home and for dinner tonight. Washed, did part of the ironing, leaving some for next week. Had our boy ready for Cub Scouts by 2 and finished cooking the dishes to be taken out – ready to leave by 5:15, home by 8:30 and finally got to read the Delta including your article.

"Sunday, 18th – Day of Rest???? Attended Sunday School and Church services, fixed lunch, started working on doll clothes (for a special donation to be turned in this evening for an orphanage) at church. Visited friends for about an hour. Had to see their new grandson and their family. Back home to fix dinner, ate and I went back to the doll project while my husband cleaned the kitchen up and did the dishes. Attended M.Y.F. (we're counselors) and back home and visited friends till 10. In bed by 11.

"This doesn't include extra phone calls which had to be made or the little jobs you do without thinking. Mending for an example. It's merely the highlights of our time and what we do with it, just a typical week.

"I do enjoy your articles (usually) but why pick on the housewife, we work too you know."

So there, I have my answer!

Gumperson's Law

December 14, 1962

This is a good time to think about the law of perverse opposites – or, as it is known to most laymen, Gumperson's law. It will refresh your understanding of the universe and steel you for the year ahead. A year that is not going to be any better than the last one, as you know perfectly well. Why not? Gumperson's law is still unrepealed.

For those of you who are unaware, Gumperson's law neatly explains a number of irritating events that might otherwise be put down to mere chance. It is Gumperson's law, for example, that causes blue grass to grow in the cracks of concrete sidewalks, but not on your lawn.

It accounts, too, for the fact that you can throw a burning match out the window of your car and start a forest fire while you can use two boxes of matches and a whole edition of the Sunday paper without being able to start a fire under the dry logs in your fireplace.

The law, stated simply, is that the contradictory of a welcome probability will assert itself whenever such an eventuality is likely to be most frustrating. Readers familiar with these matters will perhaps recognize another version of the law: The outcome of a given desired probability will be inverse to the degree of desirability.

A brief elucidation of the law, with details on its origin and development, is presented herewith for the benefit of the lay reader.

Dr. R. F. Gumperson, internationally famous physicist, began serious work in 1938 on a phenomenon long known to scientist, but up until then considered as mere curiosity. This was the fact that the forecasting record of the weather bureau, despite its use of the most advanced equipment and highly trained personnel, was not as good as that of The Old Farmers Almanac. After four years of research, Dr. Gumperson enunciated his now famous law and was able to make a series of predictions later confirmed by other scientific workers in the field. Some of the better known of these include the following:

- That after a raise in salary you will have less money at the end of each month than you had before.

- That the girl at the race track who bets according to the color of the jockey's shirt will pick more winners than the man who has studied the past performance of every horse on the program.

- That children have more energy after a hard day of play than they do after a good night's sleep.

- That the person who buys the most raffle tickets has the least chance of winning.

- That a child can be exposed to the mumps for weeks without catching them but can catch them without exposure the day before the family goes on vacation.

- That the dishwasher will break down the evening you give a dinner party for ten people.

- That good parking places are always on the other side of the street.

Dr. Gumperson served as a consultant to the armed services during World War II and evolved the procedure whereby the more a recruit knew about a given subject the better chance he had of receiving an assignment involving some other subject.

There is no knowing to what further glittering height Dr. Gumperson's genius would have led him had it not been for his untimely death in 1947. Strolling along the highway one evening, he was obeying the pedestrian rule of walking to the left facing traffic. He was struck down from behind by a Hillman-Minx driven by an English visitor hugging the left side of the road.

Santa Myth

December 28, 1962

This is the last year that Santa will visit the Hornbeck home – – and it just won't be the same hereafter!

For 16 years I've tippy-toed on Christmas Eve, learned to talk in husband whispers, kept secrets better than any spy in the intelligence service and have become quite adept at deceptive counter-measures, and now it's over, at least until there are grandchildren.

Oh, of course, there will still be secrets, but I'll miss the visits of the red-shirted gentleman. When Son No. 1 outgrew the myth, there was yet Son No. 2. And, just when it looked like there would be no more Santa visits, along came Daughter who kept us in conspiratorial fervor these past nine years.

So, Ann has been pushed into the hard, cruel world. Santa has gone the way of Cinderella, and the fairy who leaves money under the pillow for the lost tooth. But, not the dream – let's pray she never loses the dream, or love, or the gift of sharing, or even hope. As long as she has these, perhaps Santa will continue to exist, at least as a pleasant memory.

For us, this is a New Year, for Ann and others like her, a new world – I hope a world of peace and love and goodwill.

Tele-sacroiliac-itis

January 4, 1963

I'm afflicted with another case of tele-sacroiliac-itis which occurs only on New Year's Day. It's a common disease, suffered by many football fans with symptoms of pain lasting not more than two days.

Tele-sacroiliac-itis is an aching back, caused from lying horizontal on a couch from 11:30 a.m. until 8:30 p.m. with only an occasional walk to the refrigerator and a meal served from a TV tray. The pain can be severe, depending on the hangover from the night before, or slight if one went to bed shortly after midnight.

The strain on the spine also depends on the many and varied positions one assumes while eyes are glued to the Orange Bowl, Sugar Bowl and Rose Bowl games. The pain may be worse if heightened by tension, in my case, my aching back is achin' all because of the fourth quarter of the Rose Bowl and the Wisconsin team that never gave up.

This year, the living room quarterbacks may be suffering just a little bit more from tele-sacroiliac-itis, due to the fact that there was no respite between the weekend television games and New Year's Day.

Before the pain in the back really abated after Saturday's two sessions of football, plus the bonus of West Virginia's basketball play in Madison Square Garden, there was the pro-championship playoff on Sunday. This only gave the home folks one day of rest prior to the extravaganza of New Year's Day football. And, if you were out all night greeting the new baby of 1963, you just weren't in proper shape for the thrills and excitement of college football to start with.

So, before next year, may I suggest you follow the course of a safe and sane New Year's -- stay home, toast the hour of midnight with pink champagne, and go promptly to bed. Think what fine shape you'll be in the next day for the parade, the football game, the football game and the football game!

Womanless Wedding

March 7, 1963

I don't usually devote this column space to club activities or club projects, but, in this case, the B-U Band Boosters Club has such an unusual hour and a half of entertainment planned for April 5 and 6, I feel that I should call attention to the organization's latest "gimmick".

A "Womanless Wedding" with a cast of 20 prominent men of Upshur county, directed by Prof. Sam Raines, drama coach at West Virginia Wesleyan, is now in rehearsal and it's a riot.

If you will allow your imagination to run a few minutes, picture small but mighty Sheriff Willard Wimer as the groom and husky Coach Dave Reemsnyder as the bride in all 'her' splendor standing at the altar with Deck Whitescarver as preacher.

Then, allow your eyes to travel over the rest of the wedding party, the despondent father of the bride, portrayed by Judge J. L. Jennings; the bridesmaids, so beautiful in their matching gowns, played by Coach Granville Zopp and Coach Gail Zickefoose; and the baby sister of the bride, played by L. L. Moss, Dr. Arthur Gould and I. S. Morgan will be in the wedding party as aunt and uncle of the bride.

These characters are only a few of the men of the area who will be cooperating in the production to benefit the local band and to aid in raising funds for the June 14th trip to Virginia Beach, Va. where the high school band will compete in regional contests. Approximately $2,000 is needed for uniforms and travel expenses and the parents have really cooperated in an effort to raise the funds. Of course, the parents aren't doing it all.

The youngsters themselves just successfully completed a campaign where a fabulous glue called Band-Stix was sold throughout the county. But, the message I'm trying to get across is that it will be many years before a funnier or more entertaining production graces the stage of the high school than "The Womanless Wedding".

Howard Hiner Collection

Womanless Wedding – L/R Glenn Ours, Judge J. Dowell Jennings, Willard Wimer, Dave Reemsnyder as the bride, unidentified, Gail Zickefoose, Granville Zopp. Kneeling: J. Carpenter

I got a sneak prevue one night this week when my neighbor showed me the dress that her husband will wear as one of the flower girls. The white full-skirted dress will have three petticoats to make it bouffant and the dress will be accented with a wide pink sash. 'She' will have ribbons in 'her' hair and dainty anklets and white sandals on 'her' feet. How the hairy legs will be covered is beyond even the wildest of imagination.

So, don't miss it! The stage production along with the many variety acts planned – dance routines, folk singing, a girl's trio, pantomime and impersonators, all emceed by Dale Brooks, of radio fame.

City-County Growth Projections

March 28, 1963

I Don't know how many readers caught the statement made last week by Joe Pagnillo, chairman of the planning board, to the effect that in less than 20 years Buckhannon will see a population of 16,000.

This figure has intrigued me for an entire week and, being of a curious nature, I did some research of my own to see just how and where and why 16,000 will be residing in this fair city – the fastest growing in West Virginia.

Since 1930 a small increase has been noted in Buckhannon, but substantial gains have been made since 1940 both in the city and Wesleyan college.

Before 1940, Buckhannon's economy was keyed primarily to the farm and coal industry but since World War II Buckhannon's growth and increased enrollment at Wesleyan have been somewhat dependent upon industrial development and increased governmental activities.

Just to show how the population growth in the urbanizing areas has closely paralleled Buckhannon's growth, bear with me on the short set of figures: In 1930, Upshur county's population was 17,994: Buckhannon, 4,374 and Wesleyan, 484 and the urban area (one and one-half miles outside city limits) stood at 5,652.

In 1940, Upshur county, 18,360; Buckhannon, 4,374 and Wesleyan, 484 and the urban, 7,668.

In 1950, Upshur county, 19,242; Buckhannon, 6,016 and Wesleyan, 805; urban, 8,784.

In 1960, Upshur county, 18,292; Buckhannon, 6,386 and Wesleyan, 1,145; urban, 9.211.

The estimated total population has been based on three assumptions, the first assumption being that the growing element (manufacturing, government and trade) of the economy will continue to grow at the same rate demonstrated in the past five years, and the declining elements (mining and agriculture) have reached the bottom of the curve.

The second assumption is that manufacturing, etc., will continue to grow at a rate demonstrated in the past 10 years and the mining, farm, etc. will continue at its present rate.

The third assumption is that the growing elements have reached a plateau but will continue to grow at a reduced rate and the declining elements will be minimized.

The first assumption has been used in arriving at these population increases – Buckhannon, 1960, 6,386; 1965, 7,629; 1970, 8,904; 1975, 10,178 and in 1980, 11,453.

Combining Buckhannon and the urban area, the rate of population will rise from a total of 9,211 in 1960 to 10, 967 in 1965; 12,404 in 1970; 14,561 in 1975 and 16, 680 in 1980.

It is interesting to note that the nation will reach 200 million in population by the mid-60's and statistics indicate in the decade ahead the young folks of college age will show the greatest population increase by 1965 with a population exceeding 20 million.

"War babies" will be married by 1965 with the number of married couples in 1965-70 at 750,000. Consequently, this increase in marriages mean school kids in the 60's will stretch to some 50 million. By 1970, they should make up about two-fifths of the population.

Every signpost points to shifts in population. Between now and 1970 the United States must find room for some 50,000,000 more families. By 1970, 50 billion dollars will be spent on a system of super highways to meet needs of individuals and industry. All kinds of development will take place along this network.

So, Buckhannon and Upshur County should gear for some golden years.

Howard Hiner and The Centennial Bear

April 25, 1963

There must be a little humor in everyone's life or we'd go mad, especially around a newspaper office. Howard Hiner, local lens clicker, regaled us this week with an episode while photographing the "tame?" bear and lion at the French Creek Game Farm.

It seems that while Fred Trainer, the manager, was wrestling with the Centennial Bear, Lucky got loose and headed straight for Howard's new Volkswagen and his two daughters who were standing outside. The older daughter leaped into the station wagon leaving her 10-year-old sister outside. Undaunted little Ricky took a diving headlong leap through a three foot square window in the back and simultaneously slammed the window shut just as her feet disappeared through the small opening.

The story brought to mind some of the stupid stunts one pulls in moments of stress and tension. For instance, one reporter we know rushed home to change clothes for an important assignment, threw his sport coat on the bed and put his arm through the coat hanger. In another case, one man bought a four door sedan after several years of two-door models. It seems he opened the door the other night and not until he sat down did he realize he was sitting in the back seat wondering why the steering wheel was so far away.

A local mother attended revival services accompanied by her five-year-old daughter. Imagine the mother's consternation when she happened to glance down and found her daughter amusing herself with a deck of setback cards. A local building contractor tells this story on himself. A new homeowner couldn't understand why the bathroom of his new home always felt so warm, especially so in the summer time. Just recently he approached the contractor saying, "I appreciate all the new modern inventions in my new home, but really, we don't need hot water in the commode!" Upon investigation it was discovered that the water lines had been just a little mixed up in installation.

And just within the past year we've added a new word to our vocabulary in this office. You won't find it in a dictionary. We no longer are "not hungry". Just a little less "eatified", an expression used one day by one of the office force.

Grade School Centennial Songs

June 20, 1963

Today, June 20, West Virginia will mark its birthday. One hundred years ago on that day, 35 small girls in red, white and blue dresses welcomed the first governor of the state, Arthur I. Boreman. The place was Wheeling, at high noon. The girls represented the states that had been admitted, West Virginia being the 35th.

Much has taken place within the borders of this state since that first birthday celebration. What hasn't changed is the fact that youth today love these mountains and are just as loyal to the state as those 35 small girls of one hundred years ago. To prove the point, I submit as evidence some songs written this spring by second grade students of Mrs. LeRoy Canfield at the Tennerton grade school. Now remember these youngsters are six and seven years old and quite aware that West Virginia is celebrating a birthday. Molly Stansbury, daughter of Mr. and Mrs. James Stansbury, of the Hickory Flat road, composed a four-line verse to the tune of "Where Oh Where Has My Little Dog Gone". Hum the melody and say – "Oh, how I love my home state. Oh, how, Oh, how I love it. With the hills so beautiful and the lakes. Oh, how I love my state." Jody, daughter of Mr. and Mrs. Delmer Light, used her ingenuity to compose a verse to the tune of "Three Blind Mice". Hum again – "West Virginia. West Virginia, for a hundred years you've kept us free. We're all so proud of our liberty. West Virginia is for me, dear West Virginia." Not to be outdone by the fair sex, a gentleman in the class, Randy Tenney, used the tune of "Are You Sleeping" to sing along with – "West Virginia, West Virginia. You're getting old, you're getting old. You are now a 100, you are now a 100. We love you, we love you."

By this time, the entire class was getting into the act and running out of tunes, so Terry Smallridge and Mike Hicks used the same tune as Randy's but composed original works. Terry's verse reads – "West Virginia, West Virginia, we like you, we like you. You're a very good state, you're a very good state, we like you, we like you." Mike, son of Mr. and Mrs. Brannon Hisks, wrote – "West Virginia, West Virginia, You are good, you are good. You are a good state, you're a good state. We love you, we love you." And the finale, just like her happy-go-lucky father, Joe Barker, daughter Diane sang to the tune of "Come All You Playmates". "Come all you people and listen while I tell, West Virginia is our state, and it is oh so great."

Uncle Sam & The Sutton Dam

July 11, 1963

We've become so inured to governmental controls, red tape and regulation that we don't often give it much thought until a government ruling smacks us full in the face as it did this family this past holiday at Sutton Dam.

For those of you who own boats with all the conveniences of home, refrigerator, stove, bunks and head, get out your screwdriver and pliers for you just can't have a head aboard ship, not on a government owned dam anyway. (For those of you who don't know what a head is, ask that member of the family who served with the U.S. Navy.)

Ridiculous? Perhaps. Or else, we had a martinet of an inspector. No dice, even with a chemical attachment. Absolutely forbidden. With small children aboard and a stay of four days aboard ship you can see where this leads to no small inconvenience. Especially, during the middle of the night when nature calls. I suppose the inspector expects the captain to dock at the closest port and walk all his brood 100 yards up hill to the public facilities.

If the long arm of Uncle Sam wants to be concerned with the public health and sanitation, I suggest he take a better look (or maybe we should say smell of the public facilities at say, around 4 p.m. in the afternoon after a crowd of several hundred have trekked the heights.

Better yet, Uncle Sam should station his inspectors around the 11-mile shore of the Sutton Dam and catch those speaking from ship to shore. After all, with the next good hard rain, the waste will be deposited in the clear waters of the lake anyway. And if Uncle Sam is really concerned with public health then I suggest he take another look at the contamination of Buckhannon river to the south of us. Or the state of several backyards here in town last week following torrential rains. The storm sewers couldn't handle the deluge and frankly after the waters receded I considered typhoid booster shots for the entire family based on the smell and debris left in the wake of the sewer waters.

We knew the government was being accused of too much control, but the control of heads aboard ships seems just a wee-bit far-fetched.

Welfare Tab

August 1, 1963

I'm stepping upon my soap-box again this week since I've received such a staggering amount of statistical data from the W. Va. Department of Welfare. I'm mad all over again.

This annual report is still a year late covering the period of July 1, 1961 to June 30, 1962 and according to a statement on the inside front cover "This supplement contains such statistical data as is deemed essential for public accountability."

Well, I think there is still more statistical data that would be essential for the public. For one thing, I'd like to see a public list of those receiving public assistance. Secondly, I'd like to see just exactly how this general assistance is spent. Thirdly, I'm still crying for thorough investigations into those families currently receiving public welfare checks.

The welfare tab for Upshur county is even greater than I uncovered in my investigation this past winter, it now stands at $736,875.55.

Now we're right in line with the counties of Clay, Greenbrier, Lewis, Monongalia, Nicholas and Webster when it comes to the distribution of free money.

Of this staggering amount, $15,714 was levied for the year by the Upshur county court and an additional $25,525.74 was received in state funds, the rest came from the federal government.

Included in this almost million dollars worth of relief are public assistance awards of $677,236; general assistance of $22,445; boarding care amounting to $9,371,19 and the cost of administration and service in the local office of $27,823.36.

This may look like a hodgepodge of figures but add it up yourself, after all, you're paying the tab and any good bookkeeper likes to see where his money is being spent and the value received.

Another breakdown was expenditures of $138,371 for an average number of 329 cases of old-age assistance. Aid to the blind included $4,052 spent for seven persons and $30,814 for 86 cases of aid to the permanently and totally disabled. We have no bone to pick with the state or federal government concerning these expenditures. These I consider necessary and an obligation until time eternal.

What does concern me is how much actual help is being received by the 31 children in Upshur county whom the state lists as state wards, along with the 14 juveniles on probation and the two listed as parolees. Are they really receiving the kind of training that will make them useful citizens in the life ahead?

This "statistical data" shows Upshur county welfare agents dealing with 25 children with parents; nine living with relative; 23 in boarding homes and two on trial adoption. This is quite a caseload for the two or three qualified persons in the local office of the DPA. In fact, I'd almost surmise that it's too much of a caseload.

So, you say, she's sticking her nose into a problem that she doesn't understand, she's biased, she's doing no good. Perhaps. But you, the public, had better do more than just write letters to the editor. You had better raise your voices in a louder clamor before you're supporting two in four families on relief, rather than one in four families as it stands now!

Antique Newspapers #2

August 8, 1963

We're in possession of several old, old newspapers this week. Must be that everyone took a notion the same time to clean out the attic.

In at least one case, three of the newspapers were almost lost along with a valuable collection of glass negatives which were stored in the basement of J. W. "Bill" Campbell's home at Tallmansville. A recent storm caused back waters to rise to the first story of his home.

Two other newspapers were handed us last week by Mrs. Hazel Burdette, evidently owned by the late Rev. Mr. G. W. Burdett who was serving as pastor of the First United Brethren Church of Huntington when the Pt. Pleasant Register of August 30, 1924 featured the founding and growth of the North Pleasant EUB church.

The second newspaper is a remarkably preserved copy of the "Religious Herald", edited by William Sands and published in Richmond, VA…

Bill Campbell salvaged three copies from his wet basement, one of which is The Corner Stone, the sixth edition of Volume 1 and dated June 29, 1893 and published in Wheeling. The second copy is The State Weekly and Gazette of Parkersburg, and dated January 18, 1912. This copy was number 40 of volume 2. Neither paper evidently realized a long life.

The lead story of The Corner Stone deals with the "Unprecedented Bravery of Buckhannon Officials". "Jail Birds walk out and Eat on the Way – Munificent Rewards Offered for their Capture, running clear up to $25.00."

These were the headlines. The story:

"Buckhannon evidently has another force on hand. She has been accustomed to these things in dealing with illegal sellers of intoxicants, and it will not surprise the people to know that those convicted at the recent court have sauntered out of their bondage with only a paltry sum offered for their capture.

We clip from the Buckhannon Delta:

"The four prisoners, viz: Pat Stanton, his son Johnnie, a Swede, whose name we did not learn, and Harry Triplet (colored) who were serving out a term of imprisonment for keeping speakeasies, escaped jail on last Sunday morning about 2 o'clock. They did not leave town until near daylight, as they were seen near town just after daybreak, and did not seem in any hurry to get away as they walked slowly and conversed with every person met and took dinner at Mr. Bly's about four miles east of town. They say they will not be taken, and presume they would give any person who attempted to molest them a warm reception, as they were well equipped with firearms, so the Delta's informant states. The Sheriff has offered a reward to $10 each for the apprehension of Johnnie, the Swede and Triplet and $25 for the safe return of Pat."

Well, well, so Buckhannon has not always been the quiet country village that our grandpappy would have us believe!

The Corner Stone made hay of this story from the hinterlands as it was dedicated to temperance and printed for the protection of the Church, State, Home, and School.

The publishers, Frank Burt and Benjamin R. Burt, may have been against liquor but that didn't stop them from running a clever little lottery. A half-page advertisement said an "elegant ($10) guitar" would be given to every person signing 30 subscribers to The Corner Stone. Twenty subscribers meant a fine military drum. But better yet, for 200 subscribers a boy or girl would receive a $135 strictly high-grade light roadster bicycle. The ad boasted of 28-inch wheels, pneumatic tires and a weight of 30 pounds.

The State Weekly of Parkersburg plastered its front page on January 18, 1912 with the story of the "Terrible Suffering all Along Path of Flood". But a bulletin from Parkersburg noted that the Ohio River was falling after having crested at 45.1 feet.

J. D. Cox has been sworn in as governor of Ohio and attendance records were broken when Billy Sunday extended his first call to "hit the sawdust trail" in Columbus, Ohio.

In the October 26, 1912 issue of The State Weekly, "Colonel Roosevelt was placed in an auto ambulance at Mercy Hospital in Chicago, Ill. And driven to the station from which his train left at eight minutes after eight for Oyster Bay. "The wound still discharges a little serum but there is less inflammation, but the point where the bullet is located is still sensitive to pressure." (You will recall Roosevelt was a victim of an assassin.)

The annual conference of the Methodist Episcopal Conference was coming to a close in Elkins and Mrs. G. W. Pullock, wife of the Buckhannon Presbyterian minister, was elected state president of the Woman's Synodical Society in Buckhannon.

The Joseph Horne Company of Pittsburgh advertised coats of Scotch and English cloths, admirable for automobile and tourist wear, for $15, $16.50, $18.50, $20, $22.50 and up to $75. The Big Store on Market Street in Wheeling was having a sale of high grade winter suits for men and young men at $10. And, the inevitable was advertised, "Children Cry for Fletcher's Castoria". So, tempus fugit!

Letter To Dean Q. Wilson – WVU

August 15, 1963

TO DEAN QUINTUS WILSON, SCHOOL OF JOURNALISM
WEST VIRGINIA UNIVERSITY:

Dear Dean Wilson:

Forgive me, but I must use this weekly allotment of white space allowed me to both praise you for a worthy job with the "budding reporters" of your 'J' school and condemn you for what I believe is an injustice to the females of the Fourth Estate.

The public is aware by now that the W. Va. Press Association is making monthly awards to state newspapers for excellence in reporting, columns, pictures, advertising, etc.

I have been lucky on several occasions to win words of commendation for this column. For this, I am grateful.

But, I must protest, too! Why must you always designate this column as best in women's columns? I notice you don't stipulate as to best men's writing or best men's column!

In the 21 years of experience in this profession ranging from East St. Louis, to Parkersburg, to Clarksburg, to Bluefield, and back home to The Delta, I have found myself doing a man's job for which I received a man's salary. I was not hired because I was a female.

I have found, too, that I have more or less the average amount of education or experience as any man; I receive the average amount of complaints and praise as any man; I pound the same beats, including the rugged police and hospital beats, as any man; I cool my heels in the advertiser's business place just as any male salesman; I write the same amount of copy and answer the telephone as often as any male, and even now, have been known to swear on occasion like any dyspeptic editor and feel too the pangs of a growing ulcer.

I'll grant, I have been guilty on occasion of using my femininity to stand on a soap-box. At other times I've acted the role of a proud mother and written columns about my children, but would not a male columnist and father write too of his offspring?

The words of criticism or praise in my efforts to write this weekly column came principally from the male readers, which would indicate a column of interest to both men and women!

Perhaps, unfortunately, it has been my experience to find few dedicated newspaperwomen! The rest have been often indifferent, biased, prejudiced and mostly lazy.

Here again are exceptions to the rule, only two women in this state have I known personally whom I felt were dedicated - the late Marian Walls, of Bluefield, and Marie Wood, of Parkersburg. Both were splendid reporters, not women reporters. Like they, I've never become inured to the suffering and tragedy that must be written. Like any male, we too have seen the victim and the murderer, the mangled bodies of the auto wreck victims, the drunk in the hoosegow, the beaten body of a child and the coal-pitted bodies of those miners caught in underground explosions.

No, I do not like the classification of male and female, not in this business of writing.

If I found myself with a wall covered with certificates of awards for merit, they would not mean nearly as much as a slip of paper inserted one night in my typewriter by a male reporter not so many years ago in Bluefield. Those lines read:

"Our Sunday Editor is quite a pearl –
Even tho she is a girl –
She's mean as hell and somewhat cross—
But she is still our lordly boss—
Still, with all her faults
She is a joy -
We wouldn't trade her for a boy!"

Ready For School

August 29, 1963

It's that time of year again -- fall, school and football season. It all means that this lazy summer is over and it's back to the routine of meals, clothes, food, sleeping hours, new clothes, food, expensive books, soaking of aching football muscles in Epsom salts and more food.

I might as well consider stock in a grocery store for Son No. 1 and Son No. 2 will be attending the same high school. This may have its bad points before the year is over depending on just how much brother likes to tattle on brother.

Although anxious to see school start, I must admit I'm not looking forward to the fights over whose shirt who is wearing; first in the shower; who likes ham or who wants egg salad sandwiches for lunch; who limps or hurts more after football practice.

Little mother, Ann, who thinks she can calm all critical situations involving boys and mother, was ready for school Monday evening. At least she and the neighbor girls were playing school on the patio. Tuesday morning she was up and dressed and ready for school by the time I left for work and that is no mean feat as it usually takes two good hours just to unwind the hair curlers. The magic of this first school day won't last all winter, much to my regret.

Ah, yes that wonderful time of year, fall. Just think it won't be long now before high heating bills, slush of the winter snow upon your good carpet, heavy, damp jackets, the lost gloves, the muddy boots. Ah, yes, fall!

Prejudice

September 5, 1963

The day of the Big March is over. All across the land trouble had been predicted. But, even with over 200,000 black, white, ministers, laymen, the old, the young, the rich, the poor, there was no disorder.

The only arrests were those of white men. One who professed to head the Nazi party in America, another who threw stones and a third who carried a gun in his car.

For all those who watched on television, regardless of what personal opinions one possesses, we could not help but be impressed. And I asked myself if my skin were darker would I have had the courage to walk and still maintain discipline, well-mannered discipline.

The Big March had already left my mind when I happened to pick up a little 16-page magazette the other evening and the words "petty prejudices" jumped out at me. It's worth reading:

Anyone who reads the daily papers, watches television, or listens to the radio, has become familiar with the word "discrimination". It has become so closely identified with racial bias that this definition pops into the mind of the average person at the mention of the word.

Moralists long have told us that this type of discrimination would eventually stunt our economic growth, poison our national mind and erode the very roots of our democratic form of government. However, little was done to alter the situation until it became politically popular to do so, a decade or so ago. Legislation now helps to protect the minority victims of this type of prejudice.

We encounter many other types of discrimination in our daily lives in which the victims are not so well organized, and therefore will probably never be shielded by law. The question is, who is the real loser, when this type of venom is unleashed?

We are prejudiced against people who have not been successful enough.

We resist ideas we know to be better than our own.

We are biased against persons from other professions.

We are prejudiced against those with political convictions differing from our own.

We resent those who try to do too good a job, or those from a higher or lower occupational rung. We snub those we consider social inferiors.

We may discriminate against salesmen because their company is too big, or because it is too small, or merely because we have not dealt with them previously.

Possibly the most inane and tragic of all, we discriminate against men in industry, merely because of their age. We tell the mature worker when he has become unemployed through no fault of his own, and who has spent at least half his life gaining valuable job experience, that at age 50 or even less, he is too old.

These are petty things but they do indicate a state of mind in which we are generally prejudiced against new acquaintances and, just as seriously, new ideas.

Who are the real victims, then, of these types of mental toxin? The answer is that we are. We can't expect any legislation to be passed which commands us to open up our minds to new people, new ideas, and the daily changes in the world around us. It is up to us to learn not only to accept them, but to be on the lookout for them, and adapt to them.

Let us fear no one, respect everyone, and become the richer for our efforts.

Saturday Morning

September 26, 1963

I'm one who pretty well believes in "live and let live". What may seem like an idiosyncrasy to me is probably only too clear to the so-called eccentric individual.

Clothes don't interest me exclusively but cleanliness does. I don't care for golf but thousands are consumed with a passion for the sport. I'll do without lunches to spend ten dollars for a good book but thousands never look at even the front page of a newspaper. I have friends who are the world's worst gossips on the street where they live, but yet they have no curiosity in the world itself. I like history but can't add a column of five double figures. Even my fourth grader has left me far behind when it comes to fractions. Baseball doesn't particularly interest me, until the World Series rolls around, but I'll move heaven and high water to speed Saturday and Sunday afternoon lolling in front of "the big eye" beamed to a football game. This all leads up to the fact that maybe I have an idiosyncrasy. I like to sleep late on Saturday. By late, I don't mean until noon, just nearly so. It happens that I get every other Saturday morning off in this six-day work week and my biggest delight is throwing the alarm clock into the farthest corner the preceding evening.

Consequently, I don't appreciate the business phone calls I receive on these particular Saturday mornings. In fact, I'm downright hateful to the party on the other end of the line. Moreover, I consider it an imposition, poor taste, inconsiderate, extremely rude and a lot of other unprintable things, to be pulled out of bed for anything less than Main Street burning down. As you've probably gathered, I had just such a telephone call this past Saturday morning. And, to top it off it was a morning after I'd been up until 1 a.m. frying hamburgers and French fries for a couple of hungry football players after a game. Furthermore, the caller was one of those disgusting individuals who is probably full of vim, vigor and vitality even at the crack of dawn. Me? I'd just soon no one spoke to me any earlier than 10 a.m. and after at least four cups of black coffee and the morning paper.

Eccentric? Me? I guess I am when it comes to sleep but it must run in the family. I have a sister who'll sleep by an open window and wake up with snow piled on her bed.

So, I won't mention your idiosyncrasies, if you'll leave mine alone!

Letter To Bill Evans – re: Zopp

October 17, 1963

AN OPEN LETTER TO BILL EVANS, SPORTS WRITER OF THE FAIRMONT TIMES:

As the mother of two football players on the Buckhannon-Upshur high school team, I consider myself qualified to answer your vindictive attack on Coach Granville Zopp in your so-called "Sport Talk" in Monday morning's issue of the Fairmont Times.

You claim that "formal protest from a committee of physicians and surgeons concerned with athletic injuries in Monongahela Valley football will be made to the principal of B-U concerning the lack of concern reportedly displayed by its coach over the well-being of his players in last Friday night's game against Fairmont West."

You also state, "Some fans were highly critical of the young Buckhannon coach for what appeared to be his point-hunger."

You also claim that "the committee, which desires to remain publicly anonymous because of professional ethics, but which will sign its name to the protest, told this department that on one occasion – a visiting player appeared to have been knocked groggy. He was bleeding at the nose and obviously in some distress."

Now, Mr. Evans, I'll answer you charges.

Mr. Evans, how come, if Zopp doesn't have his players' health at heart, that vitamin pills and flu shots are provided, along with a proper meal preceding every game?

Mr. Evans, how come, if Zopp doesn't have his players' health at heart, that Buckhannon can continue to score and still be as fresh and in top physical shape the second half of a game as in the first?

Mr. Evans, how come, if Zopp doesn't have his players' health at heart, my son can play Fairmont West and still be in shape enough to get up at 4 a.m. the next morning to go fishing with his granddad?

Mr. Evans, how come, if Zopp doesn't have his players' health at heart, that he telephones many times during the season to check on Dave as well as Bill, who has spent the season on the bench?

Mr. Evans, how come, if Zopp doesn't have his players' health at heart, he provides special equipment for those boys with bruised ribs, pinched nerves, or crippled knees?

Mr. Evans, how come, if Zopp doesn't have his players' health at heart, he sent David to a specialist in Clarksburg to see about a knee injury?

Mr. Evans, how come, if Zopp doesn't have his players' health at heart, he went to the hospital with David and paced the floor for X-ray results?

Mr. Evans, you're talking through your hat. Frankly, I think you are a fake.

One thing for sure: You built up West Virginia University in pre-season writing like no team has ever been built up before. Now, when the Mountaineers aren't living up to your predictions you've been selling them down the river.

Either you are full of baloney or the instigator of the biggest hoax ever perpetuated by a sports writer – to sell tickets to a Mountaineer game.

You also claim that a Buckhannon player appeared to be groggy and bleeding from the nose and received no proper attention.

Mr. Evans, that player was Bill Mackey, who received a bloody nose.

As to proper attention, the assistant coach, Charlie Beer, was with the boy immediately. And just incidentally, that bloody nose was received because of the tremendous beating the kid took all night from the two Fairmont players keyed on Mackey. Three Fairmont players were keyed on Oldaker too during the game but you'll note from the score that it didn't stop the rest of the backfield from scoring. It has been my experience in only 20 years of reporting to your 50 years, that the diatribe is nothing but a cry-baby attitude for the most terrific beating Fairmont West has taken in 30 years.

Secondly, a man of your repute or lack thereof in journalism should have learned long ago to check facts before publishing rumors.

Thirdly, Buckhannon hasn't met a team this year that has been in good physical shape due to proper conditioning. Thank Zopp for having the well-being of his players at heart with emphasis on proper physical conditioning.

If the Marion County Medical Society is concerned about the welfare of Buckhannon players, let me point out that not one player has been sidelined with an injury this season. Can other coaches of the Monongahela Valley Association say the same? You talk about point-hunger. Any time a play is perfectly executed it means a touchdown. This year, Buckhannon happens to have a powerhouse – the first time since Freal Crites coached the Buc-Ups. He too, believed in conditioning and it paid off with points.

My son happens to be quarterback on Buckhannon's team and, as an illustration, may I point out that last Friday night he went for a touchdown that not only surprised the fans but David as well. If you remember, he was using a quarterback sneak to pick up a first down on Fairmont's nine-yard line. The hole opened up and, to his surprise, he was in the end zone. Is that point-hunger?

Why Mr. Evans are you so concerned about B-U being point-hungry? I see in Saturday morning's papers where Bridgeport scored 61 points over their opponent. Martins Ferry ran up 68 points over Wheeling Linsly. And how about Welch 45 over Mullens 7; Bluefield 33 over Man 0; Charles Town 42 over Berkeley Springs 7 and Weirton 33 over Tridelphia 13?

You said fans were critical of the high scoring. What fans? From where? And since when did fans start to coach high school football games?

We have some in Buckhannon who would like to – but thank goodness, Zopp has let it be known that he is the coach. Naturally this has caused some disgruntled "Monday-morning quarterbacks" to do some stabbing and jabbing. Buckhannon doesn't need this kind of fan any more than it needs your kind of sour grapes.

Furthermore, it has been my experience that whenever a committee wishes to remain anonymous that means either there is no so-called committee or a committee of "gutless, disgruntled cry-babies".

There was a man named Bill
Whose football team stood still
He wrote for The Times
Some damn fool lines
Just because he was ill.
SOUR GRAPES?

Welfare

October 31, 1963

Once more the Department of Public Welfare is under fire and once more a political football. Governor Barron is considering a special session of legislature to find $7.5 million or lose $48 million in federal aid.

West Virginia was given notice this past week that unless it strengthens its welfare administrative procedures, the Kennedy administration may not be so generous with its "handouts".

The warning amounts to this - too little in West Virginia is used in reviewing explicit cases. For instance, Pennsylvania has been spending $13.99 and W. Va. – $4.47 per case.

According to federal authorities "too many children are growing up knowing only the welfare state". Under new federal requirements a case worker cannot handle more than 60 cases each. In this state the number of cases handled per worker is 227, highest in the nation.

So we turn to the legislature. Unless the legislators cough up $7.5 million, the entire federal allocation for public welfare will be withheld and the welfare program in this state will collapse. Democrats can't afford to see this program fail!! But, where will W. Va. legislators find $7.5 million? It will be interesting to see if the working family is once more soaked with a temporary tax.

The burden of taxation in this state is already more than most can bear. In Upshur county, with three employed heads of families now working to support one DPA family. I hardly see where my salary can be stretched another dollar to support heaven knows how many more unemployed.

I sincerely believe in case reviews. Stringent case review might reveal what the man-on-the-street has been saying for too many free-loaders, too little enforcement of regulations, too much apathy and too much political manipulation in human misery.

Have the politicians thought about creating some jobs and then making it mandatory to work?

Government Regulations

November 7, 1963

While Publisher Frank R. Mills of The Chronicle-Herald of Hoopeston, Ill., has his tongue firmly planted in his cheek, there is nevertheless "More Truth in Poetry" in his commentary on the eagerness of senators to protect us from practically everything.

"Out to our house when Grandma pours my breakfast food" he writes, "I get a bowl heaped high in the middle. Because of the variety of our worked-over mix-n-match china, sometimes I get a little bowl and sometimes a big one.

"This arrangement has never bothered me particularly, at least, I have learned it unwise to evidence any complaint, lest my hair be parted with a bowl, large or small.

"Now this is all to be. Washington is to decide what is a bowlful, and what size bow, state size of a 'serving' and make the manufacturer print it on the package, so you'll have no excuse for making a mistake.

"This wonderfully outstanding and forward-looking piece of legislation holds high promise. No longer may our friendly restaurant slap out a half-cup while picking your pocket with short measure. The government will require a loadline printed right inside the cup so the customer may see he's getting full measure. And further, the inspector-general of all coffee pots will see that he doesn't chisel on the amount of coffee beans, for that would be grounds for penalties.

"There are some other points of interest in the new law. The government will determine which side of the package of breakfast food (or soap) is the front, and right there must be printed the exact contents in big type. Flat boxes might make the package look king-sized, so that is frowned upon. Picture of a wash-lady cannot show a happy smile unless the manufacturer can prove she is happy. Nothing deceptive is to be permitted…

"I'm thankful our Congress is working on this useful and profound legislation. If their time was not so taken up, they might be monkeying around with missiles in Cuba, the Berlin Wall, and Krushy's latest 'peace' offer.

"Besides that, I stand a peachy chance of getting rich, should it become necessary to imprint a few million Joan of Arc and Stokely labels with the proper information in what constitutes a serving.

"One thing I decry about the new regulation. It brings into sharp focus the stupidity of Mrs. Average American Housewife in a most uncomplimentary manner. Husbands have quietly recognized for years that wives can't recognize a bargain when they see it. That they never badger the butcher, pinch either peaches or cocoanuts, or take back something they don't like for a refund. Further, they just love to be short-changed, and return time after time to a merchant or a product they didn't like.

"Now, we must frankly recognize their lack of intelligence, love them for what they are and protect them always."

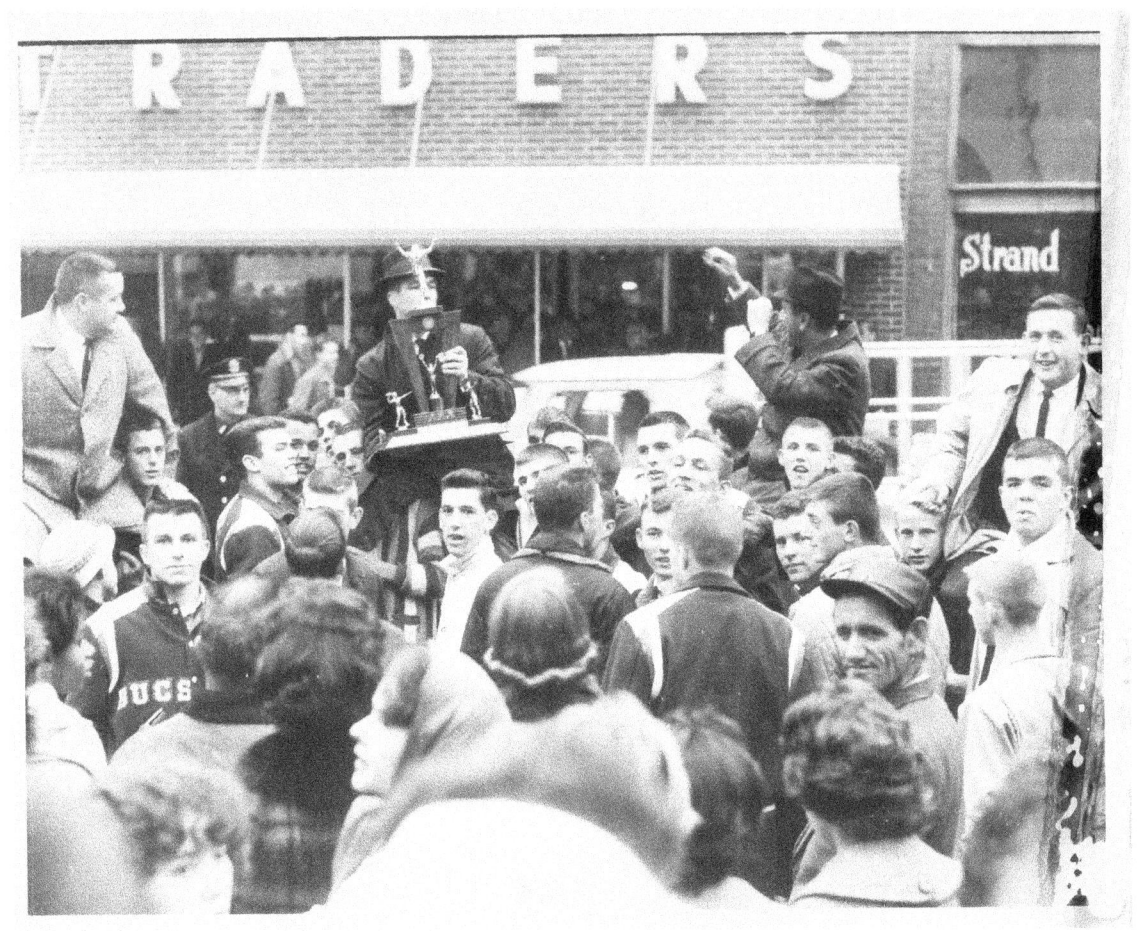

Howard Hiner Collection

Football Champions

November 21, 1963

I went back to high school last Thursday. And, it was a great day! It was "High School Football Team Championship Day". I sat in the audience along with all the other parents, grandparents, aunts, uncles and boosters and thought to myself "What a short season this has been and how wonderful for the coach and boys."

And, I thought too, how hard everyone has worked for three years to make a state championship possible. It was good to hear all of the compliments, all of the congratulations, all of the tributes, and better yet, to see for myself the beautiful trophy and the looks of pride on every boy's face.

Yes, it was a great day! It was a sentimental day for the soon-to-graduate seniors. It was a day of reminiscing. It was a day of presentations; the cheerleaders, Claudia Been, Judy Vincent, Patti Smallridge, Cheri Ellis, Hallie Davidson, Jeannie Trainer; the unsung heroes, the assistant coaches, Gail Zickefoose, Bud Newbrough, Frank Feola; the board of education, the principals.

And, there's more to come. Friday night will be the Championship Dinner and more praise, all deserving. As someone said Thursday, not one of the 45 boys on this football team would be ineligible to play any sport due to poor grades. And, along with the memories will be the individual medals.

Yes, it was a great day and a great team!!

Death of J.F.K.

December 5, 1963

President Lyndon B. Johnson in his Thanksgiving plea to his fellow citizens for their help, their strength and their prayers, pointed out manifold blessings that many may have forgotten in the full week of emotional upheaval that began with a sniper's rifle shot in Dallas on November 22.

And there is profound truth in his statement of Thanksgiving evening that "a deed intended to tear us apart has bound us together." In the vast confusion and numbing shock of assassination, unthinkable in our time, it had seemed this nation was, for 100 minutes without a chief executive. And then, in the space of an oath, given in the cabin of the aircraft to which President Kennedy's body had been brought, President Johnson contained the distraction of grief with his first executive order. "Let's get this plane to Washington" he said.

In his address to the joint session of the Congress in which he had served 32 years, almost to the day, President Johnson declared that belief in the integrity and independence of the Legislative branch "is deep in the marrow of my bones". And he said: "With equal firmness, I believe in the capacity of the Congress, despite the divisions of opinions which characterize our nation, to act wisely, to act vigorously, to act speedily when the need arises."

With this his fellow countrymen will generally agree. But, in calmer hour, the President will realize that it is because of those "divisions of opinion" and not "despite" them that the Congress is wise and capable and the nation strong. Just as the Republic goes on, so does the source of its strength, the two-party system.

The order-of-the-day, if we read it correctly, is "Carry on!"

Resolutions

December 31, 1963

This is the season of goodwill, peace, friendliness, and New Year's resolutions. I'm braver than most, I not only make resolutions, I print them for the world and all to read and then flaunt in my face.

But since I usually show more intestinal fortitude than sense, here goes.

Patience. They say you can't show an old dog new tricks but surely I can practice patience with Ann, the youngest, who talks constantly when I prefer silence; jumps when I have a cake in the oven; sings during my favorite newscast and wants attention when I'm enthralled by a novel.

Understanding. Is there a parent anywhere that understands teenagers? But, there will be understanding, and more control of temper and dessert oftener than once a week. At least, it looks good on paper and the thought is there, if not always practiced.

Frugality in expenditures of both time and money. Time for the making of doll clothes, time for talk, time for that special salad, time to sew on that elusive button, time to find the bottom of the basket of un-ironed laundry, time for visits to neighbors and friends.

Yes, if I would do all these, I would be a saint, completely out of character, but give me credit for courage. My resolutions are in black and white. How about yours?

Margaret Kyle's Rose Thief

January 9, 1964

We've all been reading a great deal on this "hate business", brought on of course, by the tragic death of President Kennedy. We've all been urged to learn a little more about forgiving and forgetting and being just plain good neighbors.

We read and listen, sometimes half-heartedly, and feel perhaps that the sermon and the preaching don't touch us or anyone we know.

But, unhappily, Buckhannon has one of the meanest thieves in my memory. This thief didn't rob anyone of actual cash. This thief robbed a local resident of something much worse – her pride, her pleasure, her peace of mind, her faith in mankind and her joy in just living and working in her own backyard.

Margaret Kyle, a retired school teacher, and her sister, Eunice, who teaches art in the local high school, spent their Christmas vacation in New York City, seeing several Broadway shows, visiting, and just enjoying the sights and sounds of the Big City.

They returned home Sunday while the snow was still several inches deep in the yard. Friday morning, you remember, spring like weather arrived and Margaret strolled out into her rose garden. She had in mind to do a little picking up here and there, a mid-winter clean up, you understand. It was then that the enjoyment of her Christmas vacation was shattered, the New Year had already ruined through the work of a thief. A thief, who stepped into the yard during Margaret's vacation, and professionally cut her six dozen rosebushes to the ground.

Every branch is gone, except one. Gone too, of course, is the approximately $100 invested in the plants. But, more important, gone, too, are the hours of pleasure she spent in nursing the roses to maturity, the pleasure in watching her handiwork grow, pride in her ability to create and joy in the knowledge that this spring and summer neighbors and friends would have benefited from the color and fragrance of her roses.

Yes, hate is a terrible thing, and it's so hard to forgive and forget. I'm wondering, this act of stealing, did it satisfy the thief's need?

Tucked In Bed

January 16, 1964

There's just no livin' anymore with those teenage boys at my house, and no discipline, either. Take Monday night, for instance. As usual, shortly before bedtime I'm half-standing at my dresser, doing those things to my face and hair that all women do before retiring, half-standing, 'cause I've had a heck of a wearing day.

Dave and Bill enter, supposedly to talk one of them starts clowning, wrestling with the other.

I say, "Stop it." They say I've raised my voice. I say "Stop it I've had a rough day." Both agree I'm tired and should be in bed.

And lo, both have picked me up and I'm in bed, shoes, slacks, shirt and all.

I shout, I laugh, I get hysterical. Too weak to resist, the blankets are tucked tight. Two pillows under my head and a book over my face.

Afterward, I lie there trying to catch my breath, gusseted like a mummy. I think all is calm and suddenly Bill sticks his head around the door, blows a whistle and shouts, "Everybody up!" Now you just picture yourself in this idiotic situation. There's no point in shouting. I learned a long time ago to just grin and bear it. Otherwise, I might get hurt.

Take this summer. I wanted peace and quiet one evening. Again. I was told I had raised my voice. I got madder and a little louder. The next thing I know, one son has my feet, the other my arms and I am swinging high and higher. I get madder, kick viciously and all I get for my trouble is a higher swing. Suddenly the situation appears ridiculous even to me.

This time I burst into gales of laughter and guess what? I'm suddenly dropped on my backside. It took me awhile to get out of bed the next morning but I eventually recovered.

You won't believe this, but I'm too brittle for such shenanigans. The boys won't listen but one of these days, you just wait and see. I'll be limping up Main Street with an arm in a cast and then you can believe it, there's just no livin' anymore with my teenagers--and no discipline either!

Welfare and Birth Control Pills

January 23, 1964

The most sensible, but perhaps controversial, solution to the county and state problem of welfare has come from a local doctor. It will cost $1.15 per month and will solve many of our problems. Since the 1930's some form of relief has been given to those unable or unwilling to provide for themselves. Recently, it has been chopped meat, bacon, peanut butter, lard, butter, rice, corn meal, cheese, flour, dried milk and beans.

Beans aren't enough!

If just one essential element were added to the surplus commodity list, prosperity would be here. Through the magic of pharmaceutical medical research, birth control pills can be given to the mother once a day for 20 days each month at a cost of $1.15 per month to the state. This, surely, is cheaper than the doubling of surplus commodity rations to needy families, an action that means expansion of the West Virginia program from a $22 million to a $44 million operation. Surely the program of birth control would be cheaper than the state paying our doctors $25 per delivery of a baby, an unwanted baby, another baby for the taxpayer to support, another generation of welfare recipients.

This state needs fewer babies and fewer $25 checks. Welfare recipients don't want a dozen children any more than the average tax-paying family. After three or four children, a mother on the relief rolls is usually crying for help. The local doctors cry, too, when a 13 year-old girl shows up in the office pregnant which is occurring more frequently in this country.

If the welfare recipient doesn't like the corn flour, he tosses it away and bakes bread with the white flour. But you don't toss away an unwanted child!

If only 50 percent of the recipients used the packet of birth control pills, inserted monthly in the box of surplus commodities, this state and county would be 50 percent that much better off.

While the state legislature is in session, how about suggesting to your senators and your delegates to spend a little more on birth control by adding this essential commodity to the list. Surely, a wise investment.

B-U Students On TV Toss Up

April 2, 1964

Not too long ago, someone mentioned to me that Buckhannon was a good town in which to rear children. In the next breath, the person said it was a shame that something nice couldn't be written in the newspaper about good kids, not just the bad ones.

That conversation came back to me last Wednesday evening as I watched Buckhannon-Upshur "pour it on" in the second round of the TV Toss-Up finals for a $2,000 scholarship.

For the uninformed or for those persons who resist "the idiot box", area schools have been matching wits each Wednesday over WBOY-TV for $250 Wesleyan scholarships and are now in the finals for $2,000.

Last Wednesday, these Buckhannon kids were tremendous. They swamped Washington Irving of Clarksburg to the tune of 250 points to 50. Most of the time Mike Jack, Carolyn Griffin, Jim Ashworth and Steve Coonts were able to answer the question before it had been completely asked. Sharp? Yes, these kids are sharp. And, it's evident that all are well read, exceptionally well-read. None are straight A students, just possessed of good, ordinary, horse sense.

I don't know how the team will do in the future or if B-U will achieve the $2,000 prize. These four students have already shown me that I need no longer worry about the state of world affairs. Multiply these four by all the 'bright four' in every high school of this nation and my future outlook seems much more optimistic.

And, it's so much more exciting to write about good kids than the political scene, or the DPA or the county roads, or the breakings and enterings, or mine closings, or the lack of support of the Girl Scout program, or the failure of the school levy.

Yes. Buckhannon is a good town in which to rear children. It's a shame elders set such a poor example.

Gibson Library

April 9, 1964

It isn't a great, grand, towering edifice, rich in endowment or adequately staffed, but the Charles W. Gibson Memorial Library is rich in friends and dedicated workers. A memorial to the vision of an Upshur county cattleman, the public library opened in October, 1942 and operates on a budget of less than $4,000 per year but its usefulness is demonstrated in the fact that over 1,000 books are circulated per month.

Buckhannon is richer because Charles W. Gibson had the wisdom to bequeath his money for the construction and operation of the library and richer, too, because this town has been blessed by the dedication of a librarian, Mrs. Rachel Barlow. The widow of a Baptist minister, Mrs. Barlow has worked untiringly since 1946 for the betterment of the library. The culmination of all her efforts will be realized this Sunday when the Charles W. Gibson public library receives a $1,000 award from the Book-of-the-Month club.

What will $1,000 buy? It will buy approximately 300 new books to add to the already 15,000 volumes now housed in the modern, one story building at the intersection of Meade and East Main streets. But, the $1,000 also buys a future and a hope that there will be other awards and other endowments. The library is always pathetically short of funds, not because there is any lack of local cooperation, but rather because we are not always aware of the need.

Mrs. Barlow and two college girls as part-time workers make up the library staff. Their salaries are paid from an endowment from the Gibson estate of $500 annually and from the $3,000 a year realized from a levy supported every three years by Buckhannon voters. The taxation amounts to less than a penny on a dollar. The Buckhannon Lions Club gives $75 a year in interest on a library endowment fund and another $100 comes from cash donations of Buckhannon's Woman's Club, the AAUW and others. From this sum, books and magazines must be bought, utilities paid, repairs made - an ever growing list of needs but all handled capably by the library board, six volunteers appointed by the city council and the superintendent of schools.

Serving three-year terms, with two new appointments each year are board members, Dr. George Glauner, Mrs. James Colemen, Mrs. David Reemsnyder, Dr. Lewis Chrisman, W.T. O'Brien, and C.B. Curry, along with Superintendent Charles D. Munson.

Their job isn't easy, but o' how grateful they are to the individuals and the civic organizations who try to ease the burden of maintenance! The Rotary club, for instance, which buys the paint for a face-lifting now and then. And the Lions who spend a night applying the fresh paint. The Historical Society, the Junior and Senior Women's clubs, the DAR, Moose Club, Jayceettes and the two garden clubs who buy many, many books and subscriptions each year. And the Stonewall Jackson regional library which maintains a revolving depository of 300 books, one-third of which are replaced each month and which answers special requests for books. I may have missed some, but these organizations are just a sample of the awareness that a need for knowledge exists.

This Sunday, the $1,000 check will be presented at ceremonies at 2:30 p.m. in the First Baptist Church. There will be open house the balance of the afternoon at the library. We all can't bequeath endowments or donate cash, but we can show our support of the library by attending these events.

Whirligig by Herb Welch

April 23, 1964

For the first time in history, the number of a Buckhannon-Upshur football player has been retired, never to be worn by another B-U gridman, and his game jersey has been placed permanently in the locked trophy case of the school.

High School Coach of the Year, Granville Zopp, head coach of the 1963 AAA state champion B-U grid team, bestowed the honor upon Dave Hornbeck, and tri-captain of the team, Saturday night at an annual B-U junior and senior high father-son athletic banquet.

His voice muffled with emotion, Coach Zopp told the more than 200 at the banquet that Hornbeck is one of the finest boys he has ever coached – "very dedicated and a boy of great courage."

Coach Zopp related the story of Dave's triumph over many obstacles, including a deficiency in speed which continued to plague him even as he was quarterbacking his team to the state championship. Thus his coach indicated that there were others of no doubt greater football ability on the squad. And yet it was Dave who was singled out for the unprecedented honor. Why?

Zopp summed it all up when he declared that Dave's dedication and his will to win were the greatest of any athlete he has ever coached.

"When Dave graduates from college and if he settles down in Buckhannon," said Zopp, "he'll make one of the best citizens this town will ever know."

Dave is the son of Mrs. Betty Hornbeck, this newspaper's Girl Friday six days a week and for this reason only it has been awkward if not impossible for THE DELTA to give Dave the recognition he deserved for his leadership of the team.

Make no mistake about it—his team mates were on Dave's side throughout the season and they were just as proud as we were when Coach Zopp singled Dave out for the special honor.

To them, just as to Coach Zopp, No. 16 in the backfield represented David Hornbeck, good citizen as well as good football player.

Somehow, it seems to us that Coach Zopp's emphasis upon character represents football at its finest. Granted, it poses the greatest of challenges to young Dave, who in life won't always find himself on the winning side as he tries to live up to his coach's estimate of him.

But at the same time, it could be that the No. 16 battle-scarred jersey in the high school trophy case will spark like determination to succeed in football—and in life—on the part of other boys in the years to come.

And if No. 16 exerts a good influence on just one other boy, then Coach Zopp's action in retiring the number will have been justified.

Mental Illness

April 30, 1964

If you had asked me several weeks ago how many people in this county were interested in mental health, I might have answered a dozen. "O, ye, of little faith," said He, for over 35 Buckhannon residents turned up recently for a meeting of the Upshur County Committee on Action for Mental Health.

And, believe me, Dr. Alexander H. Baranski, superintendent of Weston State Hospital jerked our eyes wide open and yanked us upright in our seats with some facts and figures on mental illness and mental health.

Does the reader of this column know or care that Weston State Hospital houses 2,238 patients from a 35-county area? Do you know or care that this includes 100 criminal cases and 102 TB patients, who have no business in the state hospital? Do you know or care that West Virginia spends $2.79 per day per patient, (this includes clothing, food and medicine) as compared to $4.40 per day for patients in Huntington State Hospital and 50 per day per patient in the state of Ohio?

According to Dr. Baranski, 50 percent of the patients never should be sent to the state hospital. If we realized that we live in the year 1964 and not in the 17th century, all of us would be concerned that often the mentally ill are taken to the hospital in chains and often times by a sheriff or deputy, indicating a criminal case instead of a physical disability. A patient may not be curable but treatable, but then so is a bleeding ulcer or a broken arm.

It should be our prime concern in the 20th century to begin treating mental illness as a disease. We all need some education when it comes to recognizing mental illness, fighting prejudice, gossip, shame, and to learn not to be afraid. It should be our concern when a school guidance counselor becomes alarmed at borderline cases she discovers at school, attempts to find help and there is no help!

It should be our prime concern to bring pressure upon our legislators to improve on admittance requirements to state hospitals. It should be our concern to improve upon facilities, realizing that there is need for rehabilitation centers in counties, and mental health centers with out-patient clinics, all of which, take money.

Since money, or enough money, hasn't been forthcoming from the state legislature, ridiculous as it may seem, Dr. Baraski and his staff must now use their valuable time, which could be used for better patient care, to arrange a bazaar, proceeds of which will be used to buy additional items necessary for the comfort of patients.

But, since the staff finds itself so handicapped for funds that the bazaar is necessary, then the public should support his plan. Weston State Hospital will observe Mental Health week on Saturday, May 2, at which time there will be tours of the hospital from 9 a.m. to 10 a.m. and again at 1:30 p.m. to 4 p.m.

There will be entertainment for the patients and public in the form of music, dances, artistic displays, and pony rides for children. Items to be sold at the bazaar will include patients handicraft along with items donated by various church and civic organizations, such as jewelry, aprons, tea towels, baked goods, etc.

Anyone having contributions may contact Mrs. Gerry Kiddy, director of the recreation department of the hospital.

If you don't care, you should! If you do care, for heaven's sake, support that bazaar, either with your presence or with a contribution!

Vote For School Levy

May 7, 1964

Experts theorize that only two of every 10 students now in elementary school will graduate from college. If this prediction comes true, in six or seven years the labor market will be flooded with job-seekers.

By 1970, when many of these begin graduating, the American labor force will already total about 100 million. Twenty-six million of this total will be young workers entering the labor force during the decade of the 1960's. Three million will be women entering or re-entering the working world. These facts, for no other reason, should make Upshur county voters sit up and take notice on May 12th when they march to the polls to vote for or against the school levy. It has been my experience that we get just what we pay for. If we are not willing to pay our share for a vocational trade school, I see little hope for the future but more federal control and higher taxes to finance a poverty program which is estimated to cost nearly $940 million for the first year. Original estimates call for a five-year, $5 billion program, with $500 million each year coming from existing programs and $500 million in new authorization.

If you think for just one minute that this money isn't coming out of your paycheck, heaven help America if the "hope for our people is the federal handout! According to figures released from the State Department of Education, during the 1962-63 school year, 20,552 students in 177 high schools were enrolled in programs of vocational and technical education. These courses, also taken by 11,711 adults, were offered in 53 counties. Fred W. Eberie, acting director of the Bureau of Vocational and Adult Education, says the biggest need is for vocational schools. The schools, relatively new developments in the field of vocational education, draw students from a wider territory than is embraced in the normal school system.

State vocational educators have recommended eight state supported vocational-technical centers, each serving an area of two or more counties. These centers would offer an instructional program covering the secondary and post-secondary grades as well as adult education. Your vote on May 12 in support of the school levy means that Upshur county can become a center for vocational-technical training. It will also prove that we as citizens realize that vocational and technical education are sound investments in West Virginia for youth and adults alike.

Zopp Resigns

May 21, 1964

Buckhannon had its years of glory! Buckhannon proved it could play in the Big League. This football team was one to be reckoned with. This time the raw material was molded and gouged and pushed and pulled into one of the sweetest, smoothest-runnin' machines that the Big Ten or this state has seen in a long, long time - 40 years to be exact.

The sports fans will argue for the next 40 years, pro and con – it wasn't the coach, it was the boys, and vice versa. We can straddle the fence and say it was a combination of both.

But me, I lived football under Granville Zopp these past three years. Through a son, I learned to eat football, drink football, sleep football—I was all but playing on that field. So, I say it was the coach. He took raw untutored players and made a machine that marched up and down that football field and gave sport fans a thrill they may never experience again. I'm afraid we'll never know another Zopp. And, it's a shame! Controversial, sure. But he built men. There were no cry babies, they weren't mama's boys, they were smart, bright young men, in the classroom and on the field. He put a snap in every boy's step, confidence in every boy's heart, and the will to win in every boy's mind. The greater the odds, the bigger the opposition, the harder they fell.

Zopp put fear in every coach's heart in the Monongahela Valley. Zopp brought big-time football to Buckhannon and this valley and he served notice he was out to win. Now, we've lost the best to greater pay, greater opportunity. It would be unfair of us to expect him to stay. But, I imagine tonight there are several dozen coaches in this area who are having sighs of relief. Now their jobs are insured. Once again they can sit on their "fannies" and go back to the lazy brand of football that has plagued this valley for many, many years. We won't have Zopp, and the Big Ten will have Buckhannon to use once again as a door mat.

I hope the board of education can find another Zopp! We need him!

To Granville go my thanks for football thrills, my best wishes for his future and congratulations for making possible this One Year of Glory!

Summer Camps

June 11, 1964

If there are any mothers who think that vacation time has arrived now that school is over, they must not be thinking ahead to the various summer camps. The thought of camps may conjure up visions of blankets and clothes for many but around my house it conjures up just one long, long parade of inoculations. And how do I get my three in that parade?

I haven't gotten so far along as to get the doctor's appointments and as far as what shots were given when has long escaped me. It's incidental that it is also time for a visit to the vet for the dog's shots.

Three kids and a dog can make summer rather maddening for mothers when camp officials have had a full nine months start to prepare rules and regulations for attendance.

Psychology has never been one of my strong points and I'm undecided as to whether it would be better to go to the doctor's office en masse, (it said that misery loves company) or should the trek be made individually.

June and July will find the youngest attending two Girl Scout camps and the annual 4-H camp. I will be able to cope with her as she's smaller to lasso. Son No. 1 and Son No. 2 will be a different story. Since both manage to put off until the night before any final plans or arrangements and since both have long outgrown me in height and weight, the situation may become critical. I would be willing to wager that Son No. 1 will be standing in the college registration line next fall still receiving necessary shots unless my apparent desperation moves him to action sooner out of a sense of pity for his old, graying mother.

Son No. 2 has already reached the point of no return. He will be among the 50,000 Scouters attending National Jamboree and although he's known for several months that shots were necessary, it is my guess that he believes he will be one in the 50,000 who can escape the inevitable.

The brochures always boast of the "wonderful experience" for the camper. Not one even mentions the "experience" encountered by mothers prior to camp time.

Welfare & The Pill – Part #2

June 18, 1964

O, the wrath that was heaped around my head last January when I dared suggest birth control pills be distributed to welfare recipients! And, on the suggestion of a local physician, too. The anonymous phone calls and the anonymous letters (mostly in anger) reminded me of a quotation from some time or other, "Not one man in ten dares say what he thinks; not one man in ten thousand dares put it in print and sign his name!"

In less than one week after making that suggestion, Associated Press came out with a story to the effect that there is a slowly, but steadily, developing trend in the United States to provide birth control services to welfare recipients at public expense. In the state's May primary election, one gubernatorial candidate came out in support of the pills. Also, in May, Kanawha county government leaders, physicians and ministers overwhelmingly came out in favor or the birth control pill clinics which the Kanawha-Charleston Health Department plans to set up this summer as a means of fighting poverty. Just last week, the Methodist Conference went on record in favor of birth control clinics and the W. Va. Synod of the Presbyterian church recommended last Tuesday that the state supply birth control materials and information to welfare recipients on a voluntary basis.

For many years, birth control assistance has been available through the health departments of seven Southern states: Alabama, Florida, Georgia, Mississippi, North Carolina, South Carolina and Virginia. New York has recently become the 11th state to adopt such a program. The District of Columbia soon will follow suit. I'd say these examples of support are top arguments for the adoption of birth control pills for West Virginia welfare recipients. As the Presbyterian put it, the proposal would provide "a morally sound program of letting every child born in a family be a wanted child." A woman who gives birth while receiving welfare assistance not only adds one more person to the relief rolls, but also contributes to conditions slowing her family's return to self-sufficiency. It might be wise to remind you one more time that federal, state and local welfare now costs us $40 billion a year which is $4,700 for each of the 9.3 million families the government estimates are in need. President Johnson would add $300 million to welfare programs or a little over $30 per family. If we still have poverty in this country, it is not because we have been niggardly. If $4,700 per family won't solve the problem, $30 more is not likely to! Birth Control pills might.

Topless Bathing Suits

June 25, 1964

It's been said that anticipation is greater than realization. We shall see what we shall see when the topless bathing suits first hit Buckhannon. My 11-year old has already emphatically stated "I won't wear one." That gives me hope, for I'm sure that more than morality will be sagging when the topless suits hit the beaches.

One large department store in New York City admits that swimsuits will be bootlegged from under the counter. The merchandise will neither be displayed nor publicized but available for those exhibitionists who desire to buy.

A park supervisor has already taken a stand on the controversial issue declaring that any women caught in a topless swimsuit on a public beach will be pinched. I have no doubt of that!

Our local city attorney, Bob Wallace, says he knows of no actual city ordinance banning topless swimsuits, but he will personally investigate every sale.

Of all the local stores polled this week, only one dared say the merchandise would be available if manufactured, but then, I'm not sure but that it was said with tongue in cheek. One merchant laughingly exclaimed: "He'd wait and see," before stocking the topless swimsuits.

According to Miss Sally Koon, manager of the Centennial Pool, public opinion no doubt will be varied. "The reaction would have to be measured if 'one' appears at the pool," she stated.

Deflation may be just around the corner. As one local yokel put it, "if you have a yen to bare the bosom, go to a nudist colony."

Yes, this is an Enlightened Age, as predicted, the bare backs, the plunging necklines and now, topless swimsuits. Shades of Cannes, what next?

Transient Aid

July 9, 1964

Tuesday morning, for the eighth time this summer, the Rev. Mr. Henry Austin, pastor of the First Baptist church, was called to town to look into the needs of a migrant worker, his 11 children, wife and car, all parked in front of the courthouse on Main Street.

Through no fault of the husband, he was stranded in Buckhannon, without a place to rest, nor money for food or gasoline for his car. The family, all field workers, were enroute to Indiana, after laboring in the vegetable crops throughout the South.

Buckhannon is not different than any other community in this United States, in that it will often times be called upon to "feed the hungry, give to the thirsty, clothe the naked, heal the sick, and give rest to the weary."

The point is this, Buckhannon has no facilities or agencies which provide necessities in times of emergencies such as in the above case. The Salvation Army is located in Clarksburg and our local chapter of the Red Cross does not function. Neither does the state or federal government make any provisions for the needy in this sense.

But, is this just a church problem or just a community problem, or could not both the church and community work together in setting up a fund to provide for emergencies? Must the Rev. Mr. Austin or his church alone bear the brunt of the problem? They do have a deacon's fund of not more than $50 which is little enough and certainly does not begin to meet the need.

The Buckhannon Ministerial Association is without funds. It operates the entire year on collections taken during Holy Week services and a Thanksgiving offering.

So, what's the solution? Can the Chamber of Commerce be expected to help, the several civic organizations, or individuals? If you have the answer will you please contact the Rev. Mr. Austin? He'd like a solution too!!

How To Cook A Husband

July 23, 1964

The following recipe was interesting to me so I thought I'd pass it along to Delta readers this week. I borrowed it from the Moorefield Examiner who in turn had borrowed it from Ann McClure's Cookbook, published in 1823.

HOW TO COOK A HUSBAND:

"A good many husbands are spoiled by mismanagement in cooking, and are not so tender and good. Some women keep them constantly in hot water. Others let them freeze by their carelessness and indifference. Some keep them in a stew with irritating ways and words. Some wives waste them shamefully.

It cannot be supposed that any husband will be tender and good when so managed, but they are really delicious when prepared properly. In selecting a husband, you should not be guided by the silvery appearance as in buying a mackerel, nor by the golden tint as if you wanted a salmon. Do not go to the market for him as the best ones are always brought to the door. Be sure to select him yourself as tastes differ. It is far better to have none unless you patiently learn how to cook him. Of course, a preserving kettle of finest porcelain is best, but if you have nothing better than an earthenware pipkin, it will do with care. Like crabs and lobsters, husbands are cooked alive. They sometimes fly out of the kettle and so become burned and crusty at the edges, so it is wise to secure him in the kettle with a strong silken cord called Comfort, as the one called Duty is apt to be weak, Make a clear slow flame of love, warmth and cheerfulness. Set him as near this as seems to agree with him.

If he sputters, do not be anxious for some husbands do this until they are quite done. Add a little sugar in the form of what confectioners call kisses, but use no pepper. Season to taste with spices, good humor and gaiety preferred, but seasoning must always be used with great discretion and caution. Avoid sharpness in testing him for tenderness. Stir him gently lest he be too flat and close to the kettle and so become useless. You cannot fail to know when he is done. If so treated, you will find him delicious and digestible, agreeing with you perfectly; and he will keep as long as you choose unless you become careless and allow the home fires to grow cold. Thus prepared, he will serve a lifetime of Happiness!"

Neighbors

August 6, 1964

It occurred to me this weekend that I'm very fortunate to have neighborly neighbors. This is something most of us take for granted and probably never really appreciate unless we hear a story of unneighborly neighbors.

I'm referring to a story of the elderly people (I wouldn't call them neighbors) who fuss with the children as they play ball, who refuse to give the ball back when it lands in their yard, who call the police constantly about imagined harassment and who have erected "No Trespassing" signs.

How glad I was Saturday night that this couple didn't live in my block. Picture the sound of 17 teenagers on the patio dancing to music, which isn't good unless loud. Not one irate telephone call did I receive.

On my street, even the dogs don't fight and the parents never, never, never, interfere with the youngsters' "spits and spats." Three of us have a sort of babysitting service too. If any of us want to park a daughter overnight while we go out for an evening, the service is available.

Three families cooperate in keeping a vacant field between us mowed, although I'm afraid it's more cooperation for two of them than it is for me.

How many of you have neighbors who worry if they don't see lights at night and check to see if anyone is ill?

How many of you have neighbors who labor in the strawberry patch and then drop off a quart or two every day or so?

How many of you can sit on the porch and watch the neighbors work in the garden and then come home from a day of work and find the fruits of that labor in your kitchen, green beans, new potatoes, cucumbers, carrots and cabbage.

Yes, my neighbor is wonderful! We don't want "No Trespassing" signs! We like each other.

Welfare – Commissioner Report

August 27, 1964

As one who has lambasted the State Department of Welfare on more than one occasion, you can imagine my elation at picking up Friday morning's newspaper and finding a startling announcement from Bernard Smith, welfare commissioner, revealing that aid rolls have been purged of 50,000 persons and state welfare grants trimmed $4.3 million.

But elation changed to deflation when I noticed what just may well be election-year double talk.

Smith noted for instance, that welfare appropriations had tapered off sharply to $44.3 million this past year. That's so, but the fact remains that welfare appropriations have climbed to that point from $33.5 million in 1960-61.

In Upshur county, the average monthly caseload in the old age, aid to the blind, disabled, dependent children and general assistance categories declined by 32 to 838 in fiscal 1963-64, but net cash grants were up slightly by $797- to $744,864. This is still an increase!

In checking with the local superintendent, I was told that only two ineligible families were found in Upshur county following an investigation. None or very few were dropped from the surplus commodity rolls.

True, the regular Aid to Dependent Children caseload was down in Upshur county from 292 to 278 in 1963-64, but the average monthly caseload in the Work and Training Program segment was up from 134 to 145. It's still costing money regardless of what initial it's called, although I'll concede if able-bodied fathers get in the habit of working. Some do go into private enterprise.

The new welfare approach may be paying off in some counties but I can't see it here in Upshur. Decreases are noted here only in old age assistance, from $137,076 to $125,895. But notice that in all other categories there is a definite increase in aid to the blind, aid to dependent children, aid to the permanently and totally disabled and general relief.

Aid to the blind is up $556; aid to dependent children is up $6,449; aid to the permanently and totally disabled is up $1,424 and general relief is up $3,549.

Smith attributes the increase in over-all welfare cost to such new programs as the work and training and the food stamps, as well as increased personnel and better pay for caseworkers.

A beginning caseworker, for example, is now paid $435 a month where in 1961 the pay was $290. And, at the same time, in Upshur County the average monthly caseload was down from 870 to 838 cases. So why more personnel?

In another questionable statement, Smith's report shows the surplus commodity rolls in the state were reduced approximately 100,000 but some of those removed became immediately available for the work and training programs. It stands to reason that where there was a reduction in one, the cost was added to the other.

Just this week the U.S. Department of Commerce revealed that in Upshur county 46.7% of families earn $3,000 or less a year than the national average of 21.4%. The Poverty Bill signed into law last week by President Johnson is supposed to alleviate a lot of this.

But, according to Theodore H. White in his "The Making of the President," "when men are unemployed, any job looks good, and government in many West Virginia counties is the chief source of jobs…Politics in West Virginia is not only part time jobs but full-time gossip, and it gets more intense as one descends to levels from the statehouse to the county courthouse, where the local bosses are established, barons of little realms, forming and breaking their alliances.

"Politics in West Virginia involves money-hot money, under the table money, open money, and …"

Somehow money from Washington reaches some of those truly suffering, but poverty still exists and until the public demands treatment of causes of social problems, rather than money payments as we've been doing for the past 30 years, the welfare grants will continue to climb, despite the sugarcoated hog-wash dished out of Charleston.

Not Raising Hogs

September 3, 1964

This is a letter Rep. Edgar F. Foremen, Texas Republican, reports having received from a constituent:

"Dear Sir:

My friend over in Terrebonne Parish received a $1,000 check from the Government this year for not raising hogs. So I am going into the not-raising-hogs business next year.

What I want to know is, in your opinion, what is the best kind of farm not to raise hogs on and the best kind of hogs not to raise? I would prefer not to raise razorbacks, but if that is not a good breed not to raise, I will just gladly not raise any Berkshires or Durocs.

The hardest work in this business is going to be in keeping an inventory of how many hogs I haven't raised. My friend is very joyful about the future of his business. He has been raising hogs for more than 20 years and the best he ever made was $400, until this year, when he got $1000 for not raising hogs."

If I can get $1000 for not raising 50 hogs then I will get $2,000 for not raising 100 hogs? I plan to operate on a small scale at first, holding myself down to 4000 hogs which means I will have $80,000 coming from the Government. Now, another thing; these hogs I will not raise will not eat 100,000 bushels of corn. I understand that you also pay farmers for not raising corn. So will you pay me anything for not raising 100,000 bushels of corn not to feed the hogs I am not raising?

I want to get started as soon as possible as this seems to be a good time of the year for not raising hogs. One thing more, can I raise 10 or 12 hogs on the side, while I am in the not-raising-hog business just enough to get a few sides of bacon to eat?

                                              Very truly yours,

                                              J.B. Lee, Jr.
                                              Potential Hog Raiser

I Remember Buckwheat Cakes

September 8, 1964

Someone mentioned the Buckwheat Festival one day last week here in the office and I realized just how fast have flown the years.

As a child, I spent many a summer vacation in Preston county on my grandmother's old home place at Amboy - DBE and P (days before electricity and plumbing). You can laugh about the Sears, Roebuck catalogue if you wish, but it was used page by page at the outbuilding which always seemed such a long, long walk.

But most vividly, I remember those buckwheat cakes and maple sugar syrup, the like of which I haven't consumed since. The maple sugar was always shaped in molds and the "starter" for the buckwheat batter always sat on the back of the mammoth wood-burning range.

Not that I wish to go back to the days of DBE and P, but somehow the buckwheat cakes aren't the same. But, then, I'm not noted for my culinary accomplishments. If food doesn't come frozen, boxed, or half-baked we just can't eat at my house.

I have a daughter almost 12 years old who has never been near a cow let alone seen one milked. She's never ridden a hay wagon, or run from a nasty, mean ram corralled in a pen, or seen a spring house with the cement waterway for the buttermilk and the rich cream, or seen newly-born puppies, or felt a warm egg just laid.

She's never watched the spooky shadows cast by the kerosene lamps or had that feeling of security only after "kivered up" in a feather bed. But then, neither has she gone to bed with the chickens and gotten up with the roosters. Few of us do these days.

Ah, yes, time flies! Her children won't understand either her stories of movies, TV, slow-flying jets, or housework 30 years from now. By then, she'll be far into the push-button, automatic, jet age. But I do hope they have buckwheat cakes, too.

Little League Football - #1

October 29, 1964

Alright, convince me! Why must we have a little league football program?

Oops! I can hear some of my readers saying "There she goes again, sticking her nose into something she knows nothing about."

Can you honestly convince me that "the winning pressure" is good for boys 10 to 13 years old? Whatever happened to "Go, Sheepy, Go" and "Kick the Can?"

Isn't this program just another form of entertainment for adult spectators? Why can't we allow our little boys to be little boys? Must they be men from birth!

Aside from the mental pressures imposed on youngsters, what about the physical effect. The American Medical Society is definitely against programs of this sort.

Fact of the matter is, the state medical society this past spring recommended a longer conditioning program for high school athletes. They asked that a track program be started on August 1st instead of the present August 15th. When do our little boys start their training?

Are we tend to ignore the fact that medical doctors have pointed out that there now exists a higher rate of suicide among young people? Much of this is due to the extreme pressure exerted they say, by teachers and parents. Our mental hospitals are overcrowded, authorities say, due to "pressure to excel."

Aside from the mental and physical pressures, let's consider the money angle. Having lived in a town (Bluefield) which supports the young football program, I know from experience that it costs at least $800 per year per sponsoring organization to properly equip a team of young boys. I know this because I had a son playing in this league at 11 years of age. Mitchell Stadium in Bluefield was as crowded on Wednesday nights as if WVU and VPI were contestants.

Now, convince me that a parent will enjoy seeing their 11-year-old stretched out "cold" on the ground. And, it does happen, game after game. I've seen it and I don't like it any better now than I did then.

If a sponsoring organization spends $800 per year, will that money he diverted from the community projects already supported by the club, such as glasses for the needy and the support of the city library? Would the sponsoring organizations give $800 to Boy Scouts and Girl Scouts and the Crippled Children's Society? You can bet your boots they wouldn't!

Nor will $800 a year be spent on a fine set of parallel bars, mats, etc. for gymnastics. If the public is so concerned with the physical well-being of its youngsters, why must it be football,? Why not the Olympic-style gymnastics.

No, you won't get my support for a little league football program, although there isn't a mother in town who enjoys the game of football more than I do. I cut my teeth on silver footballs won by my father in his schooldays.

But there should be a time to be young and a time to be middle-aged and a time to be elderly and a time to be an inquisitive little boy!

Note: Incidentally, these views are not necessarily those of The Delta's. And, I'll be fair about this and offer my space in this newspaper for any rebuttal, although we aren't regulated by the FCC as is television.

Little League Football - Rebuttal

November 5, 1964

The Buckhannon Jaycees would like to take this opportunity to explain just what little league football is and how we expect it to operate.

Betty, first we wish to thank you and the Delta for this space and opportunity. We respect you for the statement in your article that the views expressed were strictly your own.

Now to try and present the facts about our intended little league football program. First, the program, to get started, will take $4,000 which we hope to get from the sports-minded people in our fine town. This money will be used to order uniforms, insurance, medical supplies, and all other football incidentals needed to start the program next year.

The program is designed to include about 120 Upshur County boys between the ages of 10 and 13. It is designed to give the youths physical fitness training and to teach them the fundamentals of football. The B-U football coaches have given the program full endorsement and are actively participating in the formation of the league. After a suggestion from the school coaches, the Jaycee's decided not to become affiliated with the Pop Warner Football Program, but to start an independent league for Upshur County alone.

Youths wanting to participate in the league must first secure permission from their parents, physicians, and school principals.

Tentative plans call for the league to furnish insurance, headgear, shoulder pads, padded pants, and socks for each member of the anticipated four team league. The participants will be required to furnish their own jerseys, tennis shoes, and mouth protector.

The league will be governed by a board of directors, who will in turn, secure a director, who will handle all game scheduling, obtaining officials, and otherwise, run the entire program. Coaches for the league will be given courses of instruction from the high school coaching staff to insure that each of the boys is trained properly.

Betty, let's consider the money angle you questioned. After the initial drive for the $4,000, we hope the league will be self-supporting. We plan to make it so, by asking the spectator for a twenty-five cent donation for each game, and Betty, if we have a fraction of the crowd indicated by you, "Mitchell Stadium in Bluefield was as crowded on Wednesday nights as if WVU and VPI were contestants," then we should never have to ask any sponsor for $800.

In answer to another question, the Jaycees will continue all of their community projects as will other organizations, and this program will in no way take money away from the other worthwhile projects.

Let's stop and look at this program realistically. You have a boy who played in this program at Bluefield. Why don't you ask your own son if he thinks this program has helped him in his football career, I think you know what he would answer.

Now, boys are going to play tackle football at this young age if they have any interest for football at all, and we believe it would be better for boys to play in an organized league where they have good equipment, training in physical fitness, proper medical care and proper instruction in the fundamentals of how to play the game. We believe this is much better than tackle football in the backyard or vacant field without proper supervision and equipment.

Leagues of this type and in this age group, have been operated successfully since 1930 and well over a million boys have participated without a fatality. (Those figures are from information furnished by the Pop Warner Football Foundation).

Last, but not least, the Jaycees as kickoff sponsors for this program, family-wise, represent a large number of the boys who are or will be able to participate in this program, and if we felt that it was not a good mental or physical program for our children, it would not have been endorsed by our organization.

Robert R. Post, President
Buckhannon Junior Chamber of Commerce

Punt, Pass & Kick 1964   Howard Hiner Collection

Little League Football - Reply From Fred Boyles

November 12, 1964

Every once in a while I wonder just why I'm in this newspaper business, especially last week. The election didn't quite go the way I would have liked, and B-U lost to Victory, and the A&P mat was late on press day and we can't park in our parking space due to paving and our sports writer and his wife suffered a tragic loss in the death of their five-hour-old baby. Then on Friday morning, came a delightful letter. It was a critical letter concerning a recent stand I took on little league football, but still was a nice, friendly letter, too, not the hot-tempered differences usually expressed. It was such a delightful letter that I must share it with my readers:

Dear Betty:

Last week's stand on Whirligig on little league football was quite interesting. Of utmost interest was your desire to let curious little boys be curious little boys. Having once been a curious little boy, I know there are lots of things curious little boys are curious about before they should be. Perhaps it would be better to have them curious about how to punt, pass, and kick properly and allow their other curiosities to grow with their minds, bodies, and maturity. No? Good ball players must be subject to strict discipline, of which there is a gosh-awful shortage reflected in our delinquency rates. This form of discipline is not harmful, it will probably be all that some youngsters will be exposed to before they get big enough to suddenly realize there's a big bad world around them to make themselves a big bad name in. Recalling a stand you took on an issue in the past, that of issuing birth control pills to relief recipients, I noted a recent article in a prominent magazine that the use of such drugs could upset the normal reproduction cycles to the point that woman would be subject to pregnancies even at the age of 65 and 70. This would relieve the burden of relief roles naturally as the prospective mother would finance her child with her social security check. But the little league football program would be helpful in getting the noisy little brats out of the rest homes and let mama die in peace. This is not in rebuttal as per your invitation but I just couldn't resist offering the thoughts.

Respectfully,
Fred M. Boyles
P.S. You go ahead taking your stands, they're admirable even if everyone doesn't always agree.

"Little Girls" by Alan Beck

December 3, 1964

This is the time of year when I begin thinking and buying for the 'youngens' in the family and suddenly I realized I didn't have 'youngens', only two grown up boys and an almost grownup lady.

Then it was that I wondered, where have the years gone? And, why haven't I been much more patient at times?

Because, little girls are the nicest things that happen to people. They are born with a little bt of angel-shine about them and though it wears thin sometimes, there is always enough left to lasso your heart even when they are sitting in the mud, or crying temperamental tears, or parading up the street in mother's best clothes.

A little girl can be sweeter (and badder) oftener than anyone else in the world. She can jitter around, and stomp, and make funny noises that frazzle your nerves, yet just when you open your mouth, she stands there demure with that special look in her eyes.

A girl is Innocence playing in the mud, Beauty standing on its head, and Motherhood dragging a doll by the foot.

Girls are available in five colors, black, white, red, yellow, or brown, yet Mother Nature always manages to select your favorite color when you place your order. They disprove the law of supply and demand, there are millions of little girls, but each is as precious as rubies.

God borrows from many creatures to make a little girl. He uses the song of a bird, the squeal of a pig, the stubbornness of a mule, the antics of a monkey, the spryness of a grasshopper, the curiosity of a cat, the speed of a gazelle, the slyness of a fox, the softness of a kitten, and to top it all He adds the mysterious mind of a woman.

A little girl likes new shoes, party dresses, small animals, first grade, noise makers, the girl next door, make-believe dancing lessons, ice cream, kitchens, coloring books, make-up, cans of water, going visiting, tea parties, and one boy.

She doesn't care so much for visitors, boys in general, large dogs, hand-me-downs, straight chairs, vegetables, snow suits or staying in the front yard. She is the loudest when you are thinking, the prettiest when she has provoked you, the busiest at bedtime, the quietest when you want to show her off, and the most flirtatious when she absolutely must not get the best of you again.

Who else can cause you more grief, joy, irritation, satisfaction, embarrassment, and genuine delight than this combination of Eve, Salome, and Florence Nightingale? She can muss up your home, your hair, and your dignity, spend your money, your time, and your temper, then just when your patience is ready to crack, her sunshine peeks through and you've lost again.

Yes, she is nerve-racking nuisance, just a noisy bundle of mischief. But when your dreams tumble down and the world is a mess, when it seems you are pretty much of a fool after all, she can make you a queen when she climbs on your lap and whispers, "I love you best of all!"

- Alan Beck

"Little Boys" by Alan Beck

December 17, 1964

After a recent column dealing with the niceties of little girls a reader writes. "Sure little girls are nice. I've seen some big girls who were nice, and darned cute, too!!! Little boys may be neither nice nor cute, but certain charms they possess and for them I demand equal time."

So, this time, Alan Beck of the New England Mutual Life Insurance Company, explains "What is a Boy?"

Between the innocence of babyhood and the dignity of manhood we find a delightful creature called a boy. Boys come in assorted sizes, weights, and colors, but all boys have the same creed: To enjoy every second of every minute of every hour of every day and to protest with noise (their only weapon) when their last minute is finished and the adult males pack them off to bed at night."

Boys are found everywhere, on top of, underneath, inside of, climbing on, swinging from, running around, or jumping to. Mothers love them, little girls hate them, older sisters and brothers tolerate them, adults ignore them, and Heaven protects them. A boy is Truth with dirt on its face, Beauty with a cut on its finger, Wisdom with bubble gum in its hair, and the Hope of the future with a frog in its pocket.

When you are busy, a boy is an inconsiderate, bothersome, intruding jangle of noise. When you want him to make a good impression, his brain turns to jelly or else he becomes a savage, sadistic, jungle creature bent on destroying the world and himself with it.

A boy is a composite, he has the appetite of a horse, the digestion of a sword swallower, the energy of a pocket-size atomic bomb, the curiosity of a cat, the lungs of a dictator, the imagination of a Paul Bunyan, the shyness of a violet, the audacity of a steel trap, the enthusiasm of a fire cracker, and when he makes something he has five thumbs on each hand.

He likes ice cream, knives, saws, Christmas, comic books, the boy across the street, woods, water (in its natural habitat), large animals, Dad, trains, Saturday mornings, and fire engines.

He is not much for Sunday school, company, schools, books without pictures, music lessons, neckties, barbers, girls, overcoats, adults, or bedtime.

Nobody else is so early to rise, or so late to supper. Nobody else gets so much fun out of trees, dogs, and breezes. Nobody else can cram into one pocket a rusty knife, a half-eaten apple, three feet of string, an empty Bull Durham sack, two gum drops, six cents, a sling shot, a chunk of unknown substance, and genuine supersonic code ring with a secret compartment.

A boy is a magical creature - you can lock him out of your workshop but you can't lock him out of your heart. You can get him out of your study, but you can't get him out of your mind. Might as well give up, he is your captor, your jailer, your boss, and your master, a freckled-face, pintsized, cat-chasing bundle of noise. But when you come home at night with only the shattered pieces of your hopes and dreams, he can mend them like new with two magic words, "Hi, Dad"!!

- Alan Beck

Babysitting the Iguana

January 28, 1965

You mustn't think I'm complaining. It's just that I don't understand why normal occurrences can't happen in the Hornbeck Household.

I mean, most people when they go on vacation ask their relatives or friends to board a cat, or a dog, and even canaries and parakeets. But not my nephews! No, it's just my luck to be asked to board an iguana.

That's what I said, an iguana! An oversized lizard or undersized dinosaur, depending on what frame of mind you're in when you look at it.

And, look at it is all I'll do. It's a pretty little thing, if you like lizards with beady eyes and pink, blue, green, purple and yellow head. He has a name....Iggy. That's a help in case he slithers away into a closet or a dresser drawer. I'm sure he'll answer to "Here, Iggy, here Iggy!" Fact is, I'm not sure Iggy has the sense to come out of the dark because he sure isn't smart when it comes to eating. A vegetarian, Iggy hasn't discovered anything good by lettuce.

Iggy doesn't make a sound. In fact, he doesn't do anything but perch on his branch of driftwood in his cage and roll those beady eyes. His favorite spot is resting atop the drapes over the floor furnace vent for, after all, he is primarily a desert animal and requires warm temperatures. O, yes, he will curl comfortably across your shoulder giving solace and comfort amid your trials and tribulations. Gee whiz, dogs aren't man's only friend!

He can do something else, too. In case, you grab him by his tail (an 18-inch tail at the moment) he'll leave the tail behind and grow another one. But, if he loses so much as a toenail, that's lost for good and ever.

Yes, I'm sure we'll all grow to love Iggy before this week is over. Please, week, be over!!

The City Plan

February 4, 1965

The Plan has been provided. Now, it's up to the citizens of Buckhannon to study, to understand and to support "The Town of the Future."

What is The Plan? It is a long range physical improvement program for the city and its urban area. After many, many months of cussing and discussing, work and more work on the part of city officials and members of the planning commission, The Plan provides a guide and solution to such local problems as housing, population, traffic, community facilities, and existing land use.

The proposals are supported by a series of procedures which include a Capital Improvement Program and Six-Year Budget, subdivision and zoning standards.

The comprehensive plan, as prepared by a nationally known consulting engineering firm, is well worth the time it takes to walk to City Hall and study, even for 15 minutes.

Roughly and in plain talk, this is what the plan says.

1. Economically, the city of Buckhannon is not dependent to any great extent upon other trade centers, is primarily self-sufficient, dependent upon Wesleyan College and becoming more dependent upon industry. Incomes in Buckhannon were considerably lower in 1959 than the state average but future employment opportunities appear most optimistic in services, personal and otherwise, as incomes and population increase.

2. Population. In spite of a decrease in the state population, the city realized its greatest increase during the decade of 1940-1950. By 1980 a city population of 16,686 is forecast. Buckhannon can accommodate the anticipated growth with the establishment of proper land use development and controls including housing and building codes and subdivision and zoning ordinances.

3. Land Use. Analysis of neighborhood land use indicates more than one school in some areas and none in others. Recreational facilities are generally lacking. Traffic problems are of great intensity. Central Business District shows a major on-street parking problem.

4. Housing. The dwellings are for the most part in excellent condition and well-maintained. A concentrated area of blight is located next to Wesleyan but will be removed as the college expands. Other areas of blight are located next to industrial plants. Nearly 48 percent of the housing is over 30 years of age which indicates that a housing program should protect the overall quality of housing through a legal enforcement such as a housing code and wide-spread home improvement programs.

Howard Hiner Collection

5. Public education school facilities indicate peak capacity and already crowded conditions. By 1980 it is estimated that 1,843 students will be enrolled in elementary grades; 1,124 in junior high; 723 in high school, plus county enrollment of 1,427 in junior high and 1,120 in senior high.

6. Recreational facilities are found to be conspicuous by their absence. The need for a well integrated school recreational program for every age group is badly needed.

7. Public Buildings. The city building located within the core of the Central Business District is badly in need of major repairs and expansion is impossible, therefore a new site and building must be studied. As population increases, additional fire stations should be considered in the south and east of the city. Jail facilities and off-street parking at the county court house are critical. Police protection is less than the recommended minimums.

8. Traffic. Volume flow of traffic is a rather serious problem throughout the city. Solutions to the problem would include complete removal of on-street parking on Main Street; traffic bypasses; construction of off-street parking facilities; traffic light synchronization; channelization of traffic lanes and one-way streets.

9. Parking. Facilities for parking in the Central Business District is considered extremely hazardous during peak traffic hours. A thoroughfare and traffic plan has been suggested.

10. Utilities. The anticipated growth in population will place increased demands upon the utility systems. The most serious problem was found in the storm sewer systems. The level character of the area topography has caused sanitary sewage collection problems. Numerous lift stations have caused sanitary sewage collection problems. Numerous lift stations have resulted in rather high cost of service and pockets of development without public sewer service. On the other hand, the treatment plant has additional capacity and is located in a manner permitting future expansion. Too, the method of refuse collection and disposal is acceptable.

So, there is The Plan in a very small nut-shell. Shall we get to work?

New St. Joseph's Hospital

February 11, 1965

Sister Amalia, amiable hospital administrator, conducted a tour of the new St. Joseph's hospital one day last week for members of the local press, and my comment is, "Fabulous!"

Upshur county residents should be counting their blessing that such a modern, progressive facility will open its doors come next August.

The ultimate in comfort will be assured in the T-shaped, $1,300,000 fireproof, brick, concrete and steel building. Sister Amalia, who knows every nook and every cranny, was almost ecstatic as she explained the private and semi-private rooms which will have life-saving oxygen piped into every room, telephone, air-conditioning, private showers and baths.

The beautiful tiled walls can appear either blue or green depending on the light and sunshine. There are escape windows in every patients' room, two elevators which are equipped to hold the bed and patient for easy moving.

But, most important of all, will be the easy access to the emergency entrance with an emergency room just steps away, where time is often so precious. Both operating rooms will be on the ground floor, and a badly needed recovery room will be adjacent where all oxygen, all the fluids, all the suctions, all the medicine one would ever need will be available. Nearby is located the laboratory, the x-ray rooms, clean-up room, high-speed sterilizing facilities where an instrument can be re-sterilized in a matter of seven minutes. The patient will be moved from operating room, to recovery room and essentially to his own room, all on the same bed, eliminating unnecessary handling of the patient.

Also, on the main floor will be located a doctors' entrance, doctors' lounge, library, chapel, pharmacy, switchboard, business office, gift shop, cafeteria facilities for the public, dining room for the sisters of the Pallotine Order of Missionary Sisters, who operate the new hospital, storage rooms and deep freeze facilities next to a most modern, well equipped kitchen. Here are patients' prescribed diets will be systemically placed on trays as they move along on a conveyor belt. All beds will be on the second floor, including two wards, private and semi-private rooms, the maternity wing, nurses stations and large cylinder drops to basement for dirty linens and trash.

(-),(-),K. Huffman,(-), J.C. Huffman,MD (-), Mayor J.D Hinkle, Jr.   Howard Hiner Collection

The maternity ward is directly over the operating rooms and here again are sterilizer and scrub rooms, storage, doctor's rooms, isolation, labor rooms, delivery rooms, nursery rooms, and the valuable formula room. Ten beds for mothers are provided with folding walls to expand or decrease as need exists for maternity rooms. The third floor will not be in use unless an additional $165,000 can be found to equip and furnish this floor. It is roofed and wired and would eventually have room for 25 more beds when funds are available.

Even the basement is a marvel of engineering. Here is the telephone equipment room, more storage, emergency power system, trash and laundry receptacles, laundry and sewing rooms, the morgue, physical therapy room and dressing room (if funds are available) and miles and miles of electrical and sewage conduits, switches, breakers and two mammoth boilers to hear the modern facility. Yes, truly a modern marvel. All of which will mean a need for more nurses, more nurses aids, housekeepers, maintenance man, etc. But if one has to be ill, best be ill in comfortable and pleasant surroundings.

The Great Society

March 11, 1965

That the world is small and news travels fast is illustrated with the following. A local resident received the clipping from a California resident who scissored it from the Pine Bluff, Arkansas Democrat newspaper.

Here goes: In his State-of-the-Union message to Congress and a vast TV audience, and in his more recent addresses, President Johnson delineated in roseate language a resurrection of the Fabian dreams of the long, long ago.

He portrayed for the people of the United States, and promised them an era in which prosperity abounds, poverty is banished, music and arts flourish, the air is sweet, streams are pure and unpolluted, beauty dominates the cities and country sides, everybody is well-fed, hospitals and medicine are free, doctor bills are no more, everybody has a job and is well educated, and crime and sickness or sorrow are unheard of.

This era, this great millennium is labeled by Lyndon B. Johnson, the modern messiah, as the "Great Society."

What do the people have to do to enter this Land of Promise? Not a thing, except surrender their lives and hopes and freedom and fortunes to the federal government, and leave to posterity an unpayable, multi-billion-dollar debt, and the certainly of serfdom.

The hard facts of this "Great Society," now praised throughout the land by Socialists and pinks and politicians, both Democratic and Republican …the hard facts are that it will tend to reward the indolent and lazy while penalizing the industrious and frugal. It will not permit the self-reliant and independent to remain that way.

It will compel them to pay for services they neither need nor desire, and to help carry the load of those who prefer not to be self-supported.

If the "Great Society" is permitted to grow, unhampered, our erstwhile Free Republic will succumb to the welfare state. It eventually will make paupers of us all, deny the individual the right to be left alone. The government will dictate and regulate and control the lives of all.

That, ladies and gentlemen, is the "Great Society" the Fabian Dream, the Socialist's goal, the sluggard's pap, LBJ's political pabulum and palliative.

Every day for weeks and weeks we've been reading in the newspapers about President Johnson's "war on poverty." We have been told - and still are being told – that help will go to those in need. West Virginia has been played up as a "disaster area", ripe for sumptuous poverty help.

But look who's getting the lion's share of poverty hand-outs!!

An editorial in the Martinsburg (W.Va.) Journal gives the details. Here's the score:

West Virginia is to get $423,811 for the "war on poverty". But the fabulously wealthy state of Texas, which happens to be the home of President Johnson, will get $9,776,483.

The population of Texas is almost five times that of West Virginia, but it is going to get 23 times as much as "poverty stricken" West Virginia.

Minnesota, which is the home of Vice President Humphrey, has just about twice West Virginia's population, but is assigned $1,449,407, or more than three times as much as West Virginia will get for the "war on poverty".

New Jersey, which has always been regarded as one of our wealthier states, is being allocated the top amount - $12,456, 361.

Kentucky is to be the recipient of the second highest - $10,416,242.

President Johnson's own proud state of Texas ranks third, with Oregon in fourth spot – at $8,219,670.

The Journal's editor made this comment: "Oregon's population is just about the same as West Virginia's, but they must be really hard-up there financially to qualify for 20 times the amount set up for us.

"The next time President Johnson or Vice President Humphrey or even David and Chet come carpetbagging around West Virginia and expressing sympathy over our sad plight, West Virginians can hold their heads high and tell these 'do-gooders' to clean up their own backyards."

The Monkey, The Bird, The Jerk

March 18, 1965

It must be that I'm nearing the Fabulous Forties that I've suddenly lost all patience with the current trend in music.

Have you been exposed recently to those atrocious programs on TV, "Shindig" and "Hullabaloo?" Gorgeous George, the wrestler, was at least able to protect himself when he wore his long, blond, curly locks. But, what in heaven's name protects those boys who look like girls…The Righteous Brothers, Fantasticks, the Blossoms, and shin Dogs, etc. In my neighborhood we would have stoned them to death!

Wednesday evening I settled down in front of TV with my knitting all prime for my program "The Virginian", when I was firmly but politely told that the cowboys had to ride further West…"Shindig" was scheduled.

I suffered for 15 minutes of "Bird dog, you're on the wrong trail" and "Eight Days a week, I ain't got nuthin' but love, baby" and "Wake up, Little Susie, the movies over and it's four o'clock in the morning. What will your ma say, What will our friends say…Yaaa, Yaaa, Yaaa."

I don't know what Little Susie's ma and pa said, but you can bet your last dollar I would have met someone at the front door with a horsewhip along with bread and water and solitary confinement!

At least I have some tolerance now for my parents who suffered through my squealing over Frank Sinatra, my swooning over Glenn Miller's orchestra, and the Jitterbug. My generation didn't turn out so badly….we came through a depression and won a war.

But, I look at Son No. 1 and Son No. 2 and wonder how nice looking, intelligent boys of 17 and 18 can possibly, possibly prepare for future years of sane moderate living after a training ground of The Monkey, The Bird, The Jerk and The Clam.

Son No. 1 is now sporting a goatee and envisions himself as another Col. Lee, gyrates The Jerk as he dances to the dinner table and back, and still passes a music appreciation course in college.

Son No. 2 emulates Son No. 1 and still makes better than average grades, attends a speed-reading course once a week at the college and ushers at church.

Daughter One and Only emulates Son No. 1 and Son No. 2, loves me, loves her dog, loves her brothers (sometimes), loves school, Scouts, 4-H, friends and neighbors, but swings the most wicked hip on the block when it comes to The Monkey.

Dr. Spock says stay young with your children, but I'll be darned if I will…..I've too much sense and am much too tired for The Bird, The Jerk, The Monkey and The Clam! Yaaa, Yaaa, Yaaa.

Mental Health & Retardation

April 8, 1965

"Ten years ago, we would not have openly discussed mental health or mental retardation," said Dr. Stanley Martin, Monday night at the joint meeting of the AAUW, Buckhannon Woman's Club and the Upshur County Mental Health Committee.

How true! But with progress often comes understanding. And no one person could better qualify in the role of understanding than this state's capable director of Mental Health, Dr. Mildred Bateman.

Explaining so calmly, a turbulent problem, Dr. Bateman pointed to the local responsibility, our burden in the prevention and control of mental health.

How far we've come in 10 years! The wall of suspicion is no longer unscalable, there are cracks in the wall. Where West Virginia's program has been Spartan (destroy the weak), today West Virginia attempts the work of the Athenian (heal the sick). Where this state heretofore has provided asylums as a respite for the community, today we are attempting to practice the basic idea of preventive medicine.

This state still has a long road toward treatment and care of the mentally ill. It will require interested people, attention, knowledge and financing.

Monday night, the people of Upshur County, representatives of many organizations, provided interest and attention. With the completion of the new St. Joseph's hospital this summer, facilities will be provided for the mentally disturbed. Two hospital rooms, instead of the local jail, will be available.

But, the greatest step forward was revealed by Dr. Bateman. This year's legislature budgeted $1,800,000 for distribution among six state hospitals. The greatest percentage of money goes for personnel services, current expenses such as food, clothing, vital medicine and the maintenance and elimination of present hazards at Weston State hospital, the state's oldest and largest institution. (This facility is over 100 years old and houses 2,300 patients.) The department of alcoholism, which was started one year ago with the magnanimous sum of $25,000, was allotted $100,000.

Most important, this year's legislature changed the archaic procedure of patient admittance to state hospitals.

Now, individuals under the care of private physicians, can be admitted without necessity of court approved boards and without nights spent in county jails.

Furthermore, civil liberties of a patient are safe-guarded, the patient now has right of appeal in competency hearings and children may be admitted on basis of need, not age.

These laws, according to Dr. Bateman, are in line with modern methods of medicine. Another major piece of legislation was the passage of the County Officials Bill whereby any county which undertakes a local program of mental health, will be allowed deduction from assessments for hospitalized patients.

Perhaps many of us have not been aware that each county is assessed $150 per year for each patient institutionalized.

This bill is expected to move West Virginia and the counties toward a program of complete mental health centers, full-staffed, and with consultation programs and a full range of services.

Yes, we've come a long way! But don't be complacent. Do you know that not one college in this state offers degrees in occupational therapy, recreational therapy, or psychiatric technicians? All so very badly needed in the care and treatment of the mentally ill!

In a few days it is expected that West Virginia will be approved for the VISTA program. One hundred and sixty eight volunteers will be sent to this state to provide out-patient care, homemaking services in homes where there is a mentally disturbed member, and for work in hospital settings.

Yes, we've come a long way. There's an air of optimism, awareness, declaration of purpose, encouragement, recognition of need and a cooperative spirit!

Libraries

April 29, 1965

"When you go to the library you can go anywhere in the world. You can even go to another planet," so said a Pittsburgh, PA nine-year old last week when asked to tell "What the library means to me."

Yet nearly half the public schools across the nation don't have libraries. Some of the nation's largest cities are without a single public elementary school library, according to Jack Harrison Pollack in an article in last Sunday's Parade magazine.

The sad state of America's horse-and-buggy school libraries in today's Space Age was recently described to the House Education Committee: "Schools often have a small room with Jerry-built shelves, holding a shabby assortment of books. You might find an old mutilated encyclopedia or two and few other tattered reference books. The unappetizing mess is probably under the part-time supervision of a teacher or volunteer without library training. In some schools the janitor is on the organization chart but not the librarian."

What is the reason for this shocking discrepancy between what our children require and what they actually have at their disposal?

One reason is the vast number of administrative problems schools have to deal with. Another is overcrowding and lack of space. And despite all the evidence in favor of school libraries, many short-sighted taxpayers, even some educators, consider them "frills," "luxuries," "extras."

Buckhannon and Upshur county can consider themselves more fortunate than most. Accredited librarians are employed at both the junior and senior high school. The Charles Gibson Memorial Library is tax supported through levies and in cooperation with civic organizations. And, headquarters for the Stonewall Jackson Regional Library is located in Tennerton on Route 20. Also, we are fortunate to have the use of Wesleyan's library.

But, a good example of economizing in the wrong way is the failure of the Harrison county court last week to budget its usual $12,000 per year for maintenance and support of the regional bookmobile.

Harrison county has had to cut its budget since the county budget was not approved in Charleston due to a deficit. Money may be scarce but I hardly see where the region will be economizing if that $12,000 is withheld.

Lewis and Upshur county courts each support the book-mobile with $6,000 per year. Hardly enough unless Harrison reconsiders and gives its help.

Will our county children be able to say, "I think that library's should not be taken away. America like's library's so doz eobty eles", or "I notice the nothing noise that fills the air."

And Gail Ann Bending who went to the library before she could read. "And now that I can read I like it even more."

School Lunches – Freight Costs

May 6, 1965

This may not come as a surprise but did you know that things labeled free aren't always free? For instance the surplus food commodities shipped to schools.

The food is free but it appears that under a 1954 policy system within the Department of Public Welfare freight bills are handed school boards after transporting commodities to local warehouses. As of April 20th the Upshur County Board of Education had spent $815.24 this school term in freight charges. This for the privilege of using school-owned trucks to pick up commodities at the local warehouse which in turn are distributed to school lunch programs throughout the county.

The nearly $1,000 freight assessment could well be used for a better purpose, it might even provide better meals for youngsters. In Randolph county, a principal at Coalton claims the freight assessment costs his school $200 to $500 per year. In Ellamore, where the school lunch program is financed by the PTA, it costs the organization $11 each time the food is delivered. Understandingly, this works quite a hardship in the small community where school patrons are few and far between.

It is also understandable that PTA groups should be disturbed and concerned when it seems that one state agency is charging another state agency for the use of state-owned trucks. According to the executive secretary of the DPA, these charges are essential to keep distribution of surplus foods to school lunch programs alive.

His letter of explanation says: "The funds from this handling and hauling charge go into a special revolving fund which is used only to meet warehousing, certain vehicle, personnel and other expenses directly related to the distribution to schools and eligible institutions. There are not sufficient funds from other sources to cover these costs."

The DPA claims that studies have determined that without this current assessment method, boards of education would have to receive, store and deliver all foods made available to their schools through their own warehouse and trucking facilities, something which would cost an estimated $400,000 a year.

The current assessment procedure involves annual costs, as shared by all the boards, of about $90,000. It still seems to me that there is duplicity since the commodities are distributed to central warehouse for the use of not only the schools but for the underprivileged populace as well.

My question is whether school systems are paying for transportation of food which is also distributed to citizens? Just asking.

YWCA Activities Committee
Front L/R: Katy Whitescarver, Dorothy Short   Back L/R: Lorene Kerans, Lea Bell Light
Howard Hiner Collection

Forming The YWCA

May 20, 1965

Last fall I spoke out against the establishment of Little League Football in Buckhannon. Little time was wasted before this newspaper received letters both pro and con on the subject. The opponents of the program at that time were unanimous in crying aloud: "The boys already have plenty to do. When are we going to do something for the girls?"

Well, as a result of those letters that time has arrived. As of Monday night an organizing committee has been formed for the establishment of a YWCA. Hopefully, the program will include girls from the age of 6 to 60.

As all infants, this program will need adult support.....Talent, time and money. A YWCA official has been in Upshur county on two different occasions and says the financial and leadership resources are here. The question is tapping these resources.

A temporary YW office will be set-up in the United Fund offices in the Potter building. It will be manned by volunteer women workers. The dues for one year have been set at $3 with the hope that generous persons will donate an extra membership or two so that no girl will be turned away. Public support will determine the kind of program which can be offered. Don't look for a grandiose building, although the committee hopes in future years that a building can be obtained. Programs may range from folk dancing to gourmet cooking, here again, determined on the amount of public support.

The Young Women's Christian Association is well-known throughout the world as an organization which helps girls and women find meaning and purpose in their lives.

As you make out your check for a membership either for yourself or your daughter it might be well that you remember the YWCA Purpose: To build a fellowship of women and girls devoted to the task of realizing in our common life those ideals of personal and social living to which we are committed by our faith as Christians. In this endeavor we seek to understand Jesus, to share his love for all people, and to grow in the knowledge and love of God.

Open house has been scheduled for Monday, September 13. I hope you will be among the chartered members.

Putting In The Garden

June 3, 1965

My two rows of corn and four tomato plants have become the joke of the neighborhood. It all started innocently enough. If you had lived in a city your 'growin-up' days, you wouldn't know anything about a garden either. But since everyone in my neighborhood raises a garden, Son No. 1 and Son No. 2 and I decided it must be a status symbol. (Frankly, I'd rather raise rows and rows of flowers.)

Thanks to the owners of the vacant field next to our house, the ground was plowed. The owners put out a few rows of potatoes and then suggested we use the rest of the garden. That's when I first put my foot in mouth, by suggesting two rows of corn and four tomato plants.

After the laughs died down, Son No. 1 began to work the soil. The next-door neighbor flew out the door, and suggested that his garden Rota tiller be used first. Son No. 1 complied, and then began to mark the rows. Next-door neighbor flew out his door once again, and suggested that his hand-plow be used. Son No. 1 complied, and then started downtown to get the seed corn. Next-door neighbor flew out of his door for the third time and suggested he has more than enough seed corn….use his. Son No. 1 complied and planted his corn. Next-door neighbor flew out his door for the fourth time and said we must have some fertilizer. You guessed it, the neighbor supplied the fertilizer.

By this time, next-door neighbor's wife has stuck her head out the window and said "let that boy plant his corn the way he wants to!" Next-door neighbor went downtown to get his haircut in a huff and puff and Son No. 1 covered over the seed and the fertilizer and called it a day. We now have four rows of corn and the only investment in the entire project has been Son No. 1's time.

We also have eight tomato plants because of the generosity of the neighbors who for some reason had more than enough plants in their own gardens, or else they were ashamed for us to have only four plants.

Come football practice along about August 1st, guess who will be hoeing the four rows of Corn! It won't be Son No. 1 or Son No. 2!

Summer Job For Kids - Protesting

June 17, 1965

Recently I had an idea for summer employment for the college kids - those who can't find work to get themselves through another year of higher education. It's also an idea for the high school kids who are tired of picking strawberries for 10 cents a quart, or washing windows at 50 cents an hour, or washing cars at 75 cents, or mowing large lawns for a buck.

The poverty stricken are being taken care of and the wealthy don't need the money, so why don't all the college and high school kids sign up as demonstrators for this long, hot summer?

Why don't you agree to march against something. For instance, march against the war in Vietnam, the Marine landing in the Dominican Republic, the investigation of the committee of UnAmerican Activities, a student's right to free speech, or the price of beef, all at $2 an hour.

For $3 an hour you can agree to carry a sign. For $4 you'll sing and for the magnanimous price of $5 you'll throw yourself under the wheels of a "paddy-wagon."

With all the protest marches in progress and all those who can certainly think up between now and the start of school next fall, an intelligent kid could finance himself royally for next year's term.

Merchants Remodeling

June 27, 1965

If Buckhannon isn't nominated for the All-American City award I'll eat my hat! The thought occurred to me last Friday as I ran the obstacle course on the south side of Main Street. The fever of remodeling is spreading like wild fire or a contagious disease. Nothing has happened to that "pride of every mountaineer."

Starting at the west end of Main street, is the remodeling, painting, and new flooring in the former Dr. Rusmisell offices in the Potter building. Step carefully for right there is where that first brick might fall.

Three doors down of course is the gigantic remodeling and face lifting of the Adrian Buckhannon Bank which it is hoped will be completed by August. That area has been roped off for days because of the hazardous construction work. No one complains, everyone is just anxious to see the finished project.

Friday, I stepped across the corner and another rigging blocked the street. This time men were replacing a plate glass window at Opals Dress Shop. It seems that a woman narrowly escaped injury during the Strawberry Festival Parade when she was crushed, pushed, or crammed through the display window.

Three doors more and the sidewalk was almost entirely blocked at the Acme Book Store. At this business the entire front has been scrapped and workmen are busily engaged in modernizing. Joe and Dave Oldaker have knocked out walls and expanded into the rooms which were formerly occupied by the Thrash Insurance Agency.

The only inconvenience here is to Joe, who can't spend as much time fishing as he'd like to.

Just a hop and a skip onward and the Alkire Tire and Supply, Ashland oil dealer, has excavated a huge area to re-install new storage tanks and gasoline pumps.

So, believe me, watch your head and your footing for Main street is dangerous….but it's wonderful!

Aboard Ship With Sis

July 15, 1965

In case anyone noticed the absence of this column last week, it simply was due to the fact that it has taken me a week to recuperate from a Fourth of July weekend aboard "ship" at the Sutton Dam.

Let's face it, bruised and battered Betty is not the athletic type. My sister is! And, though I love her sincerely, she may be the death of me.

It is utterly inconceivable to Sis that anyone, even those fat and forty, cannot skim saucily over the water on skis. Let me explain here and now that she has a Master's Degree in physical education, knows dances that I can't even spell, was a former high school cheerleader and still wears the same size clothes as she did in college. She not only water skis but also spends two weeks each winter in Canada on snow skis.

She is a fiend for outdoor living. In fact, when we were girls sharing the same bedroom we spent the better part of the cold, winter nights lowering and raising the window. She liked the invigorating night air, I hated it. Many a morning the snow has lain two inches thick atop the bedspread on her side of the bed.

This all brings me to the point of this column. That weekend aboard "ship" Sis and my brother-in-law insisted that I ski. There must be a touch of dare-devil in my personality after all, for I readily agreed…too readily. I wanted to 'chicken out' the minute the life preserver was being strapped around my waist. I mentioned casually that the water was 25 feet deep. I was informed that it was 10 feet deep. Right then and there I began to wonder who would take care of my three orphaned children.

Sis, in the meantime, was grinning like a Cheshire cat still in the water waiting to coach me after she has ended her stunt of water ballet on two skis and then the finale of one ski.

It is beyond me how she manages to get five-foot boards on feet that want to go in opposite directions, and at the same time cling to the tow rope. After minutes of instructions and exertion, I demanded Sis go back to the boat and I would manage.

There she sat in the stern with that darn camera to record for posterity every ridiculous angle and every stupid mark of awkwardness that I displayed. Every time I thought I was in position, knees drawn to the chest, skis together and pointing skyward, arms straight, and tow rope between the skis, I'd dip to the left, head downward in 100-feet of water, feet and skis all askew on the surface.

This went on for several minutes until I was at the point of exhaustion. My 12-year-old daughter sat in the boat with an expression of disgust. She was no doubt wondering in embarrassment if anyone else had a darn fool mother like her mother. Brother-in-law was getting dizzy from circling the boat around and around to get the tow rope back to me as I struggled ungracefully in the water. Finally I managed to come to the surface, thought I had it made. I forgot to hold my arms straight and I smacked the water with the grace of an elephant.

That was it. I had had it. I quit with the promise I'd try tomorrow. Thank God, it rained and there was no tomorrow!!

I'm Worth $329 Per Week

July 22, 1965

The Federal Labor Commissioner came out last week with the statement that I am worth $159 weekly in my role as dietician, cook, maintenance man, chauffeur, laundress, nursemaid, and housekeeper.

Ha! Ha! Ha! That man evidently has not lived in a home with two teenage sons and a daughter. According to his figures, I put in 99.6 hours a week at household duties. As a seamstress, dietician, or cook I earn $2.50 an hour; as maintenance man $2.25; as chauffeur, $2.20; laundress, $1.90 per hour. As a nursemaid I'm worth $55.36 in dollars and cents value; as cook, $32.75 and as housekeeper, $26.25.

Never once did he mention my role in the telephone answering service. Nor did he mention my role as garbage man which includes the scrubbing of the cans. How about the two times this summer I had to mow the lawn because the boys were too busy with physical fitness programs and summer basketball. Doesn't that classify me as a gardener?

There's a special category in my household which I have named 'pick-up the shoes, pick-up the books, pick-up the newspapers, and pick up the mud.'

What about the counseling service? That includes fuss between the girls next door and daughter or patching up the quarrel with the boys' best girls.

Don't I also have a role as official hostess when the weekend guests arrive who may vary in age from 12 to 20.

Statistics are fine, but frankly, I can't be hired for less than $329 a week!

Baxa Restaurant

July 29, 1965

It's a long way from cooking in a logging camp to the new modern, attractive restaurant that Ed F. Baxa and his family are opening next week. I think it would take a lot of courage too, for a man of 69 years to invest the amount of money it has taken to equip and furnish the superb Baxa Restaurant which is a definite asset to the county and state.

But, Ed F. Baxa has lots of family help. Joining with him in the operation is his son, Charles, who moved here from Miami, Fla., last year to be a strong right arm.

Baxa Restaurant should be serving luxurious dining for many years because Charles has five children, and Ed's brother, Arie, brings alone three more, all of whom, no doubt, will be coached in the maintenance and operation of the business.

Ed Baxa started cooking when he was 15 years of age in a logging camp for the Croft Lumber company at Alexander. Those were the days when the lumberjacks fired the cook if they didn't like his cooking. Ed survived any criticism and went on to own and operate a Baxa Restaurant on North Kanawha street, with the help of brother Arie, until 1953 when the location was sold to Dr. Wease Ashworth for office space.

In the meantime, Baxa and his wife, the former Josephine Laura Robey, of the Brooks Hill community, bought the Keim hotel on North Kanawha street shortly after World War II and four years ago added an attractive, modern 18-unit motel.

But, there was a need for a restaurant. And, it wasn't until the Latham building was available that Baxa could fulfill his dream of a nice, modern, attractive restaurant close to his motel-hotel.

One year and six months ago, the site was purchased, the building gutted, construction started, and next week the Baxas are open for business.

The three-story building is modern from top to bottom. Since there are so many Baxas, living quarters were built on the second and third floors.

Charles and his wife, the former Sarah VanDiver, a native of Georgia have a 12-room apartment on the second floor. They need that much room for there are five children, Eddie, 9; Kathy 7 ½; Pam 6; Jackie 4 ½ and Lulu 3.

Charles graduated from Buckhannon-Upshur high school, went on to the Eastman School of Music and University of Rochester, N,Y., and then along came World War II. He served with U.S. Army post bands throughout the nation, returned to home and graduated from West Virginia University School of Pharmacy.

Mr. and Mrs. Arie Baxa live in another one of the apartments with three of their four children. Arie cooked for years at the 4-H State Center at Jackson's Mill and returns to Buckhannon from hospital cooking at Harrisonburg, Va.

So, you see, the restaurant is a family affair, a nice family and we're proud they belong to Upshur county.

Buckhannon-Wesleyan Swim Team

August 5, 1965

Summer's favorite sport, that of swimming, is going "great guns" this season with Buckhannon-Wesleyan's young swim team placing second in last Saturday's Tri-County Stealey Invitational meet in Clarksburg.

Only two years old, the local team has shown fantastic progress since they jumped into second place from last summer's fifth place among the eight competing teams.

Swimming is old but the art of competitive swimming with proper coaching is something brand-new as far as this area is concerned. The parents and swimmers can be grateful for one person, Mrs. W. David Williams, of Mt. Hibbs, a relatively newcomer to Buckhannon, who started the instruction a year ago and who has been the force behind the team's affiliation with the Tri-County Swimming League and the AAU.

The team has also been fortunate in that Wesleyan college has an indoor pool available for practice and the willingness to cooperate in all that team members do, even to some financial backing.

Three team members will travel to Ona, near Huntington, for the annual AAU age group state meet on August 14. This is a remarkable feat when one thinks that coaching has been available for only one year. Winning trophies Saturday at the tri-county meet were Jeff and Cathy Willis, and Danny Williams, the eight-year-old son of the swim coach.

Approximately 40 youngsters are working with the team winter and summer. Buckhannon lags behind when it comes to the 15 to 18-year-old class since very few teenagers are taking advantage of the year-round sport. As the interest grows, so perhaps, will the interest among teenagers. The coach, Cathy Williams, has three sons swimming on the team. She's calm, cool and collected when it comes to shepherding the 40 young people plus her own boys, which means she loves her work.

Cathy attended Morris Harvey college for one year and then transferred to West Virginia University where she graduated in physical education in 1947. Her interest in swimming dates back even before college days when she was swimming instructor during summers at Girl Scout camps and at the Charleston and Edgewood Tennis Clubs in 1949 and 1950. She also did some instructing at the 'Y' in Charleston and as a teacher in St. Albans high school.

Swim teams are only about five years old in the state of West Virginia. The Stealey Invitational Meet is only three years old so Buckhannon isn't too far behind in originating a swim team. Who knows, an Olympic swimmer may be the result of the volunteer work of Cathy Williams.

Howard Hiner Collection

Welfare – Free Contraceptive Foam

August 26, 1965

If you're willing to be led as flock of sheep and disgusted at my jabs on current state of affairs, read no further! I'm on my soapbox again this week and all because of a news release from the Department of Welfare. Quote: "Federal commodities distributed to needy person, institutions and special projects in West Virginia for the past fiscal year has a value of more than 19.3 million dollars, 3.8 million more than the preceding year."

They must be kidding! I've seen nothing but glowing reports out of Charleston concerning the economic growth and progress in the past several weeks.

Then, how come, more and more, 3.7 million more dollars are being spent in surplus commodities? Yet, the State Health Department quibbles about the advisability of free birth control pills in the monthly distribution of food.

While the average taxpayer is oblivious to the situation, it is obvious to a St. Louis firm, which last week began a unique program of birth control by mail.

Beginning this month, the Emko Company will use mailboxes in homes throughout the state to send birth control literature along with order forms for free supplies of Emko foam, a medically-approved contraceptive.

And, you know that the president of the company says? Quote: "West Virginia has more than its share of poor people. And these are the folks who need birth control help the most, but do the least to obtain it. Birth control is at least one answer to the problem of poverty in this state. "

"Secondly, we believe the State Department of Health has moved too slowly in authorizing birth control facilities in health clinics in West Virginia."

"And, we think that West Virginia would be a good example for the nation, to demonstrate the need for tax-supported birth control facilities in all health and welfare agencies."

Amen and amen, but who listens?

See Cass Railroad

September 30, 1965

Don't let another Sunday go by without gathering up the family in the "wagon" and traveling to Cass for a train excursion which will delight the "youngens" and bring back memories to the elders.

The Cass Scenic Railroad is a tourist attraction that the state can well be proud of and which I understand will grow in improved services come another year or two.

I would recommend that you select a better Sunday than the rainy one we chose two weeks ago. At least the downpour didn't dampen anyone's spirits aboard the reconverted log cars as we huffed and puffed up Cheat Mountain, pushed and pulled by an old Shay engine.

The train will be operating there each Sunday throughout October and with the advent of the fall season the view should be spectacular.

As added pleasure is the narration, while speeding along the track at eight miles an hour, by W. E. Blackhurst, author of several books concerning the lumber industry of West Virginia, whose latest work "Of Men and a Mighty Mountain" depicts life in Cass when the hoarse whistles of Shay engines were as common as the sound of birds.

It would be advisable for one to read this latest book, which records the fast vanishing history of lumber town boom days, before riding the scenic railroad as it will give the passenger much background material concerning one of the eastern United States. At one time 3,000 men concentrated their effort and skills in the massive assault against Cheat Mountain.

Once atop the mighty mountain, picnic tables and a refreshment stand are available for those who wish to carry along their lunch. Otherwise, the reconverted company store has food available. Also displayed are relics of another era along with two museums, wildlife and Civil War items.

All in all, it's an enjoyable Sunday drive and an opportunity to enrich one's interest in state history.

City Traffic Problems

October 7, 1965

This office has received one personal visit and two telephone calls this past week concerning speeding on Camden Avenue and Fayette street. One caller was rather appalled at the number of car accidents within the city limits, believing it to be all out of proportion in relation to the number of cars.

With the cooperation of Mrs. Elizabeth Poundstone, city recorder, I did some checking at city hall and found some interesting facts. Let's be fair about this problem. There are more people who own cars, and more and more people are two and three-car families. In Upshur county, there has been an increase this year of 5.5 percent in the ownership of vehicles over the previous year. Traffic is on the increase so naturally accidents will increase proportionately. Sometimes we may feel that the average driver knows nothing but to turn the key in the ignition, aim and steer. Another complaint has been that the local police officers are not doing their job. To my amazement I find that there is only one patrolman and one squad car on duty nightly from 5 p.m. until 1 a.m. On weekends two patrolmen in one squad car are on duty.

Will you please explain to me how they are expected to patrol the area which now comprises Buckhannon city limits in this manner? We get exactly what we pay for and monthly salary we pay our policemen certainly is not enough for this day and age. The increase in population and area would warrant the addition of at least two more policemen.

But, where is the money coming from? The fact of the matter is that the city budget has been cut $5,000 for the next year. In the past fiscal year (from July 1964 to July 1965) it may surprise you to know that a total of 143 accidents were investigated and citations given in 404 cases of traffic violations. Does that sound as if the local law enforcement officers are not doing their job? We as citizens are also responsible. This is a community problem, not a headache for the police department or city council alone.

In the accidents and violations investigated, 41 persons were injured with most of the accidents occurring this past January for a total of 19. Fewer accidents occurred in June, only three.

Major violations were speeding 84; improper passing 68; running stop signs 65; failure to yield right-of-way 34; reckless driving 32; failure to have vehicle under control 24 and driving intoxicated 11.

I'll grant these statistics may be appalling. Something should be done, but what? One suggestion is the publication weekly of names and address of all traffic offenders. This is being done in Kanawha county.

Welfare – Physician Ratios

October 21, 1965

At a recent state medical meeting, interesting maps were presented to doctors pointing to some startling statistics concerning welfare client caseloads.

With a population of better than 18,000 in Upshur county, we are fortunate that eight doctors reside in the county. But we are unfortunate in that the county ranks high in the percentage of population of the Department of Public Welfare's medical program.

Percentage-wise, Upshur county ranks high with 19.1 to 21 percent of population receiving free medical care from already over-burdened physicians. This compares to counties such as Berkeley, Jefferson, Ohio, Brooke, and Hancock who have seven percent or less of the population on relief rolls.

Pinpointing it even more, there are 42 welfare patients for every 1,000 patients treated by a doctor in Upshur county or 689 welfare patients.

Interestingly enough, one local physician tells me that these clients will have far more office calls than the paying patient because it is all free. Secondly, due to poor nutrition the welfare client is more likely to be ill, and thirdly due to less intelligence, less likely to take care of himself or his children, health wise.

To complicate matters even more, the physician and the pharmacist must fill out forms, file and submit statements to DPA within certain periods of time. All this work means the employment of a bookkeeper in the doctors office in addition to the nurses and or receptionists.

Even after statements are submitted to the DPA the physician may wait months for payment and when payment is made checks will show only the eligibility number. This entails even more time, for it is much easier to find patients by name rather than number in the doctor's files.

When asked what was the solution, one doctor threw up his hands in despair, "We're so over burdened with paperwork it's impossible to find time to read the medical journals. And just wait for Medicare."

Creeping Socialism

November 4, 1965

Senator Stephen M. Young of Ohio tells an amusing story about a modern 'rugged individualist.' This is the man's background:

While going to public schools, he lived with his parents in a low-cost housing development in Hamilton county, Ohio. He rode the free school bus and enjoyed the free lunch program. Following graduation from high school, he entered the Army and upon discharge kept his National Life Insurance. He then enrolled in an Ohio university, receiving regularly his GI check. Soon after graduation he married a Public Health nurse and bought a farm in southern Ohio with the aid of an FHA loan. Later, after going into the feed and hardware business, in addition to farming, he obtained help from the Small Business Administration when his business faltered. His first baby was born in the county hospital. The hospital was built in part with federal funds under the Hill-Burton program. As time went on, he bought additional acreage adjoining his farm and obtained emergency feed from the government. He then put part of his land under the Soil Bank program and used the payments for not growing crops to help pay his debts. His parents, elderly by now, were living comfortable on the smaller of his two farms with the aid of their Social Security payments. Lacking electricity at first, was finally served from lines supplied by the Rural Electrification Administration. A loan obtained from the Farmer's Home Administration helped clear some bottom land and obtain the best from it. That agent suggested building a farm pond, which the government stocked with fish. The government guaranteed him a price for his farm products. The county public library delivered books to his door. He banked his money in an institution which a government agency had insured up to $10,000 for every depositor. His son attended engineering school at Ohio State University and received financial assistance under the National Defense Education Act. His daughter is taking her nurse's training with assistance from the Nurse's Training Act. About this time, our hero purchased business and property in the county seat and began taking a proprietary interest in the local chamber of commerce. He became an ardent foe of excessive government spending programs and high taxes and finally wrote Senator Young the following letter:

"I believe in rugged individualism. People should stand on their own two feet. I oppose all these Socialistic trends you have been voting for and demand return to the free enterprise system of our forefathers. I and my neighbors intend to vote against you next year."

Men & Women 1882-1966

January 20, 1966

Had a note this week from one subscriber asking "When're you going to resume the Whirligig? It's even better than the editorials against sin and corruption in high places." With just that one note of encouragement and the fact that the heavy pre-Christmas advertising is at an end and I've caught up with correspondence and some reading, I'd like to share the following with readers:

-1882-

Eighty years ago women wore hoopskirts, bustles, petticoats, corsets, cotton stockings, high buttoned shoes, ruffled cotton drawers, flannel night-gowns, puffs in their hair, did their own cooking, caking, cleaning, washing, ironing, rearing big families, went to church Sundays, were too busy to be sick.

Men wore whiskers, square hats, Ascot ties, red flannelled underwear, big watches and chains, chopped wood for stoves, bathed once a week, drank 10-cent whiskey and five-cent beer, went in for politics, worked 12 hours a day, and lived to a ripe old age.

-1966-

Today women wear silk stockings, short shirts, low shoes, no corsets, an ounce of underwear, have bobbed hair, smoke, paint and powder, drink cocktails, play bridge, drive cars, have pet dogs, and go in for politics.

Men have high blood pressure, wear no ties, and some no hair, shave their whiskers, shoot golf, bathe twice a day, drink poison, play the stock market, ride in airplanes, never go to bed the same day they get up, are misunderstood at home, work five hours a day, play 10, and die young.

Timber Industry

February 3, 1966

What I know about the timber industry, you could stuff in a Kleenex and put in your hip pocket and have room to spare. But, when three men walk into a meeting of Lions Club members and start talking about better than a million and half acres of timber here and the possibility of new industry then I'm willing to learn a lot more.

Such was a case last Thursday night when representatives of the B & O Railroad disclosed findings in a recent resources study which could lead to the location of major wood industries.

One speaker, Jack T. Locomb, the railroad's industrial forester, was no stranger to this area having been a former resident of Buckhannon. In his report, the area of Lewis, Upshur and Barbour counties was called "The Land of Forest Fortune."

It's no wonder it's a fortune when you realize that the area made up of 1,401,280 acres of forest land which can be converted into hundreds of items ranging from paper, toys, baseball bats, skis and boats to caskets, fence posts and floorings.

Of historical interest, the period around 1910 was considered the "heyday" of the West Virginia sawmill industry. At that time the watershed of the Cheat and the headwaters of the Middle Fork rivers embraced a remarkable virgin forest of 195,000 acres. Upshur county was known then for its large, high quality yellow poplar, black walnut and chestnut. Whipsawed and hewed boards and timbers, still to be found in the old weather-beaten barns, bear witness to the quality and size of that virgin timber.

Since that time, despite heavy timber cutting, destructive cable skidding, uncontrolled forest fire and the chestnut blight, the predicted timber famine has not occurred. In fact, today there are more acres of commercial forest land in this area than there was 50 years ago, particularly in the southeastern corner of Upshur county, near Alexander.

At the present rate of consumption and growth, the Weston-Buckhannon-Elkins area is growing approximately 12 ½ million board feet of saw timber more each year than is being harvested.

For example, present forest industries include some 64 sawmills, only 14 of which saw in excess of 8,000 board feet per day. The larger mills are located at Buckhannon, Pickens, Elkins, Parsons and in the Tygart Valley. George Miles, Pioneer Lumber, and Frazee have band mills sawing 18 to 30 thousand board feet per day.

Wood-based industries already operating in the area include charcoal at Parsons and Belington, dry kilns at Belington, Parsons, Elkins, Buckhannon and Dailey, cabinet shops at Belington and Philippi, planing mills at Buckhannon, Belington, Parsons, Beverly and Elkins, flooring plants at Belington and Elkins, laminated industrial flooring at Buckhannon, dimension mills at Weston and Dailey, veneer mill at Elkins; laboratory cabinets and furniture at Beverly; moulding at Beverly and Buckhannon, and rustic rails at Ellamore and Parsons.

So, with the potential such as this, yes, I'm willing to learn a lot more about "The Jolly Green Giant Who Lives in Forest Fortune."

Whirligig by Son No. 2

February 10, 1966

It had to happen sometime. There I was sitting calmly in a chair reading the latest Whirligig masterpiece when I suddenly came onto the concluding sentence, "Jolly Green Giant in a Forest Fortune," I cried, "oh groan!" Mother came running into the room. "I suppose you've found something wrong with my column again," she said, "Alright what is it this time?" "I don't believe this Green Giant bit," I answered. "Come to think of it, the crop of CORN is awfully high this year!" "Ok?," she screamed, with eyes glaring and mouth frothing, "why don't you write this column one week and see if you can do better."

"I accept," I said, envisioning my debut as a great journalist, "but on one condition: you have to put my picture where yours usually is!"

"Agreed, buddy-boy," she retorted, a sly grin slowly forming, "I want to see you squirm!"

Readers of this column are certainly familiar with mother's frequent reports on the state of the Hornbeck household involving Son No. 1, Son No. 2 (that's me), and Daughter. Well there has been a slight addition to the household. Seems Son No. 1 grew up, entered college and brought home a wife, wagging her tongue behind him. That brought the total membership of the house to five, two men versus three women. That's just about even sides, I'd say. Of course, sometimes I have to fight all the others, including Son No. 1, alias Husband. I'm tormented from all sides. Daughter, our little mother, asks me to make my bed and will I please not dirty any more dishes. Son No. 1 asks me to make my bed and when am I leaving so he can take over my room. Sister-in-law asks me to make my bed and why do I have to keep bothering my dear brother?

Mother comes home from work, surveys the day's mess, asks me to make my bed, take out the garbage, burn the trash, shovel the walk, scrub the tub, pick up my clothes, and why do I have to keep bothering my dear sister?

Oh, well that's a bachelor's life! But, I've managed to survive, in spite of insurmountable odds. At least I've completed one challenge offered me although I'm not about to follow in my mother's shoes. Come to think of it, I never could wear high heels.

Federal Funds

February 17, 1966

It should be quite obvious to Upshur countians that this is an election year. Federal funds are raining upon the county like "manna from heaven" if one takes a look at the headlines used weekly in one's newspaper.

The latest grant is $49,590 financed by the U.S. Department of Labor to train 16 unemployed workers as highway engineer aides, whatever that means.

Now I go along with most of Johnson's war on poverty where he seems to want to give everything to everyone (although I haven't been the recipient of any extra) but I flatly refuse to accept the fact that the government is using my hard-earned cash to finance adult education classes in needlecraft, beginning knitting and hat making.

This talent won't earn anyone a dime! The remedial reading program announced last week by the Board of Education--- that I will support wholeheartedly. But, knitting, no sirree!!

Furthermore, if one must learn to knit and sew and construct hats, I have a suggestion. For the price of a membership in the YWCA and the cost of the yarn and material, anyone can attend classes weekly at the YWCA home. And, it won't cost the taxpayer a cent.

The biggest budget in history will cost $568 for every human in the United States next fiscal year. It will raise the total national debt to $321.7 billion.

This "manna from heaven" is a perfect example of how the government puts money in one of our pockets, then promptly takes it out of another. And if the drive toward a total welfare state continues, the takeout is going to be vastly larger than the put in.

New Décor at St. Joseph's Hospital

February 24, 1966

No more sterile white but modern, sunny, light, airy tones of yellow, turquoise, blue, green, beige, brown and tangerine dominate the décor of the new $1 ¾ million fabulous St. Joseph's hospital when dedicated March 3.

On a private tour last Thursday it was most evident that the ultimate in scientific, architectural and structural planning has gone into the sorely-needed hospital facility which will open for patient care March 8 following open house on Saturday and Sunday, March 5 and 6.

Described by some as a miniature Medical Center, the air conditioned, fireproof structure is one that the county can well be proud of. If one must be ill, one might as well be ill in luxury.

Even the hospital visitor is considered with a gift shop operated by the auxiliary, the use of the cafeteria for those who must sit and wait, and the interdenominational chapel for those who must wait and pray.

No patient rooms are on the first floor. Here are offices and storage, kitchen facilities, dining areas, reception rooms, emergency entrance, emergency operating room, two other operating recovery rooms, pharmacy and medical records rooms, central linen supply and medicine supply area, laboratories, and examining rooms.

If anything has been overlooked for comfort and convenience in medical treatment, it is not obvious. The most modern facilities include conductive flooring in operating rooms even to a machine known as a Conducheck which gives the doctor a green light before entrance to the operating room where there is no chance of static electricity.

An ingenious intercom system eliminates the many steps for every nurse. Doctors and patients can talk back and forth to each other, to other patients and to the nurse at the nurses stations.

In this world of new communication systems, even the doctors benefit with the use of a Televoice where the physician can repeat the patient's history into a phone which is recorded downstairs on tape and transcribed eventually for permanent record.

Patients will have a choice of a four-bed ward, semi-private or private room. In each are facilities for oxygen which is piped to every room, push-button beds, individual baths, music and television.

All 53 beds are on the second floor and include the pediatric ward, the maternity ward, one security room for the acutely disturbed patient, and even an isolation and nursery room.

Thirty-five beds can be placed on the third floor which will take $180,000 more to complete. But here too, future planning is evident because all plumbing, air-conditioning, wiring, heating, etc. is set to go.

But, see for yourself, take advantage of the tours during open house, this hospital is beyond my description and the Sisters of the Pallotine Order, the W. Va. Diocese, doctors and the townspeople are to be commended for their long effort.

Mental Health Clinic

March 24, 1966

For 19 long years a citizens group has actively and sometimes inactively "hung on" waiting for the day, planning, cajoling, studying when an out-patient clinic on mental health would be readily accessible to residents of Upshur County.

Committee personnel has changed at times but the actual realization of a 19-year-old dream came true Monday night when Dr. Cornella B. Wilbur, superintendent of the Weston State hospital, promised the loan of a part-time psychologist, psychiatrist, and social worker for Buckhannon.

Beginning April 4, a mental health clinic for Upshur County will open for two days a week in space provided by the County Department of Health in the Edmiston building.

The clinic will handle cases referred to it by hospital and by local doctors. Patients will pay as they can on a voluntary basis. The local citizens group will seek federal funds to set up a voluntary mental health program as a demonstration project, which is hoped to be a model for the entire state.

The savings in treating patients at home in familiar surroundings is untold. As Dr. Wilbur pointed out Monday night it is naturally cheaper to treat patients at home rather than hospitalization. The savings of $4.78 per day cost per patient at Weston State hospital is infinitesimal as compared to the saving when a mother is at home with children who otherwise would be "farmed out" to foster homes or when the farmer is restored to employment and once again a productive tax-paying citizen.

Startling though it may be, 40 Upshur county patients are now being treated at Weston state hospital. Another 80 patients were in and out of the hospital during 1965. Yet another 120 possible need treatment as that total has been admitted during the past 20 years, some patients admitted as many as 16 times.

So wouldn't you say there is a need for a voluntary mental health clinic in Upshur county? For once can't we use foresight instead of hindsight and at the same time save considerable sums of money in the hospitalization of mental patients?

Big Money in Poverty

April 7, 1966

The word has gotten around among civil servants in Washington that the big money is in poverty." Rep. William H. Ayres, of Ohio, made this statement last week attacking the "fantastic leakage of funds" through the War of Poverty.

In an analysis of salaries paid through the Office of Economic Opportunities report:

The antipoverty war is budgeted in fiscal 1967 for 6,484 permanent Federal employees whose annual salaries will total $53,500,000.

1,557 poverty fighters will draw yearly salaries of $10,619 or more, greater than an Army colonel's base pay. 25 poverty fighters will be paid more than Gen. William C. Westmoreland, commander of our troops in Vietnam. 36 poverty fighters will be paid more than Astronaut Neil A. Armstrong. And to top it all, Rep. Ayres says Sergeant Shriver has budgeted more than 300 jobs paying $17,000 a year or more, nearly double the number in the U.S. Office of Education.

But, on the other side of the coin, comes a news release from the Veterans Administration lauding the actions of Mr. and Mrs. Astrange P. Lindsey, of Crab Orchard, Raleigh county. As dependent parents of a son killed in service, they are eligible for a pension of $33 each per month.

The Lindseys, who only recently became eligible for Social Security, wrote the Huntington BA regional office saying they felt they no longer are "dependent parents," and that now they do not need the $66 per month. The Lindsey letter stated: "Attached please find the checks you mailed us as dependent parents of the above named. Since we are in receipt of Social Security benefits, we feel we are no longer dependent. Also, we have three sons now in service in Vietnam and perhaps this might help them in some way. Thank you so much for this award, but at the present time we do not need it."

The Lindsey family now consists of nine living children, seven boys and two girls. The Lindseys' action has just restored my faith in the American public!

Killed In Action - Vietnam

April 14, 1966

When he was a kid, Sammy Hartzell liked to stretch out and day-dream under a tree not far from his home in Westover, PA. It was a pleasant spot and from it Sammy could see much of the countryside. He loved the place and never got tired of going there.

A few days ago Sammy's father walked up the hill. He carried a shovel, and when he got to Sammy's favorite tree he started to dig. He was making a grave because Sammy was coming home to rest forever. Word has come from Washington that the boy has been killed while guarding the Da Nang air base in Vietnam. But the news wasn't entirely unexpected. Shortly before Christmas his sister had received a letter from Sammy and in it he had expressed a premonition of death. The letter told his sister: "Last night and most of today I've been thinking of things I've got to be thankful for. Seems like the Lord and I understand each other, and that is such a feeling of comfort.

Sammy wrote more, in the same vein. Then he told how he wanted to be buried under his beloved tree and added, "Let all our memories be good ones."

The memories of the Hartzells and all those who knew this boy will assuredly be good ones, but as we read about Sammy we wondered about some other young men. We thought of those over-educated simpletons with scraggly beards and placards who call for a peace which would throw away everything gained by the sacrifices of the Sammy Hartzells. And the exhibitionists who display their inadequacy in childish draft-card burnings and shrill outbursts testifying to their great ideals, their sublime ethics and their love of all mankind.

And that other kind of American youth, imbued with the idea that the world owes them a living and there's no point in passing up the nice things of life even if there is a war. Let the fall guys, the Sammy Hartzells, go and get themselves killed. And finally we thought of that yellow Muslim, Cassius Clay, the heavyweight champion of the big mouth-division, and his crowd.

We wonder how these miserable characters will end up in the years to come. We wonder about their memories, and if they'll be the sort that anyone can live with. Somehow we doubt it.

Grandmom Dutton

May 5, 1966

I couldn't find the proper Mother's Day card this year. The card I wanted didn't say anything about the sewing, darning, mending, altering, and washing, ironing, drying, which nine times out of ten is done on the spur of the moment or in dire emergencies for the Hornbeck household.

You see, my mother just lives one street over from our house and since I spend more time in this office than I do at home, Son No. 1, Son No. 2 and Daughter have a convenient built-in second "Mom."

The Mother's Day cards this year don't say anything about Mom slipping in when you're flat on your back with the flu, or sending over a pie when you just don't feel like baking or inviting the entire "Hornbeck posse" in for dinner after a hard day at the office.

The cards this year don't say a thing about the "surprises," like a new pair of shoes or a new suit for the boys or an accessory for your home.

And, a card doesn't mention the numerous times the car is loaned or the errand run or pick-up and deliveries completed. Mother is always there it seems whether at the high school football games in rain and snow or a Girl Scout function. She's one of those women who keeps an immaculate house and never looks like she's cleaning. She can cook all day at the church for 150 people and play a wicked game of bridge the same evening. I know she suffers occasionally with "old-fashioned rheumatism" but one would never know it unless you accidentally found the prescription on the kitchen shelf.

She doesn't argue religion or politics and never intentionally gossips.

Mom isn't a saint or a sinner, she's just a mother who tends to her own business and the business of her daughters and families. She's available for baby-sitting or for any extra duties when called upon. We don't always agree with her and she claims we're rearing poor husbands because we haven't "taught our sons to pick up a thing." She's my Mom and I wouldn't trade her for another. You see why I can't find a proper Mother's Day card this year!

Foreign Exchange Student

May 12, 1966

For several months B-U students have been actively engaged in a fund-raising campaign to institute a new program at the local high school. The foreign exchange student scholarship program has been inexistence since 1914. Schools at Bridgeport and Fairmont East have had a student exchange for some years.

Through the efforts of the Student Council, it appears now that a student from abroad will arrive in Buckhannon for his or her senior year this August. The student will live with a typical American family and believe me the local high school students are quite excited about who the family is and from where the student will travel.

But the kids need a little more support from local organizations and service clubs.

A $750 participating contribution is required of each school bringing a foreign student to the United States. This fee is the same for every chapter, regardless of the country from which its student comes. The actual operational cost varies from $900 to $2,000. The local goal has been set at $1,000. The $750 pays such direct expenses as ship or plane fares, personal allowance, medical payments, transportation within the United States, baggage cases, etc.

Various local expenses occur during the year which are not covered by the $750 or which the student cannot pay for out of his own monthly personal allowance. The most common are transportation to and from school, school lunches, school books and supplies, graduation expenses, class ring and a senior trip.

Under no circumstances is the local host family paid for hosting a student.

At last accounting a total of $716 had been raised through contributions. And, believe me, the local students have worked hard receiving money through two skating parties, a Talent Show, and the sale of stock.

So, won't you give them a little more help? Send your contributions to the high school, to chapter president, Mrs. George Rossbach or Bob Stell, chapter treasurer.

It will be interesting I should think to host a student from another country who will gain an understanding of America and Buckhannon and at the same time local students will learn more of his or her country.

Our guest will be of above average ability; sufficiently competent in reading, writing and speaking English; with personal attributes which will enable him or her to act as good representative of home countries.

During the student's year in the United States, he is to be acquainted as widely as possible with American life and the different ideals, customs, and people to be found here so that he can explain Buckhannon and American society to his friends and family when he returns home.

I Can't Cook

May 19, 1966

I can't cook. That's an honest, sincere statement as anyone who has eaten at my house can attest. Food doesn't interest me that much unless someone else is paying the check and then my brother-in-law will cringe when I order prime ribs well done instead of rare.

If and when I live absolutely alone, I know I shall subsist on sharp cheddar cheese or Swiss cheese and rye bread, scrambled eggs and toast once in awhile and maybe a bowl of boiled shrimp now and then.

Don't misunderstand me, a well balanced diet is always there on the table for the boys, but that doesn't necessarily mean I must eat it just because I fixed it. My menus read like something out of the first year 4-H cooking project book. I couldn't fix a meal if there wasn't such a thing as tossed salad. You can imagine my consternation this winter when lettuce raised to 39 cents a head. I never buy a pound of coffee as instant suffices as far as I'm concerned. (I do buy coffee during football season, but only because my father stops in after the games and absolutely refuses instant coffee.)

I was long ago reconciled to the fact that my mother and my sister surpass in kitchen craft. I really wasn't concerned, but now that I have a daughter-in-law who is fast approaching the title of superb cook, my youngsters have suddenly realized that they have been missing quite a bit of culinary art over the years.

For instance, I wasn't even able to bake and ice a birthday cake Monday night. The icing was suddenly brick-hard, refused to spread and it was only because my daughter-in-law baked a banana cream pie the next morning and placed a candle in the center that mother had a birthday symbol. Tonight when I attempt to make Dad's favorite seafoam candy for his birthday, it will probably refuse to set. Anything that ever turns out right in my kitchen is purely accidental.

Now, after 20 years in and out of the kitchen, answering the telephone, settling the quarrels and wiping up spilled milk, I've suddenly gotten a complex.

But I'm reconciled. I'll never be a cook.

Beautification Going Sour

June 2, 1966

What a pity! Suddenly Buckhannonites have lost their pride. What started out to be a beautification project has suddenly turned sour. Have you noticed the concrete planter boxes on Main Street recently? Disgraceful! They have become merely trash receptacles.

Even the planter in front of the county courthouse holds only dry, burnt, brown twigs of pine. The other supposedly planters hold chewing gum and candy papers, stubbed out cigarettes and cigar butts.

We commend the garden clubs for their efforts of a year ago, but grieve at the lack of interest from Main Street merchants who wish they could dump the planters in the middle of the street.

Isn't Buckhannon supposed to be a Petunia City? How about bright pansies or red geraniums. But, for heaven's sake, let's do something. Either keep them planted and clean or do away with the unsightly mess before conference and Strawberry Festival time.

What a pity!

Instant Housing

June 23, 1966

Isn't instant living wonderful? There's instant milk, instant pudding, instant mashed potatoes, instant coffee. Friday, I left town for just one day and there was a vacant lot across the street. When I arrived home at 5 p.m. there was a complete new instant house resting on that vacant lot.

Brought in by a tractor-trailer in two pieces, the only thing left to expedite instant housing is to have homes gently dropped by helicopter. And believe me, I'm told that is not improbable as experiments have been successful. War does bring out the good sometimes. After all, if helicopters can drop men and equipment, why not houses onto foundations.

It was amusing to me Friday evening to sit on the front porch and watch motorists drive up and down the street, suddenly notice a house where a house hadn't been that morning. Slam on the brakes, do a double-take and finally drive slowly onward, gaping in amazement.

Instant housing comes in all sizes, styles, and models…if you don't like the style after a few years or you outgrow the present model, just snap your fingers and if by magic you have a new instant house, complete with built in kitchen, appliances, and wall-to-wall carpeting.

Yes, there's instant living and instant death…the only thing left to develop is instant babies!

Jennifer is Born

July 14, 1966

I'm a special person today! In fact, a very special person and I want special treatment, at least for today. I've just joined an age-old club, the Grandmother's Club. This morning (Wednesday) at 5:30 a.m., eight pound, six ounce Jennifer joined the Hornbeck household. Son, David Dutton and wife Judi Taylor Hornbeck, presented me with a large bundle of black-haired joy.

I don't feel one day older. Oh, maybe a little older since I didn't close my eyes all night waiting for the phone to ring. This is "old-hat" to those who have been grandmothers four and five times over but "new-hat" to me.

I have those same qualms about being a grandmother that I had when I became a mother for the first time 20 years ago. It seems to me that being a grandmother perhaps carries even more responsibility.

One nice thing about this responsibility is that she can be returned more often than not to the arms of mother and father. For instance, I won't be responsible for that 2 o'clock feeding, and the wakeful nights of colic, or the DPT shots, the scratched knees and the bruised feelings.

Yes, there's something special about a grandmother and a grandchild. I'm going to enjoy this new experience. Jennifer is welcomed with love and humility. God's handiwork makes one humble indeed, and grateful.

YWCA Events

August 11, 1966

If Josie Clem, a clerk at H-P was sharp with her customers Monday; if Lana Tomblyn at Adrian Buckhannon Bank miscounted your money; if the A&P check-out counters weren't quite as genial as usual and if The Delta is full of mistakes this week, blame it all on the YWCA chartered bus trip this past weekend.

Seventy-three adults and Y-Teenagers traveled all day Sunday, with stops here and there enroute, to attend a performance of the outdoor Civil War drama "Honey in the Rock." The only discordant note in the entire trip was the fact that we arrived back in Buckhannon at 4 a.m. Monday morning. That was very little sleep for those of us who had to arise at 7 or 8 to be on the job!

Prior arrangements for the bus trip were well worth the time. If you have not attended the performance, you should. In this day and age of condemning our young people from Buckhannon, they were exceptional travelers, well groomed, mannerly and well behaved throughout the trip and during the performance. It is a group that Upshur county could well be proud of.

The year-old infant organization of the Young Women's Christian Association is still a toddler in many, many ways. During the past year, the board has made some mistakes but cannot be condemned for not trying.

It wasn't too long after formal organization that we realized little was being done for the young people. Still, we realize that we are neglecting the older women, too. This chartered bus trip was arranged with the thought in mind that it included all ages. It is the hope that many such trips throughout the state can be made during the year.

Soon, the annual membership drive will be underway once again. As required, one general membership meeting will be publicized for September 28th.

Work this past year has been exciting and several new ideas are being tossed around. Women of Upshur county should make themselves heard as to what they expect of the YWCA.

For instance, plans are currently underway for the mother-daughter banquet, new classes are being arranged for the winter months including a series of serious lectures to help inform the public of today's problems within the city, county, state and nation. We are contemplating a business etiquette course for clerks and another geared to secretaries and receptionists needs. We're wondering if the public would be interested in a creative writing class taught by one of our well-known English teachers. The board realizes the dire need for a paid full-time director at the rented property on West Main Street.

These are problems which will be solved, maybe not this year but certainly in the not-too-distant future. We do hope that the public will be patient but receptive to ideas.

As far as the past year's accomplishments, they have not been so bad. Youth dances have been staged on several nights in the fire department auditorium. Most classes were well-attended but, here again, interests ranged. The board hired Miss Suzanne Young for the summer as youth director, we are financially solvent, a beautiful style show was produced in cooperation with local merchants, Y-Teen clubs have been organized at both the Junior and Senior high schools, and the Y-Teens were active during the Strawberry Festival, selling programs, sponsoring the Youth Dance and building two floats, one of which won a trophy.

For an infant organization without constant assistance from national YW headquarters in the form of a paid staffer this doesn't sound so bad! In fact, little known to the public, is the fact that the local chapter was an experiment in that we started from nothing and without trained personnel. Since we were formally affiliated, flyers have gone out from national headquarters using Buckhannon as an example of what can be done so we have received national recognition. Miss Dorothy McAdam, eastern regional director, did visit the YW five times in the past year and each time was delighted with our progress.

Much has been done and more will be done, if we have lots of volunteers and a little more interest.

Trimble Hill

August 25, 1966

With school bells due to ring again next Monday, it was rather a coincidence that I should receive a communiqué from Mat Holt, of Weston, in relation to ceremonies of the laying of the cornerstone of Buckhannon's first school of higher education, the Buckhannon Male and Female Academy.

It seemed that Mat was glancing through an issue of the Weston Sentinel of July 2, 1847 when he found the following account of the cornerstone ceremonies.

To familiarize readers with a little of the background, the Buckhannon Male and Female Academy was the first institution west of the mountains to accommodate both sexes. It was in existence from 1847-1866 and was located behind where the Curry Chevrolet company is now located.

In the story, C.D. Trimble, Esq.'s hotel is mentioned which is commonly known as Trimble's Tavern, and was located at the corner of South Kanawha and Madison streets, on the present location of the Hunter residence.

South Kanawha Hill was known at one time as Trimble Hill for Trimble owned approximately 25 acres on the west side of the present street.

Also mentioned is Dr. D.S. Pinnell, a Buckhannon physician who owned property and a home between the present East Main street school and the present Masonic building. Col.. Henry F. Westfall lived in a log cabin at the top of Kanawha Street Hill which is now the site of the EUB parsonage. He was Deputy sheriff, clerk of the circuit court and postmaster in Buckhannon from 1832 to 1852.

Mentioned too is the performance of the Buckhannon Band.

School Budgets

September 1, 1966

"On the present course, all schools will fail to open within the next five to ten years." This statement was made last week by the member of the Randolph County Board of Education but could hold true in Upshur county and throughout the state of West Virginia.

The seriousness of the statement was amplified by pointing out that the schools of Randolph county have been going out of business for the past several years.

The complete closing of the schools has thus far been prevented by abandoning several buildings each year and preserving the skeleton force for the remaining schools, which again is the case in Upshur county.

According to the spokesman for the Randolph board, the history of education in West Virginia shows our legislatures down through the years have not provided necessary salaries to attract students to the teaching field. When the present dedicated teaching force retires there will be no more public schools until long after a crisis alarms the apathetic voting public to action.

Certain corporations, unions, and out-of-state interests have been able to control our legislatures in such a way that a logical tax on our raw natural resources leaving the state have not been taxed for the education of the young people of West Virginia.

If you doubt the authenticity of the above statements, just take a look at teacher salaries for Upshur county, they average $3,800 which is barely above the poverty level of $3,000 which is where federal money is being poured to alleviate the suffering among low income families.

If you doubt the authenticity of the statements, look at the average age of our present school teachers, about 52 years. How many new, young, bright-eyed college graduates have we been able to acquire. Why should they teach in Upshur county or West Virginia when they can make double the salary in another state.

Along with the $3,800, consider the teacher conditions, overcrowded classrooms and long hours. In fact the local high school is now on probation as the North Central Association of

Colleges and Secondary Schools frowns on the fact that many of our teachers do not have an hour's break in their teaching day. If you don't believe the association is powerful, just remember that if Buckhannon-Upshur high school is not an accredited school, graduation seniors will be refused admission to many, many colleges.

Vacancies still exist in many classrooms now that school is in its first week of operation. The local high school with an enrollment of 1,000 students will not have a school newspaper this year, because the local board could not approve extra pay for extra hours although the newspaper is self-supporting through the sale of advertising.

There has been no increase in salaries this year, but neighboring Harrison county granted another $25 per month increase, realizing we hope, the seriousness of the teaching situation.

The three-county vocational training school which has been in the planning stage for two years, has never gotten off the ground, though the land is bought and federal money exists. It is time that citizens of Upshur county realize that we need garage mechanics, carpenters and brick-layers, along with teachers, in this complex society.

And, it should be apparent that the federal money will not be available forever. We cannot look to the federal government as a glorified Santa Claus…the federal government is you and I, and I'm about to run out of money.

Overworked Doctors

October 13, 1966

Have you tried to make an appointment with your family doctor recently? If so, you probably came away from the phone muttering about the wait of three weeks for the first opening, and wondering what you'd do in case of emergency.

Don't blame your doctor. He's doing the best he can. In fact, he's doing more than he should. One local doctor, who has practiced in Buckhannon for 25 years and who is typical of our local doctors, just recently had his office secretary complete a survey requested from the American Medical Society.

He was more surprised than anyone to discover that he is averaging a 72-hour work week. If he devotes 72 hours a week to professional activities that leaves little time for family, any social or civic life.

The survey shows that 150 patients are seen by appointment each week. The office secretary tells me that it is actually 250 persons in and out of the office during the week. The appointment sheets won't show the number of shots per week, or the phone conversations with patients, the conferring by phone with other hospitals and doctors, the urinalysis and hemoglobin laboratory tests, the patients with the skin rash or other minor discomforts who sees the doctor but is never charged.

The survey also reveals that the doctor sees an average of another 50 patients per week in the hospital. An average of five home calls are made a week. The survey doesn't show the night calls or those on Sundays and holidays.

Upshur county has 10 doctors for a population of 18,292. That means more than 1,800 patients per doctor.

So, the next time you feel like rebuking your family doctor for his apparent lack of attention, or neglect or disinterest, remember, it isn't that at all, it's overwork!!

Trouble With Kids

October 27, 1966

Time was when education in this country was symbolized by the little red schoolhouse. Today, the symbol is the big yellow school bus. It used to be a pleasant sight to see the children playing in the schoolyard, oblivious to the fact that some of them had different colored skin, and different religions, and different ancestors. Now, you find them very mindful of this, properly proportioned, snuggled in cars and buses which lumber in from every direction and selected neighborhoods.

Years ago, youngsters went to school to learn the three r's readin', ritin, and rithmetic. There seems to be more emphasis today on two other r's: rock and roll.

Only in institutions of higher education is a third "r" added: either radicalism or rioting.

In days of old, school kids prayed to Our Father in Heaven. This is now against the law. The emphasis these days is on installing a proper respect for Big Brother Who Art in Washington.

When they talked about passing, students used to refer to the grades they were getting. Nowadays, passing has to do with a drag session, or zipping around a trailer truck at 80 miles an hour. As for grades, they're the things that go uphill and downhill. Students aren't graded: they're adjusted.

No longer will you find evidence of brutality such as hickory switches in schools. Only zip guns, switchblade knives, brass knuckles and other aids to conformity.

Kids used to be taught what was right.

Now all they hear about is rights.

Excelsior!!

Mrs. H. M. Darley

November 3, 1966

At the end of another "long, hot summer," it is worth noting that approximately 21,590,000 U.S. Negroes (out of 22 million) did not throw any Molotov cocktails, tip over any automobiles, smash any store windows, or otherwise rampage or riot.

Approximately 172,990,000 U.S. whites (out of 173 million) did not throw rocks or rotten vegetables, yell "black bastard," or otherwise insult or interfere with Negroes staging lawful demonstrations.

On the other hand, millions of college students did not demonstrate in protest to the war in Vietnam and countless thousands of others enlisted in the war against Communism. At home, a childless 73-year-old woman, Mrs. H. M. Darley, of Arlington, Mass., who has lived to celebrate her golden wedding anniversary, has become personally interested in other mother's sons, one of whom is a native of Upshur county, Delmus Hamner, son of Henry Hamner, of Gaines.

Delmus' mother died while he was young and he spent his school days living at the home of his grandparents. After he graduated from Buckhannon-Upshur high school, he entered the army and went to Vietnam, it was there that he got a card from Mrs. D."

They kept in contact throughout the time he spent in Vietnam and in less than an hour after he arrived home, Mrs. Darley was on the phone inquiring about Delmus. In the meantime he has made two visits to the home of Mr. and Mrs. Darley in Massachusetts.

Perhaps if more people would take an interest in our fighting boys as "Mrs. D.", the world would be a better place in which to live and lot of lovely people could find happiness in making others happy."

"Mrs. D", as she is fondly known to her servicemen around the world wrote the following tribute, which she says was inspired on one of Delmus' visits to her home.

"To the American soldiers in Vietnam. Most of all to the boys whom I have written, what it has done for them and the rewards for me, I dedicate this letter.

"Last December 1965, my work started by sending Christmas cards to individual boys in Vietnam, their names given to me by a friend.

"In a short time after receipt of my cards, the boys began to send me acknowledgements of the cards and their appreciation. In turn I sent a reply to each boy, saying I would be happy to write to them if they would like me to do so. It is needless to say what happened after that.

"Letter by letter, the friendships became strong and the desire for my letters was very apparent. I have stacks of the most wonderful letters that I have ever read in my life and that covers quite a span of years. The letters are full of devotion, gratitude and respect. Whatever help I have been able to give to the boys to help them over the rough spots, I am proud to have done. As they have told me, they consider it a privilege to have been able to serve their country. So do I.

"My rewards are many, in knowing that I have helped and made friendships of untold magnitude. There seems to be no end to it. Some of 'my boys' are home, some in the process of doing so. Some I have never had the honor to know because they have gone home to God who will take care of them, 'No more wars, only Peace'.

"I will continue writing as long as I am needed and I hope I can be of help to some new boys who will be true American soldiers.

"Thank you boys for what you have done for me in a faraway land of trouble. It was a privilege to be by your side as a fortress of strength to help you to do your duty and carry on. May the good Lord bless you and keep you safe from all harm in the years to come.

Very sincerely,

Your faithful friend,

Mrs. D."

Salute!

Babysittin'

November 10, 1966

Done any baby-sittin' lately? I hadn't until this past weekend and found I had lost my touch. Maybe I never had that proverbial touch to start with but that four-month-old granddaughter of mine was awfully slippery in her tub.

It's been 14 years since I bathed a little baby and my coordination was long gone along with any routine that I may have had. Cardinal rule No. 1, you know, is be sure and have all supplies at finger tips. Otherwise, I guess you let the baby drown while you're rushing for the swabs and the baby oil.

Also, I had forgotten that little babies can splash so far and consequently the clean clothes were wet. I had forgotten too that babies can spit food so far, even to the opposite kitchen wall. I doubt that one bottle was warmed properly, found them either too cold or too hot.

It's to Jenni's credit that she didn't protest, but put up with me for a day and a night. Somewhere along the line she got an extra bottle for she was eating fruit and cereal at 8 p.m. instead of the usual 6 p.m. dinner.

Some things haven't changed. There were still mountains of clothes to wash and dry, babies still respond to lullabies and they still enjoy the rocking chair.

But, don't tell her mother.

Instant Schools

November 17, 1966

Some time ago I was writing about instant living, instant mashed potatoes, instant coffee, instant housing and now Bill McKnight comes along with pictures and a story about instant schools.

His story fell right in place along with my visit to the junior high school last Wednesday night and a letter to the editor in last week's Delta, written by Loutellus M. Stout, well known staff member of the W. Va. Farm Bureau.

In Stout's letter, in no way critical of the school administration, he suggests the formation of an Upshur County School Improvement Association, the purpose of which would determine the facts concerning needs of the schools in Upshur county, dissemination of the information to the public, and assistance in the meeting of these needs.

In other words, why can't the local board of education have a long-range plan such as Wesleyan college has had for many, many years and West Virginia University which now publicizes its plans for its three Morgantown campuses?

The need for a long-range plan was apparent Wednesday night on my visit to the local junior high. I was quick to notice that many of the rooms had been newly painted even though the lighting was of the most antique. I was dismayed when I reached one of the basement science rooms to discover one of the filthiest, darkest most inadequate classrooms in my years of visits to schools in Harrison, Greenbrier, or Mercer counties. Four old-fashioned round globes provided the only light and believe me, in an underground basement room the lights are a necessity. To top it off, the dirty, chipped walls were of the worst color of pink which screamed at the bright green woodwork.

Now, getting back to McKnight's story. His pictures show a modern, attractive six-room school recently set-up in Hack Valley which was ready for use in two weeks with the work of three men.

Electrically heated, air-conditioned, beautifully lighted, the 58 by 100 feet school building made up of eight mobile sections was moved to the site by trailers.

Housing 180 students, six teachers, six rooms, two baths, a principal's office and a storage room, it is decorated throughout with cheerful modern green trim and green tile floors. Each classroom has two large blackboards and two large bulletin boards. There is a fire door from each room for safety's sake. And it was all possible through a federal government aid act. This certainly points to the need of a long-range plan on the part of interested citizens and the school board.

Instant schools - wouldn't it be wonderful!!

Howard Hiner Collection

Pearl Harbor

December 8, 1966

Where were you on Sunday, December 7, 1941? Usually during times of national emergency each of us can precisely say just where we were and what we were doing at that particular time.

When the Japanese staged their sneak attack on Pearl Harbor which led to the United States entry into World War II, I was a junior in high school. That particular afternoon 25 years ago, as teenagers still do today, I was lying across my bed talking, talking, and talking to a favorite girl friend, Lorna. At a precise moment the bedroom door was flung open and the blare of Dad's radio reached us. Four years later Lorna, her husband and her baby daughter died in a plane crash in Germany, a result of the infamous Sunday.

Inquiring yesterday in this office, Mary Liz was doing her college accounting. After the news, her studies stopped, she had two brothers already in the Air Force.

Millie had a month-old baby, she was just getting ready to take for a stroll. Millie and Matt walked to Zella and Stick Martin's and talked and talked the afternoon away.

E. Quentin and a bunch of fellows had just gotten to the bookstore when they heard the news. Extra papers from all the large cities were sent for so all could read the day's events.

Dana and Rita were at home, and as always Dana started worrying about the Delta and how would he get newsprint and type for publication.

As for the rest of the staff, three were not yet born and one was just a grade school student. But that day and that war still affect their lives. Three of the boys have served a "hitch" in the Army and our sons, the "War-boom" babies are now awaiting their turns.

President Roosevelt was trying to save Indo-China from the Japanese and today our sons fight at the same place to save it from communism. It has another name, Vietnam.

It seems so strange that our children must know December 7, 1941 as a date in a history book. It's so real to us, we were there.

The Ant & The Grasshopper

December 15, 1966

It was President Grover Cleveland who said "The lesson should be constantly enforced that, though the people support the government, the government should not support the people." His words came to mind this morning as I read the daily newspaper where State Welfare Commission L. L. Vincent has asked the Board of Public Works for almost double the $24 million in state funds being spent by his department this year.

In presenting his budget, Vincent in the next breath boasted that West Virginia is the only state where the caseload of welfare recipients is dropping. In fact, he noted that the caseload had declined 133,000 in the past five years.

The $24 million increase is asked by welfare for doubling of funds for medical services, public assistance grants, and higher salaries for new positions.

All of which brings something else to mind, remember the fable of the ant and grasshopper?

Once upon a time there was an ant who worked hard all day in the fields. It was summer and the ant was busy cutting grass and dragging it home. The ant had a grasshopper for a neighbor. The grasshopper sat in his doorway singing all day. When winter came the ant had a whole bale of grass. He was fined $162.50 and the surplus was seized. The grasshopper received the surplus in exchange for his food stamps.

Tales of Fantasy

January 5, 1967

It occurred to me this week that Son No. 2, though only a college freshman, made a profound statement sometime during the bustle of the holidays. His comment was that youngsters were too sophisticated nowadays. The thought cropped up because I had had difficulty in purchasing a plain, old-fashioned nursery rhyme book for my granddaughter. Son No. 2 found just what I wanted in a bookstore in Morgantown, almost a carbon copy of an edition he had as a boy.

Children just don't seem interested or else parents aren't taking time to read the favorite fairy tales and bedtime stories to which we were exposed in our "growing-up" days.

A four, five or six-year-old can hardly be enthralled with Rapunzel, Cinderella, Beauty and the Beast or the Frog Prince when he has just seen on television a Super Z-Ray Cannon that shoots genuine atomic warheads and costs only $24.95. Five-year-old Sissy has her demands too, "I have been watchin' Uncle Zuk on television and you know what, for only $39.95 you can buy me a Genuine Hollywood Screen Test Kit Including Hair Dye. And I want one."

And your neighbor Mrs. Jones, who has been denouncing high food prices, is silent at the dinner table when Junior has the floor. Seems he has been looking at cars. He can get a Caramba, with bucket seats, four-on-the floor, tachometer, stereo type system and 440 cubic inches of power, all for only $3,495 delivered.Is it any wonder that today's youngsters aren't guaranteed absorption in exciting tales of fantasy and make-believe, adventure stories, poetry, popular fairy tales, stories that teach a lesson.

But we are guaranteeing our youngsters one thing….ulcers. More and more cases are being diagnosed today by physicians. It's no wonder. Have you recently itemized all the extra-curricular activities in which your youngsters are involved? There's Little League basketball, football, baseball, the swim team, 4-H, Girl Scouts, Boy Scouts, Cub Scouts, Brownies, Senior Scouts, band practice, choir practice, play practice, Y-Teens, Kan-Teens, Rainbow Girls, Theta Rho Girls, Loyal Temperance Legion, MYF, BYF and Junior Newmans.

Somewhere in between are household chores, TV, study and some baby-sitting. Forgive me, progress is wonderful, but so are quiet fairy tales!

United Fund – Little Angel

January 19, 1967

The boys have always had their football trophies and Ann her gold and bronze swimming medals displayed around the house and at times looked at me rather askance as if to say "What has she ever done?"

Well, really, they do have cause for wondering. I mean, after-all, most mothers aren't lousy cooks, always behind on the washing and ironing, clean house only once a week, look like Phyllis Diller of Finks Run and have a reputation for diarrhea of the typewriter.

They can move their medals aside now and make room for my "Little Angel." He isn't very pretty, looks a little like Charlie Brown of the comic strip, his halo is slightly lopsided too, but the coveted "Little Angel" is prized by anyone who has worked with the United Fund campaign.

The surprise award made last Wednesday at the annual meeting of the UF was presented to me. I still don't know why. Someone said it was a bribe to either talk up or shut up. Since I have the reputation for saying what I feel, I intend to talk up….that is, about the United Fund.

It's much easier to sit at this typewriter and talk than it is to attend a 7 a.m. campaign meeting or canvass the neighborhood or wheedle and cajole someone into giving a helping hand to those who can't help themselves.

And, isn't that what the United Fund is…a helping hand? The goal wasn't reached this year. But, $4,000 over the previous year was raised. Progress has been made but it's been a rough, uphill fight all the way for the campaign chairmen. It must get rather discouraging when you note that people have money for everything but the "helping hand."

You may not be interested in every agency supported by United Fund, but surely "you care enough about one to give the very best." At least, think about it.

New Job Ideas

January 26, 1967

I'm indebted this week to Dr. H.D. Almond for a bit of information obtained from the Community Action Council. Upshur County is and has been the goal of the Chamber of Commerce and local business groups for years.

New Ideas, your ideas, no matter how impractical they seem are now being solicited at the courthouse by the staff of the Community Action Council.

No one knows yet if these or your suggestions are valuable but local businessmen will examine all suggestions. Here are a few received already:

1. Burn Upshur county slag piles in an old blacksmith furnace together with sawdust and a little river sand and make and sell cinders to the State Road Commission.

2. Graft red dogwood twigs to the 50,000-plus native white dogwood and sell at about three dollars per tree.

3. Erect plastic greenhouses, similar to Feola's along the river and use waterpower for heat, raise watercress, lettuce, tomatoes, beans, etc.;

4. Grow two to 50 acres of graveyard moss, or creeping phlox, and sell to the State Road Commission to be replanted with the seed blower when straw and grass are blown on the bare roadsides.

5. All high school students bring some toy, kitchen utensil, game, or gadget made of wood to school and have our lumber experts study the feasibility of making the product.

A thousand similar ideas from college, high school, civic men's and women's groups could create an industry and jobs.

Have you any impractical-practical suggestion? Bring or mail them to the Upshur County Community Action Council at the courthouse.

Letter From A Foxhole

March 2, 1967

The following letter "from a foxhole in Vietnam" recently came to my attention. It is from a young soldier whose mother, Mrs. Ada Casto Rutherford, lives near French Creek.

"Dear Members of Wilson Chapel WSCS:

"I received the beautiful Christmas card and I would like to thank each and everyone of you for it ever so much. It was nice of you all to think of me. I attended your church only one time, three years ago, and I met a lot of real nice people. I am a member of the Methodist church at French Creek. We have a beautiful church also. Perhaps some of you have attended my church. "When I start feeling lonely and the going gets rough I find it helps to say a prayer and ask the Lord for strength. Here is a little prayer I thought all of you might enjoy. I know this little prayer by heart now, as I have read it so many times. I have carried it in my billfold and it is a little messed up but I am sure it makes no difference as the meaning is what counts.

"God Bless all of you, Sincerely, Terry Casto."

This is Terry's "prayer from a foxhole": Lord, God, I have never spoken to you but now, I want to say "How do you do." You see, God, they told me You didn't exist and like a fool, I believed all this … Last night from a shell hole I saw Your sky… I figured right then they'd told me a lie. Had I taken the time to see the things you made, I'd have known they weren't calling a spade a spade. I wonder God, if You'd shake my hand, Somehow, I feel that You will understand. Funny, I had to come to this hellish place before I had time to see your face. Well, I guess there isn't much more to say. But I'm sure glad, God, I met You today. I guess the zero hour will soon be here, but I'm not afraid since I know You're near. The signal Well, God, I'll have to go. I like You lots… this I want you to know. Look now… this will be a horrible fight. Who knows, I may come to Your house tonight. Though I wasn't friendly with You before, I wonder God, if You'd wait at Your door. Look I'm crying, me… shedding tears. I wish I had known you these many years, Well, I have to go now, God… goodbye. Strange… since I met You, I'm not afraid to die.

The Big Flood of 1967

March 9, 1967

The post office has a motto, something to the effect that "neither rain or sleet, nor hail nor storm of night, etc," can keep the carrier from his appointed rounds, but it says nothing about flood waters.

The newspaper profession likes to think that the post office motto also applies to it, but Tuesday, flood waters kept postal carriers from their appointed rounds and also kept the Delta staff at home.

The Delta staff wasn't snug and warm and dry in every case though. Two members of the staff were inundated by high waters with water reaching into their homes to a depth of a foot or better.

One member, Gary Stone, was still on duty with the National Guard on Wednesday morning. Our fire-eater, Chuck Atkins, was still somewhat bleary-eyed Wednesday morning when he reported for work due to the fact that he had had very little sleep during the two-day emergency. Dana Deane made it by boat and set type all day. Only one employee made it Tuesday to the Central National Bank and that was Calvin Shreve, who rowed to get to work.

Mrs. John Thomas, of College Avenue, worked alone at the Kanawha Cash Market all day Tuesday since other employees were unable to get to work. Needless to say, bread and milk were long gone although one bread truck did arrive at 10 a.m. with a fresh supply.

Ken Thornhill, of Hillbillie Market in Deanville, sold out of almost everything in the store Tuesday and worked at full-speed with a minimal staff. Betty and Sam Feola were still marooned in their home Wednesday morning at the corner of Florida and Madison streets. Thanks to members of the Theta Chi fraternity their furniture was saved as the boys worked through-out the night moving everything to the second floor.

College boys also saved the possessions of Dick and Sylvia Summerfield on Meade street. All furniture was placed high and dry and, without heat, the Summerfields moved in with the William Ours for a couple nights.

Howard Hiner Collection

Many college married couples lost everything in apartments and trailers along Lumber street. One couple, the Jim Dawsons (he sells advertising for the Pharos newspaper) lost all of their wedding gifts.

Although hundreds were evacuated by the fire department, one local resident, Mrs. Ruth Whiffen, found a very wet and very lost Chihuahua on Locust street Monday night and took her in for shelter. Even the rats were seen swimming by the hundreds for their lives on Tuesday. Cattle was seen on the Hall road standing neck deep in flood waters.

To get an idea of the height of the waters Tuesday, Mrs. Hester Hodges says she has lived in her home for 40 years at the corner of South Kanawha and Madison streets and never had water in her home. Tuesday, her wall-to-wall carpeting was covered. The flood waters at one point reached the front of Central Methodist church on South Florida street.

Dr. and Mrs. W.C. Carper are wintering in Florida. Gilbert Baxa, of South Florida street, who is doing some painting before the Carper's return, entered their home Monday night and saved much of their furniture and most of their collection of treasures from the Far East. Only the valuable Oriental rugs were under water and a Clarksburg firm was picking those up Wednesday for cleaning and repair.

Mayor and Mrs. Hinkle at one time were feeding and bedding 30 people in their home on Lightburn street while groceries floated in their store at the intersection of Sedgwick and East Main Street.

The city recorder, Mrs. Elizabeth Poundstone, got her four children out of her home Monday evening and left herself at 9 p.m. but the water raised to only a few inches inside. The foundation is gone from beneath the house.

Vic Newman of American Furniture Company stated that they suffered minor damage to furnishings at the store on South Florida street but at least $50,000 in stock is lost at their warehouse near the Nazarene church on the Clarksburg road. Charlie Green at City Lumber, Inc. made a conservative estimate of $30,000 loss to shop and building on North Locust street.

Picture-taking was the order of the day on Tuesday, too. According to George Carothers, Manager of Krogers, he sold 403 rolls of film to those customers who could reach his store.

Telephonitis

March 23, 1967

The telephone is a marvelous instrument. I can't begin to visualize life without this means of communication. Fact of the matter I wouldn't be sitting in a newspaper office writing this column if it weren't for this fantastic invention.

But daily I'm beginning to doubt the wisdom of the instrument. In fact, I'm beginning to scheme and speculate as to what life at home would be without the telephone. It certainly might be peaceful of evenings. I have a teenage daughter who has a very bad case of telephonitis. This disease has also been transmitted to her teenage friends.

Unless you've reared a teenage daughter with telephonitis you have no idea how serious the complications can be. Some nights the situation becomes more than critical.

It has reached the stage that family and friends find it much less complicated to call personally at the front door than to use the marvelous telephone. The disease has reached the stage whereby I'm using a timer, set at five minutes, for all incoming calls. The disease has reached the stage where my ulcers are acting up, my nerves are frayed, my blood pressure is at an all time high and lung power increasing, all because of those incoming calls at ten-minute intervals.

The telephone company has made great strides throughout the years and without its research and science, man could not reach space. Space is where I'm sending Ann unless the company comes up with a solution, and, I don't mean her own phone and number. I mean a little gadget that automatically winks or blinks, or dings or dongs, or signals in some fashion whether the incoming call is for anyone in the household or just for the teenage daughter.

With such an electronic code, I could then ignore the ring if Ann is out for the evening. Otherwise, I would not budge from the comfortable sofa, run downstairs or run upstairs, or leave my warm bathtub, or my bed, dash in from the front porch or the flower garden.

Please, Mr. C&P, ban the teenage calls or invent an invention just for parents. Otherwise, we'll never survive the complications of this serious disease of the telephonitis. We're now at the critical stage!

The Jackson Cemetery

March 30, 1967

Someone told me one time that because we are a young country, we care little about the old or historic. I believe it. This was brought to mind Sunday as I read an article in the Clarksburg daily newspaper telling of the citizens fight to save the historical Jackson cemetery, which lies near the Holy Trinity Catholic church on Philippi Pike and is bordered on the rear by Route 50 East. It seems the Jackson cemetery has survived the vicissitudes of 160 years but Burl Sawyers, SRC commissioner, has notified the public that the proposed Clarksburg connection with the interchange of I-79 and Route 50 will destroy the cemetery.

Surely public opinion will save this cemetery.

The stones in the cemetery tell the history of the crossroads of Northwestern Virginia from 1807 until two decades after the Civil War, which brought into existence the State of West Virginia. Here lie buried four generations of the pioneer Jackson family, among them Jonathan, father of Stonewall Jackson, and Elizabeth, sister of Stonewall. Elizabeth Cummins Jackson, who came over the mountains in 1758 with her husband and on to Buckhannon in 1768 to settle this town is also buried in the Jackson cemetery. She died in 1828 in Clarksburg at the age of 105. According to Mrs. Bond (Dorothy) Davis, of Salem, the first burial on the plot of ground occurred in 1807, the year that Mary Coles Payne, mother of Dolly Madison, died while visiting her daughter, Mary, whose hand John G. Jackson had won when he was a Congressman. John Jackson and Mary Payne were married in the first wedding held in the White House, an event staged by Dolly Madison when she was the official hostess for President Thomas Jefferson.

Newspapers of the day described the wedding as a "nine-day wonder."

It is ironic that federal funds for an Appalachian Center, recently established to awaken an interest in the culture of the mountain area, will finance the dissemination of information on historic sites to be visited by tourists and historians. The left hand seemingly does not know what the right hand is doing. If the proposed I-79 route destroys the historic Jackson cemetery there will be little use for federal funds to preserve the old. The historical sites will have all been wiped out before the federal bureau can get into operation!

High School Guidance Counselors

April 13, 1967

This is the time of year when all high school seniors are getting just a wee bit jittery about college entrance, test results, money, and all the various and sundry details that go along with college life requirements.

It is also the time when a student and his parents alike should do some soul-searching as to whether college is more of a status-symbol than a necessity.

If a student has not demonstrated that he can do above average work in high school, then over-zealous parents should beware!

No one person is better qualified to judge than the high school guidance counselor. In Buckhannon's case this is Mrs. Marguerite Keller whose work cannot be endorsed strongly enough as far as I am personally concerned.

Her joy in a student's attainment of a coveted scholarship more than matches that of the student. Counseling on the importance of planning for a career and the further education necessary to qualify for it is the most solemn business of Mrs. Keller.

Yet, she will be the first to advise against college for those whom she knows will not succeed. It is a great temptation for students and parents alike when tax-supported colleges will admit any high school graduate with almost no restrictions.

On the other hand, she must be concerned about the trend among teenagers in the 18-19 year-old group towards the pursuit of fulltime jobs. In many cases the lure of easy money diverts many college-qualified students from seeing the need for further education. At 18 and 19, without serious obligations, they might think that they can well afford to take such a job, but what will happen to them 10 years from now, when their need for more money is hindered by their inability to earn it?

All of this points more and more to the brand-new idea of the Tri-County Vocational-Technical Training Center due for completion here by January 1, 1968. It should solve part of the problem….furthering of education and reassurance for those non-college students.

Loud Music

April 20, 1967

I've been exposed somewhat to modern music and the dances that go with it. It's logical since I'm the mother of three teenagers. But, I had never chaperoned a teen-age dance until recently.

I'll not do it again! I'm thoroughly convinced that all teenagers will be stone deaf by the time they are 30. If other parents wish to take the physical risk, that is their business. But I value my hearing and the well-being of my nervous system far and above any responsibility I may feel in chaperoning.

I'm convinced that our young servicemen can withstand the rigors of battle and the "brainwashing" simply because they have been trained on the hometown dance floors.

The orchestra only has one volume....LOUD! One parent suggested that the young were getting rid of their sex impulses. Frankly, the gyrations reminded me of tribal fertility rites.

One psychiatrist has said that modern music reminds him of a cross between an automobile accident and a war dance. I must admit, occasionally there is a slight foot-tapping on my part, no melody, just a beat.

Dr. Edward M. Levine, of the Illinois Institute of Technology, has his mind thoroughly made up on the subject. People who do the twist, the frug, the watusi and the jerk aren't really dancing, he says, they're looking for themselves. He brands their gyrations as symptomatic of a "....lack of identity which is .... A pathological condition."

Now weird dance fads are one thing, but allowing an entire generation or two to get themselves pathologically lost at it is something else altogether.

Maybe we oldsters should set up a therapy program for these kids before it's too late - say some instruction in the big apple, the bunny hop and the jitterbug?

Traffic Problems

May 4, 1967

Yes, Buckhannon has a traffic problem. The residents say so, the merchants say so, visitors to town say so. Local drivers find frayed nerves and nasty words don't alleviate the problem. The municipal city parking lot on Kanawha street will help. But, it won't help the constant traffic flow up and down Kanawha, Florida, Main and Spring streets.

City officials know there is a traffic problem, I know there is a traffic problem, you know there is a traffic problem. The problem won't ever be eliminated, it can only be eased.

A local citizen took the trouble Friday morning to pick me up at the office and drive me to Spring street traveling toward Madison. A natural lane exists through an alley between the old Bastable home (once a post-Civil War showplace) which now serves as a warehouse, and Koon's Welding shop. The extension of Spring street would bring the motorist onto Lincoln at the intersection of Smithfield and Lincoln streets. It is a natural lane for traffic which would ease the traffic flow on Kanawha and Florida streets.

It means perhaps the removal of two trees and not more than three feet of property, I'm told. The slight bend at the end of Smithfield street would serve to avoid any collisions since Lincoln is now a one-way street. Traffic could be closed to trucks and trailers eliminating much noise to residents. The suggestion isn't new, it won't be acceptable to many but it is a means to ease part of the traffic jam. We do have a problem. The Jaycees recent traffic survey shows it and as far back as 1964 the comprehensive plan as presented by Michael Baker, Jr. Inc., consulting engineers and planners, pointed out the seriousness of the situation.

In fact the plan states "traffic flow volumes are a rather serious problem throughout the city. Factors contributing to this problem include channelization traffic light synchronization and on-street parking facilities and location of regional highways within the retail trade center. Central Business District traffic circulation is considered difficult because of the high frequency of use of the alleys within the street system and absence of a sound traffic circulation pattern including one-way system."

This is food for thought!

City Police

May 11, 1967

There's no denying that Buckhannon has shown exceptional progress in the past few years with paved streets and alleys, new water, waste and sanitation facilities, new city building, perseverance in the flood control project, aid in acquisition of new industry, and cooperation with roads, school and civic endeavors.

A progressive city police department goes along with a progressive city. So it is that the local civil service commission is looking for respectable applications for two vacancies on the police force.

Not so many years ago in Buckhannon, a policeman's job meant a seven day week, 12 hours a day, one day off a month and a low, low salary.

'Tain't so this day and age. A policeman's job today is respectable. You won't get rich but who does in this era of high prices and high taxes. Today's policeman works a 40-hour week with a starting salary of $325 per month and paid vacations. There is a clothing allowance. Additionally, the job now comes under Civil Service rules which means unless one flaunts the regulations one has a job for life.

So, let's not strap a gun on just anybody! How about some respectable applications from respectable fellows for respectable city employment.

That Darn Dog!

May 18, 1967

Darn ungrateful dog! I've fed her, paid her taxes every year, and bought dog food that was nearly as expensive as what we eat, kept count of the rabies shots and had her wormed. She's been bathed and brushed and had every consideration from the family.

Then in her old age (she's almost eight years) she decided that she wanted a final fling. First hint was when she started chasing around with every Tom, Dick and Harry who came to the neighborhood. As happens when one becomes promiscuous, she suddenly found herself in a family way.

I accepted the fact – didn't drive her away from my door. Even felt a little sorry for the animal and fixed up a nice box with clean spread and blanket so the maternity ward would be comfortable.

Then one evening she suddenly disappeared and was gone for 12 hours. She returned home happy, starved and thirsty. She was fed and watered and suddenly again disappeared.

Upon investigation we found she had constructed her own maternity ward under the neighbor's garage floor. She has puppies but she won't let us see them…we don't know how large a litter, we don't even know what species, we don't even know the color.

Darn ungrateful dog! I suppose she'll come whining to my door some night when she's tired of the night feedings. Anyone want a puppy? Please?

(Postscript: The rains drove mama and four pups home to dry ground. And the pups are promised to good homes. Hurrah!)

Great Society Goofs

June 15, 1967

Some great society goofs have just been uncovered! The magazine, Nation's Business, in its May 1967 issue tells a tale of how the nonplanners in the Great Society go about being nice to just about everybody. The story involves an attempt by the Bureau of Indian Affairs to bring the people of the Quinault tribe into the 20th century.

The Quinaults live in the lush Olympic peninsula area of the State of Washington. They make their living by fishing.

According to the magazine account, the Bureau decided to spend $200,000 to build 20 houses for 20 families. The houses would, the bureau felt sure, be the pride of the neighborhood and the envy of all.

So they set about it last fall. And by February the first of the houses were complete. They were designed for gracious living, the magazine account said. They were completely electrified, electric baseboard heating, electric water heating, electric ranges, electric refrigerators, electric washers, electric driers. The houses were indeed beautiful.

So in February, the first seven families moved in. They found one slight flaw. And by now, you've guessed it.

NO ELECTRICITY!

It seems the nearest electric power line was 15 miles away – and nobody had bothered to plan ahead far enough in advance to bring power to the tiny Indian community.

And the Republicans will love this! It seems that the Office of Economic Opportunity has come up with a scheme so irrational and irresponsible that it does disservice even to OEO.

The program covers production and marketing of the celebrated silver and turquoise jewelry made by the Zuni Indians of the Southwest. The production end calls for, of all things, teaching the Zunis how to make Indian jewelry, a skilled craft they have excelled in for centuries. With further audacity, the OEO is arranging for the traditionally hand-crafted jewelry to be machine made. The OEO is setting up a cooperative which it says will market

$150,000 worth of the "genuine" machine-made handcrafted jewelry. However, private stores are already buying more than $2 million of the original article now. The OEO has let a grant of $208,741 to "improve" the jewelry business for the Zunis.

The magazine went on to outline a few other goofs by the Great Society's octopus-like many arms. Examples:

* Luxury lodges in Oklahoma, financed by ARA, in the red $600,000. Cost $10 million.

* $3.5 million to build housing for Rio de Janeiro's slum dwellers. Nobody wants the houses because they're built too deep in the boondocks.

* WAVE barracks built in Maryland to house WAVES who'd already been transferred to Florida. Cost: $1.5 million.

* Locomotives built for Thailand; wrong gauge couldn't run on Thai railroad tracks. Cost: $1 million.

And so it goes with the Great Society.

One Sewing Machine For Sale

June 29, 1967

Try as they might, all newspapers contain typographical errors. This paper is not unique to the industry; we have them, too. But I don't think the Delta has ever had one as complicated as the following.

A fellow with a sewing machine to sell walked into a certain newspaper office to place a classified advertisement. The ad came out the next day as follows:

MONDAY: For sale: R.D. Smith has one sewing machine for sale Phone 958. Call after 7 p.m. and ask for Mrs. Kelly who lives with him cheap.

TUESDAY: We regret having erred in R.D. Smith's ad yesterday. It should have read: For Sale: R.D. Smith has one sewing machine for sale, cheap. Phone 958 and ask for Mrs. Kelly who lives with him after 7 p.m.

WEDNESDAY: R.D. Smith has informed us that he has received several annoying telephone calls because of the error we made in his classified ad yesterday. His ad stands corrected: R.D. Smith has one sewing machine for sale. Cheap. Phone 958 after 7p.m. and ask for Mrs. Kelly who loves with him.

THURSDAY: Notice: I, R.D. Smith, have no sewing machine for sale. I smashed it. Don't call 958, the phone has been taken out. I have not been carrying on with Mrs. Kelly. Until yesterday she was my housekeeper.

Please Buy My Book #2

July 13, 1967

If my step seems a little lighter, my smile a little brighter, and my disposition a mile more pleasant, it's all because I had a dream once upon a time and that dream has come true.

In case you didn't know, and I don't see how you could help but know, I have a real book printed. A beautiful book with my name in gold, very formal, very business-like, even to the copyright and all that stuff.

I can't stand on the street corners and shout "Book for sale." But, it is for sale. It's a true story and as authentic as stories can be after 100 years. "Upshur Brothers of the Blue and Gray" has meant five years of research on my part.

Sometime or other all the stories were put down on paper in some form, whether in letters or diaries or privately-printed booklets. It just took me a long, long time to read all the material about Upshur county's role in the Civil War.

And believe me, Upshur county men and women played a big role in that tragic era of American life. Buckhannon was occupied no less than 12 times by armies of the North and South. Hundreds of lives were lost because Upshur county men believed in the right to fight for whatever honor credited the blue or the gray.

The work was so much easier because historians before me had done much work and there were others here who were interested in Civil War history and lent their talents.

Not enough praise can be given to Mrs. Beatrice Arnold Giffin, grand-niece of "Stonewall" Jackson, who now lives in Topeka, Kansas. During the days of the depression, she was hired by the WPA to bring up-to-date historical material concerning Upshur county. She did a remarkable job and researchers will thank her forever for the thorough research she completed during those months. She and her sister, Miss Grace Arnold, were most cooperative.

A remarkable young man, French Morgan, who is 84 years old, and one of my favorite persons, had done considerable research on the Civil War period of history. I am indebted to him for the many hours spent on my behalf.

Talented Robert G. Smith, Jr., of French Creek, along with the late Ruhl Colerider, researched the maps of French Creek and Rock Cave as they were 100 years ago. Bob is also responsible for the book's dust cover. I thank him.

So many people helped with the loan of letters and diaries. I'm pleased that there are those who care about this country's heritage.

Now Ken McClain, of Parsons, and I will be more than pleased if the book sells. Just give me a buzz…the book is available at the Delta.

Welfare & The Pill #3

July 20, 1967

I've been plugging away at this column now for over eight years and sometimes I was serious, sometimes sarcastic, sometimes funny, sometimes right and lots of times very, very wrong about issues and problems.

Too, I've often wondered whether anyone read this weekly "drag" and whether "sounding off" on issues and problems did one darn bit of good.

This week though I was notified of a new ruling by the Department of Welfare which made me think "Gee, maybe my sounding off did help."

Remember a few years ago I suggested that perhaps this country needed some sort of a domestic corps…well, along came VISTA. Then one time I mentioned the lack of juvenile facilities at the local jail….along came a juvenile room.

O, boy, do I remember when I came out with the bold suggestion that perhaps birth control pills could be dispensed along with the surplus commodities issued to welfare clients!!

Thanks to a tip from one of the local physicians this week, I've been informed that as of July 1 the Department of Welfare is paying for family planning drugs.

It's nothing as drastic as dispensing pills with surplus commodities…that program no longer exists. It's the stamp plan now. But, the program is much more effective.

Hereafter those mothers who are not physically and mentally capable of continued child-bearing, those mothers who need no other mouths to feed at home can now obtain free of charge oral contraceptives, contraceptive creams and jellies or the diaphragms and inserters.

Maybe this state can now fight poverty at the level where it should have been fought three generations ago.

WBUC Radio

August 10, 1967

Received an interesting communiqué this week from Dale Brooks at Radio Station WVRC in Spencer. His story is about as big a set of coincidences as one is likely to find at one place of business.

There seems to be some sort of cycle of radio personnel which involves Spencer, Buckhannon and Keyser.

Brooks, co-owner and manager of the Spencer station, is originally from Buckhannon. He first worked at Keyser, then went to Buckhannon and from here to Spencer.

Joe Barker, also a stockholder in WVRC, worked with Brooks at Keyser, later joined him in Buckhannon, and then again as part owner of the Spencer station.

Dale Darnall started with WBUC in Buckhannon, later worked at WKLP in Keyser and is now afternoon man at the Spencer station. Still another man has followed the cycle...Dave Harper, who worked at WBUC in Buckhannon, and at WKLP in Keyser, is now a member of the WVRC staff in Spencer. Another familiar voice on WVRC is Paul Ellison, heard frequently on commercials and station breaks, news openings and promotions, is now at WBUC in Buckhannon, and worked with Brooks and Barker at the Keyser station.

A sixth man in the radio organization started at Buckhannon, moved to WKLP in Keyser, back to Buckhannon, is frequently heard on WVRC on commercials and his name is seen daily on Main street in Spencer...Phil D. Phillips. However, it is not the Phil Phillips who owns the store, although the names are identical. It is noteworthy that the local Phil Phillips has a grandson, Scotty, who also worked at the Spencer station and is now a director of a TV station in Huntington.

There's one thing for sure, if Buckhannon's Phil D. Phillips should move to the Spencer operation, there's a Spencer store that will get a lot of free advertising by virtue of the identical names. And, the way the cycle has been running so far, it just could happen!

World Evolution

August 24, 1967

I don't think of myself as a "cockeyed optimist" but maybe I am. Or, maybe I'm too blind and unaware of the world situation to be afraid. But somehow I can't go along with a statement made to me last week by a devoted churchman, a man in his late fifties, who explained that he was glad that his life was almost over.

There were so many changes and evolutions going on in the church and the schools and the world that he pitied his children and grandchildren who had to live in such a mess.

I was so surprised at the statement that I had no reply. As I walked back to the office I kept thinking "o, ye of little faith." Hasn't every generation predicted disaster. Wasn't the American Revolution a disaster? The Industrial Revolution? The Civil War? The Depression Years of the 30's?

Senator Byrd said this week that the American Republic is on the decline. Perhaps so.

But, all the cry babies in this world won't make me think otherwise….this nation and this world has a tremendous future. Maybe we won't have a government as we know it today. There may be even a United States of Europe, a United States of Africa and a United States of Asia, even a United World.

We have the promise of so many technological and medical advances. The challenge and protectorate of space. The strengthening of education, slum eradication, the cosmopolitan aura.

I shan't live to see it but I wish I could!

Off The Paper Spike

September 21, 1967

Cleaned off the paper spike this week and here goes with a miscellany of odds and ends gathered from here and there. We've had relatively cool, rainy weather but one Charlestonian was quoted recently as saying he remembers a summer so dry that "the Baptists were sprinkling, the Methodists were using a damp cloth, the Episcopalians just dusted 'em off and the Presbyterians were taking 'em dirt and all."

A small-town editor I once knew repeated so often to his eager but inexperienced news reporter, "Always remember that names make news", that finally the cub reporter on his next assignment came up with "Fire last night destroyed Farmer Alvin Albright's barn, claiming the lives of three cows named Bossy, Bessy, and Gertrude."

Someone telephoned me this little item the other day. It seems a Washington, D.C. couple recently had a letter from their son, a helicopter pilot in Vietnam. The first part described a pre-dawn Viet Cong mortar attack during which he took his plane up without a crew and for half an hour made single-handed rocket and machine-gun attacks on enemy positions. The last part of the letter asked his father to send a signed statement that he will need on a forthcoming leave in Hawaii. He wants to get a driver's license there but he's too young to get one without his parent's permission.

A California woman recently placed this ad in the weekly newspaper: "Wanted – Handyman to repair six leaky faucets, jammed window, knobless door, immovable closet door, water closet, unhinged yard gates, remove large tree limb broken in 1965 windstorm, repair three water hydrants without handles, etc. for bereft Golf Widow."

She added her name but gave her husband Gene's business phone number. The day the ad appeared his phone rang out of control as friends and customers, knowing his addiction to golf, applied for the job. So far, the wife has had her knobless door repaired.

Which reminds me…have you received one of those chain letters known as "From the Land of Paradise?" It reads: "Dear Friend, This chain letter started with the hope of bringing relief and happiness to all tired husbands. Unlike most chain letters, this does not cost money. Simply send a copy of this letter to one of your 'married friends' who is equally tired. Then bundle up your wife and send her to the man at the top of the list and add your name to the bottom of the list.

"When your name comes to the top of the list you will receive 16,487 women and some of them will be 'dandies.' Have faith in this letter. One man broke the chain and got his old lady back."

Pumpkintown, WV

October 12, 1967

I couldn't resist the temptation to pick up a front page news story from the Belington News this week, especially since it concerned the proposed Tri-County Airport, a project near and dear to the heart of many.

Entitled "Pumpkintown: Harley Halloween Heaven", the author of the feature had tongue in cheek while waxing the following words of wisdom. "Chances are Charlie Brown never heard of Pumpkintown, West Virginia. For if he had he would probably quit his backyard Halloween vigil and venture here in quest of the Great Pumpkin.

"Founded by Irish settlers years ago, Pumpkintown, or punkintown, as the natives say, lies on US 33 between Harding and Ellamore.

"In the 1880's, a feud broke out between two farmers over local pumpkin rights. One of the farmers planted some pumpkins and the vines climbed the fence. Rights to the fruit were hotly disputed and the case ended in the court of a Justice of the Peace. Residents have long since forgotten the winner, but the controversy was important enough to earn the name for the town.

"Even in the boom days Punkintown's population rarely exceeded it's present figure of 41. Eight houses stand in this historic hamlet, but the Midway Diner, owned by Mrs. William Patrice, gets most of the attention these days. The Midway caters mostly to travelers and specializes in groceries, food, and gasoline.

"Mailing Halloween cards could be great sport, but unfortunately Pumpkintown has no post office. However, there may be life in this Randolph County yet. For Pumpkintown Hill, elevation 2,450, has been proposed as the site of a Tri-County Airport, serving Randolph, Upshur and Barbour counties.

"So Charlie Brown in search of the Great Pumpkin may yet wing his way to West Virginia. "All aboard please for Portland, Pittsburgh, and Pumpkintown.'"

Miss Whirley

October 19, 1967

A certain retired professional man of this town, who enjoys calling me "Miss Whirley," said last week he admired my philosophy. With my usual "smart-aleck" attitude, I retorted "Philosophy doesn't pay the rent."

It took a full five-minute lecture to inform me that money isn't everything. (That's an easy attitude for those with money.) Granted money isn't everything. I'd rate good health above all else.

As I walked back to the office I studied about "my philosophy." I still don't know what it is. Just like my housework, my philosophy is erratic.

I guess it can all be summed up in the fact that writing for a newspaper has its ups and downs, (mostly downs), and we of this crazy trade keep smiling and keep writing.

And, we keep writing because of wonderful letters like the following I received from a little second grade girl, printed here verbatim:

Dear Mrs. Hornbeck,

Thank you for putting the big picture in the paper. It was very nice? I am glad you wrote it. It had a very good story about me? Love, Tappan."

I love you too, Tappan!

The Bowl Games

November 30, 1967

Each year around this time, specifically at Thanksgiving, I take a day of my vacation time and spend a long four day weekend at home. I have two reasons for saving a day of vacation for this long weekend. First, I feel I need a rest before plunging into a busy month of extra work at my newspaper office, the gift buying, the gift wrapping, the candy making, and in general, the extra holiday festivities.

Secondly, and perhaps the principal reason for my long Thanksgiving weekend of rest, is to get conditioned for the New Year's Day of football.

The way I figure it, three games on Thanksgiving Day, two on Saturday and four this past Sunday should have my eyes well-primed for The Big Day. Especially, since there will be four full weekends of professional, college and bowl games before The Big Day.

Now it isn't only important that one has his eyes accustomed to the focus of TV, but one's posture as well. After all, if one spends as long as eight hours on the couch watching TV, serious complications of the spine could develop. Not to mention muscle spasms, leg cramps, twisted neck and paralyzed arms. I've found if your favorite team isn't doing well or the game is dull, all one must do is roll over and turn one's back to the TV. Then the biggest play of the game develops. Now you won't miss a thing, because of instant replay. Don't above all pretend to sleep, because that's when the phone will ring. There's always one idiot who doesn't watch football!! Depending on your addiction to Bowl Games, it is up to you if you wish to "farm out" your cat or dog for The Big Day. This eliminates rising from the couch to allow the dog and/or cat in or out the door.

Also, there is another rule. Unless one has an ample supply of snacks, drinks and sandwiches prepared in advance, you and your family could suffer from malnutrition.

Another important point one must practice within these next four weekends is one's timing during commercial breaks. Practice, practice, practice this timing!!! Otherwise, you'll lose out even on the instant replay if you're delayed in the kitchen or the bathroom longer than the commercial – all because you didn't practice your timing. Good luck!

Statue of L.B.J.

December 14, 1967

Gary Olson writes a column for the Wesleyan College "Pharos" newspaper which on more than one occasion has caused a few laughs in The Delta office.

Since many of the Delta readers are not familiar with the "Pharos" or have no opportunity to obtain a copy, I must steal a section of Mr. Olson's spritely column for the enjoyment of all Republican readers.

It seems that the following letter is being distributed in political circles:

Dear Sir:

We have the distinguished honor of being members of the committee to raise 50 million dollars to be used for the placing of a statue of Lyndon Baines Johnson in the Hall of Fame, Washington, D.C.

This committee was in quite a quandary about selecting the proper location for the statue. It was thought not wise to place it beside that of George Washington, who never told a lie, nor beside that of Franklin D. Roosevelt, who never told the truth, since Lyndon Baines Johnson could never tell the difference. After careful consideration, we think it should be placed beside the statue of Christopher Columbus, the greatest new dealer of them all, in that he started, not knowing where he was going, and arriving, did not know where he was, and in returning did not know where he had been, and did it all on borrowed money.

Five thousand years ago, Moses said to the children of Israel, "pick up your shovels, mount your asses and camels, and I will lead you to the Promised Land." Nearly five thousand years later, Roosevelt said "Lay down your shovels, sit on your asses and light up a Camel, this is the Promised Land." Now Johnson is stealing your shovels, kicking your asses, raising the price of Camels, and taking over the Promised Land.

If you are one of those citizens who has any money left after taxes, we will expect a GENEROUS CONTRIBUTION FROM YOU for this worthwhile project.

Income Tax Laws

January 18, 1968

It's time to be thinking about those income tax forms. Which brings to mind that even after 30 years, death or taxes haven't changed for back in 1931 the Chicago Evening American printed a letter which is as true today as it was then.

The letter is from an Oklahoman to his banker, and should make you feel better about your own tax troubles.

"It is impossible for me to make a further payment on my note. My present financial condition is due to the effects of federal laws, state laws, county laws, corporation laws, bylaws, mothers-in-law, and outlaws that have been foisted upon an unsuspecting public. I have been held down, held up, walked on, sat on, flattened, squeezed until I do not know where I am, what I am and why I am.

"Those laws compel me to pay a merchant's tax, capital stock tax, income tax, real estate tax, property tax, auto tax, gas tax, water tax, cigar tax, street tax, school tax, syntax, and carpet tax.

"The government has so governed my business that I do not know who owns it. I am suspected, expected, disrespected, examined, re-examined, until all I know is that I'm supplicated for money for every known need, desire or hope of the human race, and because I refuse to fall and go out and beg, borrow or steal money to give away I am cussed, discussed, boycotted, talked to, talked about, lied to, lied about, held up, held down and robbed until I am nearly ruined, so that the only reason I am clinging to life is to see what the h… is coming next.

West Virginia Ranks Low

January 25, 1968

A newspaper office is forever getting literature and brochures from every Tom, Dick and Harry in the continental United States, most of which ends up in File 13, the waste basket.

But, a post card size communication arrived last week that opened my eyes. I think the message is important enough to pass on to the readers.

No one denies the importance of an adequate welfare program and good roads. This state ranks 10th in welfare based on local expenditures per capita, and ranks 20th in roads.

But, take a look at West Virginia's educational level. We rank 44th among the 50 states, down in the cellar along with the "poor south" Arkansas, Mississippi, North Carolina, Louisiana, Tennessee, Kentucky and South Carolina.

Is there a relation between low expenditure for public schools and educational level? Also between educational level and welfare expenditure? Just thought I'd ask!

Mental Health Clinic - #2

February 1, 1968

Ten to 15 cases are handled monthly in the local Upshur-Buckhannon Mental Health office, a model comprehensive mental health program operating out of the Appalachian Mental Health Center in Elkins.

Approximately 40 Upshur county residents are patients in the Weston State hospital. Over 130 cases of local residents were handled this past year in addition to those already hospitalized.

This new concept in mental health treatment is unique in West Virginia and Upshur county's role is considered a model program among the 10 counties now participating.

Staffed locally by a receptionist and Andrew Hinkle, the clinic operates each Thursday from 9 to noon and 1 to 5p.m. with Dr. Nina Levin, psychiatrist in attendance. The staff can be reached by phone any day at 472-2022 and contrary to some reports, one does not need a referral from a local physician or minister.

Also assisting locally are two VISTA workers, Diana Simmons, from California, and Nancy Belohlazek, of Wisconsin. The late H.H. Thompson had served since the program's inception on the board of directors for the Appalachian Mental Health Center.

The mental health center is the first of its kind in West Virginia. It offers these services:

1. Short-term intensive care in local general hospitals for patients requiring 24-hour care.

2. Outpatient services, either in the Elkins center or in outlying counties, consisting of diagnosis and therapy.

3. Day care for patients who do not need full hospitalization.

4. 24-Hour emergency service.

5. Consultation and mental health education through schools and other community agencies.

The center has a psychiatric team which brings psychiatric services to communities within a 50-mile radius of Elkins. The team travels daily by car. Upshur county is also unique in that it is the only one of the 10 counties, besides Randolph, which provides psychiatric service with the attendance here of Dr. Levin.

The mental health program covers Randolph, Barbour, Mineral, Hardy, Grant, Pendleton, Tucker, Upshur, Webster and Pocahontas. Director of the center is Dr. Juan Jusior, a psychiatrist, who came to the post from Eastern Shore State hospital in Maryland.

The traveling psychiatric team is headed by Dr. Levin and Dr. Dionisio Britton, both psychiatrists. The team psychologist is Gene Furbee. The center has a regular fulltime staff of 20 persons and the assistance of 10 Vista workers.

A major aim of the center is to prevent mental illness and keep patients out of the hospital. West Virginia spends at least $6 million a year to care for excess loads of hospital patients. About 1,400 of a total of 5,000 could continue as contributing members of their family and community if local treatment were available.

The Elkins center offers such treatment with the aim of keeping patients in their community and the government should find ways of giving more assistance to communities in long-term financing for comprehensive mental health programs. Upshur county now budgets almost $5,000 yearly for the operation of the mental health center. This is money which formerly went to the state to be used here and there and anywhere in the mental health program.

The Appalachian Mental Health Center is a giant step in the right direction for treatment of disturbed persons.

Moonshining

February 8, 1968

On several occasions, readers will remember I've jokingly written about the amount of brochures, releases, etc. received in this office which end up in the "file13", better known as a wastepaper basket.

But, once in a while something pops up on my desk which is enlightening, at least to me, and maybe to the readers.

The gem this week is a new bit of notoriety for the state of West Virginia. Yes, we have another claim to fame. We are one of the "moonshine states" in a black belt where the bulk of illegal liquor is produced in "them thar hills." We can claim status and symbol along with Alabama, Arkansas, Florida, Georgia, Kentucky, Mississippi, North Carolina, Oklahoma, South Carolina, Tennessee and Virginia.

The moonshiner, like the proverbial "bad penny" is still with us. But times have changed. We no longer have the old stereotyped moonshiner – barefoot, awkward and amusing. He went out with the buggy whip. Today many "fast buck" operators run incredible big business type structures which are fully organized systems of production, modern in every respect except for purity.

Unable to compete with the mob-type efficiency, many small operators are joining up with organized crime cartels.

Since experienced enforcement officers are wise to the old standard tricks, the "moonshiner" employs ingenious ways to hide his "white lightening." Here are a few that have been uncovered by officials during recent raids: fireplace chimneys, box springs of beds and mattresses, milk bottles painted white, secret compartments in ceilings, TV and stereo sets, gravel floor of garage, compartment in top of a doghouse, manholes in streets, concrete blocks with false centers and even toilet tanks!

One vice squad officer in Ohio said, "There's such a mass movement of Tennessee, Kentucky and West Virginia cars to and from Ohio that we couldn't possibly keep up with the liquor traffic.

They come into town with a trunkful of the stuff, park the car and leave it. The middle man unloads the car and the driver never comes near it. After some time passes, and he's sure everything has gone smoothly, he returns for the trip back south."

If you don't think there's money in moonshining, believe this! "White Lightening" flows into some cities at roughly 1,000 gallons a day. It is estimated that it costs about $1.50 a gallon to produce. The bootlegger pays about $5 a gallon and sells it for as much as $2 a pint – a $10 net profit on every gallon.

Moonshine is commonly sold in "nip joints" – any number of dingy flats, back rooms of stores and basements, dismal alley outlets and numerous other "blind-pig" places.

The going rate ranges from a few pennies up to 50c a shot. One place run by a woman sold six gallons a day, for which she paid $8 a gallon. She charged 50c a drink or $2.50 a pint, and averaged $120 daily. Gross annual profit was $43,000, tax free. Authorities said the woman also owned and rented several houses in the $10,000 range. This individual told raiding officers she gets arrested a few times a year, pays $50 for a $500 bond. $150 for a lawyer and usually is fined $100 to $300.

It was also brought out that the woman never filed tax returns of any kind. She expressed ignorance of such obligations, telling officers she thought all along that her fines were her "taxes".

Cheers!

Secretary's Prayer

02/15/1968

Recently published in the monthly newsletter from Corhart Refractories plant is this belated Valentine Day greeting to all bosses from all Girl Fridays.

A secretary's prayer… "Dear Lord, help me to satisfy my beloved, but slightly loony and unreasonable boss. Help me to have the memory of an elephant, and to be able to do six things at once, answer four phones, keep the boss from throwing lighted matches in his full trash basket, and take a letter that 'must go out' today and he'll forget to sign until tomorrow.

"Help me keep my patience when he has me search for a report in the files that he finds later in his desk. And Lord, permit me not to destroy records that he'll want three days later, even though he's ordered me to get rid of them.

"And, teach me how to say 'He's in an important conference' when he's watching a ball game on TV.

"And above all, dear Lord, when I finally retire, grant me enough strength left in my weary bones to give the big lug one big sock right in the kisser."

Teacher Pay

February 22, 1968

In light of the fact that we were appalled last week to discover that New York garbage collectors had won a pay increase to $7500 annually, it was interesting to read a recent statement from Phares E. Reeder, executive secretary for the West Virginia Education Association.

In case you care, average annual income for Upshur county school teachers is $5,440.

In Reeder's statement, he points out that during the recent 30-day session of the legislature the governor's call contained 52 items. The legislators took time to add numerous issues for consideration. The WVEA has gone on record saying "We cannot condone any legislature on such things as bingo, who should or should not pay into the "flower fund," Sunday horse racing, etc, above such educational needs as holding good teachers in West Virginia classrooms, providing ways for procuring funds for school buildings and modernizing the structural organization of the educational system. "Naturally, the small increase in pay for teachers and service personnel will help meet some of their bills, but this action is a far cry from closing that incredible gap in how West Virginia supports its teachers compared with that of the average state." (Incidentally, West Virginia ranks 44th among the 50 states.)

"We want the people of the state to know that for almost two years the WVEA has been working on an all-inclusive program of education which is being called "An Educational Design for '69." The basic parts of the program will be completed in time for candidates for Governor, Board of Public Works and the Legislature to evaluate and take a position.

We know that teachers and we believe that the general public will be most interested in learning whether those running for office will find realistic solutions to such basic problems as: antiquated and unsafe buildings, the lack of vocational and technical training, early childhood education, the high loss of experienced and beginning teachers.

"If West Virginia does not come through in 1969, this state could have uprisings in the educational ranks comparable to those of Florida and other states. Sanctions invoked in Jackson county serve as a good example."

Jim Knorr

February 29, 1968

In this day of strikes and threats of strike, few persons realize that there is one profession whereby many extra hours are devoted with no monetary benefits. In fact, the school teacher is more or less expected to devote outside hours in the interest and promotion of youth.

These extra hours are most often little noticed nor is the teacher involved given even a personal thank you from the public.

Last Saturday night was an exception. Patrons and friends of Buckhannon-Upshur demonstrated their support and thanks to Jim Knorr and a large cast of senior high school students with attendance at the musical production "Oklahoma."

Upshur county is fortunate to have a teacher such as Jim Knorr. The county is also fortunate that it has a student enrollment which expects and delights in such productions. Well over 800 persons attended Saturday night's performance, the fourth performance in three days.

It is most unusual to see such an audience at a high school event unless it involves sports. I have nothing against sports. In fact, I am one of football's most avid fans, but I've always felt that there was time and facilities for both.

Sports are great…but so are the arts. I think Upshur countians demonstrated Saturday night that they also feel there is room in our public school system for both. Support of the director and the cast was also demonstrated with the involvement of the Buckhannon Kiwanis Club, whose members gave time and talent in the sale of tickets, stage management, lighting effects, and general participation in the production.

Yes, indeed, we are fortunate in having Jim Knorr in our school system, and, indeed, we are fortunate that we have students and not "hippies."

Jim Knorr (L) and cast

Howard Hiner Collection

Jim in Vietnam

March 21, 1968

There's a young man today serving near Pleiku, South Vietnam, who this past fall left his classes at WVU, entered the Engineering Corps and in January was shipped to the Far East.

A close friend of my sons, he has been practically a member of the family since junior high days. A so-so student (who could do better) he never was in any trouble, played ball, dated, longed for a car of his own, liked people, took an interest in his surroundings, but never seriously considered the world problems or looked closely at a local election. Just a typical, All-American boy.

I'll call this boy Jim, a typical All-American name. He's been corresponding with the family since his arrival in Vietnam as a green, scared Armyman supposed to be surveying, but for the past six weeks under constant mortar and rocket shelling. His only complaint was the fact that his ditch wasn't wide enough or deep enough to hold his air mattress for a good night's sleep.

High in the Central Highlands, he talks more or less casually about the Viet Cong bodies lying outside the perimeter. In more or less the same tone he writes about intelligent Vietnamese children who hang around the base laundry, the unbelievable morale of his buddies, and the ample supply of good beer at the club and the one day of water skiing which was, almost like the days at Cheat Lake.

"Charlie" has only hit his company once since February 23rd, which was good news to me in his letter last week, although 19 guys in another company had been wounded.

What does a typical, All-American boy in Vietnam think about our involvement over there? Listen…

"I have some strong convictions about this war, maybe not fighting the communism but saving an individual person does give me some pride.

"I didn't even pay attention to this war until I got over here and now I know. Most people in the States only know what they pick up through the newspapers. Most of this is really twisted up bad.

"I read Time magazine today and was really disgusted. They said that we were set back by the Tet offensive…Ha…we accomplished more than we ever did. That 40,000 VC dead which Time claims was wrong (they claim one third that many) is a very moderate estimate. As a matter of fact, only the bodies of proven VC were counted here in the Highlands. The rest were called civilians. Proven VC means that he fired at you. If the VC wounded ratio is anywhere near American ratio's that means that another 50,000 were wounded. The VC have poor medical facilities and only one out of the five comes back to fight the war.

"Time magazine says that our program was set back and the people lost faith in us. Wrong again, The Vietnamese are proud of the way we licked Charlie and more joined the revolution that Charlie had started. Half of the ARVN's were on leave when the attack hit but they fought wherever they were. Their determination proves that they are good soldiers. My life depended on them for three weeks and they did the job."

Thanks, Jim. I wondered what we were doing over there!!

--

[Ed. Note, 2014]: Now it can be told…this young man was Jim Beer]

The Future Of Medicine

April 4, 1968

Last week, March 27th, was Doctor's Day. I mention it simply because 15 years from now you may not know your doctor.

It's true! In a recent medical journal it was revealed that office practice will soon be obsolete. Hospitals of less than 100 beds are going to have to close their doors because doctors aren't going to go to communities that are too small to support larger hospitals.

In the future there will be only hospitals of no fewer than 1,000 beds and preferably about 2,000. They'll need that many beds to support the specialists and expensive equipment that every hospital should have.For instance, Buckhannon is 62 miles from the WVU Medical Center. In ten minutes by helicopter, a patient can be loaded into the helicopter and in bed under intensive care by a specialist. Take the kid who gets a pain in his belly and they're wondering whether he's got appendicitis. Does he have to go all the way into Morgantown to find out he hasn't got it?Fifteen years from now your kid with the pain in the belly is going to be wheeled up in front of a television camera with a registered nurse who will push on the abdomen where the surgeon in Morgantown tells her to push on it. If the surgeon sees the kid wince on his television screen, he'll say, "Fine, bring him to Morgantown."

And what about the fellow who cuts his hand while working at the local machine shop and needs four or five stitches. Fifteen years from now that fellow with the cut finger will have a registered nurse dust on some glue, hold the edges together for a second, and it will stick better than stitches ever did.

You think it's improbable that patients will ever consent to transportation by helicopter to large hospitals under specialized care? Remember, we used to have a corner drugstore a block from our house and a corner grocery store that could meet 90 percent of our needs. There was an intimacy there; they were our grocer and our druggist.

Those stores have long gone out of business and out of style. Now we drive miles to the supermarket that meets 100 percent of our needs and we do it cheerfully. And, we don't know the manager from Adam.

What Subscribers Want To Read
May 16, 1968

If I couldn't steal a column now and then from someone older and wiser, this space would remain blank many, many weeks of the year. The temptation was too great again. I've stolen a Montana newspaper editor's column, written with tongue firmly placed in cheek.

He has composed a list of answers to a questionnaire on what a weekly newspaper subscriber would like to read. Here are the responses to what the average reader desires to see:

1. My name.
2. A front page article showing how crooked the city government is most of the time
3. My wife's name.
4. A feature article showing 25 ways on how to cheat on income tax forms.
5. My kids' names.
6. A local news item about the affair my neighbor is having.
7. A classified ad offering a new home for sale for $4,000.
8. More news about lawbreakers.
9. Less news about lawbreakers. I was picked up last night and I should not have to pay a fine.
10. An editorial condemning high school teachers for being too liberal with "F's.
11. A wedding picture of the groom instead of the bride when he is more handsome than she is pretty.
12. A sports picture of me when I bowled 183.
13. More advertisements on things that merchants are giving away.
14. A front page picture of my neighbor being hauled out of the bar by his wife.
15. A front page spread about the deadbeat who lives across the street from me who just had his car repossessed.
16. Forget the last one, I just got word from the finance company that they're coming after my car.
17. More letters to the editor naming the crooks we have in town.

Delinquent Notice Reply

May 29, 1968

A Buckhannon schoolteacher, who also sells a well-known and well-advertised encyclopedia, recently received a communiqué from the Mountaineer branch of her home office with a note saying "The following is a reply from delinquent notice letter which we sent out from our office. Thought you might enjoy reading it."

The local lass also thought local readers would enjoy it and here 'tis.

Dear Sir:

In reply to your request to send a check, I wish to inform you that the present condition of my bank account makes it almost impossible. My almost shattered financial condition is due to federal laws, state laws, county laws, city laws, state laws, borough laws, corporation laws, mother-in-laws, and outlaws.

Through these laws I am compelled to pay a business tax, gas tax, amusement tax, water tax, luxury tax, hidden tax, occupation tax, income tax, food tax, defense tax, property tax, and even sewer tax. I'm required to get a business license, car license, operator's license, truck license – not to mention a marriage license, dog license, fishing and hunting license.

I am also required to contribute to every society and organization that the genius of man is capable of bringing into life, the woman's relief, unemployment relief, gold digger's relief and the red ants of the Andes relief.

Also to all charitable institutions in the city, including the Salvation Army, Community Chest, Red Cross, Purple Cross, Double Cross, Scouts, Y.M.C.A., and the Y.W.C.A., and Police and Firemen Benefits; in addition, I'm expected to do my share to support research into physical diseases of the heart, lung, muscular and blood diseases, polio and diabetes.

For my own safety, I'm required to carry health insurance, property insurance, life insurance, fire insurance, liability insurance, medical insurance, tornado insurance, burglar insurance, accident insurance, business insurance, unemployment insurance, and old age insurance.

My business is so governed at the present time that it is no easy matter to find out exactly who owns it. I am inspected, suspected, disrespected, rejected, fined, maligned, and commanded until I provide the inexhaustible supply of money for every known mood, desire and hope of the human race.

And if I should refuse to donate to something or other, I am lied about, held up, pushed down, boycotted, ostracized, vilified, debased, calumniated and slandered.

I can reveal to you in all honesty and sincerity that except for a miracle which happened, I could not enclose this check. The wolf that comes to my door nowadays had pups in my kitchen last night. I sold them and here are the proceeds. Sincerely yours.

Upshur County Educational Ranking

June 27, 1968

One of the cardinal sins in the newspaper profession is the publishing of a long list of statistics. No one reads them, no one cares outside of those directly involved or affected by the figures.

This applies to me as well. Heaven knows, this office seems to receive more than its share of statistical data from every Tom, Dick and Harry in the continental United States, most of which is shucked into the wastebasket.

But last Friday, there appeared a small copy of a booklet uninterestingly entitled "Rankings of the Counties, 1968". This annual report is prepared by the director of research and special services for the W. Va. Education Association.

Ordinarily it too would have been shucked into the wastebasket. For some reason I started to study the figures. Within the pages of this unassuming booklet were some startling facts. They do involve and affect every working resident of Upshur county.

This booklet provides data helpful in determining to some extent the accomplishments of a particular school system.

Much too often, I'd heard the comment from office and store clerks that "teachers don't deserve a raise." You'll note that these people usually are making much less in salary than Upshur county school teachers. I usually write off the comment as "sour grapes." One man even had the gall to suggest, that if one was dedicated, a school teacher didn't expect a high salary. This same man sold out his grocery business when it started losing money. I notice he wasn't so dedicated to the business that he sold a loaf of bread for a penny. He had a family to rear just like most of our school teachers.

So now, bear with me, here's some facts. Upshur county has a population of 18,000, with a loss in population of 1.1 percent in the past six years. The net enrollment in Upshur schools totals 4,295 students…a net loss of 2.2 percent in just the past year. So it would appear that the state and county continues to lose population, and as more and more residents go on welfare there are fewer of us to support good school programs.

How dedicated are our teachers? The figures bear out the fact that they are highly dedicated. For instance, Upshur county ranks 18th among the 55 counties with 86.5 percent of elementary teachers with at least a bachelor's degree. And, we rank first among all counties with 100% of our secondary teachers holding a bachelor's degree.

Do we appreciate this dedication and preparation for the teaching of our youngsters? We do not! Upshur county ranks 46th among the 55 counties with a beginning salary of $4,150 for our teachers.

With barely a salary above the so-called poverty level, we then give them another slap in the face by ranking 50th among all 55 counties in crowding their classrooms to the point that they can teach only ineffectively. In Upshur county, an average of 31 pupils are placed in each elementary teacher's classroom and 15 pupils in each secondary teacher's room. The West Virginia average is 17 and 22 pupils per teacher.

Do we give the teachers any professional help in Upshur county? We do not! Lo and behold, we rank 53rd among the 55 counties in this category.

Upshur's complete unconcern for our educational system is apparent when one studies the educational attainment of its population. Only 5 percent of our population has at least four years of college. Only 26 percent has four years of high school. That leaves 69 percent of our population with an average of an eighth grade education.

Would this by chance explain the average personal income of $1,693? No education, no jobs? Forty-one percent of Upshur county households in Upshur county had incomes under $2,999 in 1966. Only 7 percent of our households had incomes of $10,000 and over.

But do not despair! Despite all the handicaps, if we get a student to continue his education to the point of graduating from high school, then the figures show that 46 percent of each graduating class enters college. But, it's evident, with the continued population loss that they are not staying in Upshur county. One can hardly blame them. Upshur ranks 48th among the 55 counties in expenditures per enrolled pupil...$377 annually. The state average is $437.

Of this income, local revenue totals $109 per pupil with an additional of $280 from state sources and $41 from federal sources.

So here it is in black and white...we are very much unconcerned.

Heartland - Central West Virginia

July 25, 1968

A nice, young college man was in this office last week promoting Heartland, West Virginia. He asked our help in seeing that the public is aware of this non-profit organization of volunteers in seven counties to encourage tourism, travel and recreational development in Central West Virginia.

I agree, I think the public should be aware of the fact that Heartland is attempting to boost your business, create new enterprises, establish new facilities and support new ideas.

Tourism holds much promise. In fact, tourist business is destined to increase in volume with a market of steady growth if it's cultivated. West Virginia and the Heartland area should plan to get its fair share.

But, I pointed out to the nice, young college man that until restaurant owners learn to use place mats in this state, I can't see where tourists will particularly care to return to the area.

If I have one pet peeve, it's eating where the waitress swabs off the table with a damp cloth (the cleanliness of which is questionable) and immediately places my silverware atop the still damp tabletop. I always have the urge to wipe off the silver on the hopefully-clean napkin.

Our local eating establishments are guilty of this unsavory and unsanitary habit. Maybe there's a health department regulation but if so, it certainly is not enforced.

In a general breakdown of the tourist dollar, 35% goes toward eating and food supplies. It might be well if the area of Braxton, Clay, Gilmer, Lewis, Nicholas, Upshur and Webster, the counties which make up Heartland, concentrate on simple cleanliness and courtesy.

Perhaps then, the tourists will visit the Strawberry Festival events, the French Creek Game Farm, the wood sculpturing of Wolfgang Flor, Indian Camp Rock, Pringle Tree, Seed Mosaics on Route 1, the Wagon Wheel Ranch Vacation Farm at Rock Cave, Shady Rest Vacation Farm on Route 2, all attractions listed in a brochure for "Adventure in the Uplands", Heartland of Central West Virginia.

Bill, Barb & The Agnews

August 15, 1968

It's really a small world. But, seldom do the paths of the great and obscure cross, except maybe in America. This family of mine was particularly interested in Maryland's Gov. Spiro Agnew's nomination last week as the GOP candidate for the office of vice president…simply because last summer his path did cross that of No. 2 Son.

The truth of the matter is that Governor and Mrs. Agnew are responsible for Bill's and Barb's wedding anniversary falling on August 28.

To make a long story short, last summer No. 2 Son and Barb were working at the beach in Ocean City along with the hundreds of other college students who wait tables, sell ice cream, lifeguard, etc. Barb's particular job happened to be a checkout girl at the largest supermarket on the beach.

One of the steady customers was Mrs. Agnew, who, being a particularly friendly person, grew to know Barb, Bill, Claudia Been and several other of their friends. To make a long story even shorter, I was stunned to receive a telephone call one night from No. 2 Son that he and Barb had arranged a little church wedding ceremony, all plans were complete, but there was one hitch…No. 2 Son needed my parental permission. Dutifully, (who am I to argue?) the permission slip was picked up at the local county courthouse, and notarized legally by one of my co-workers in this office. Suddenly, the phone calls were flying thick and fast between this office and Ocean City. The permission slip did not have a seal and the Maryland county clerk refused to issue a license!

Here is where Mrs. Agnew steps into the picture. On a routine shopping trip to the supermarket she learns of the "snafu." She takes the kids to her summer home, introduces them to the governor, who speedily places a few phone calls to this office concerning West Virginia procedures on notarizing legal documents, questions, studies the situation and Lo! on August 28 the wedding goes on as scheduled with the Governor and Mrs. Agnew represented at the ceremony by an aide.

And that is how it was! You can be sure that No. 2 Son and Barb sent a congratulatory message to the Agnews last week.

The Chicago Convention 1968

September 5, 1968

Last Monday and Tuesday I thought I was seeing a summer replacement for Rowan and Martin's "Laugh-In." Wednesday it wasn't funny anymore. A thought kept running through my brain "Born of revolution, this country is dying of revolution." And, even as the delegates became disenchanted with the so-called Gestapo tactics at the corner of Balboa and Michigan Avenue, the National Guard with bayonets, the Chicago police with billy clubs, the tear gas, the barbed wire, I felt like sobbing. Later, I wanted to vomit! Maybe we don't prefer the long hair, the sideburns, but when have we beat and bloodied a human being because of how he looked? My TV cameras focused on some pretty typical-looking American young people. We middle-aged perhaps don't understand the young or don't always agree, but when were we given a license to beat and bloody a 19-year-old because of what he believes?

Those weren't "hippies" speaking from the podium! These were respected statesmen who were also calling for the end of the war in Vietnam and in our streets. How did a machine grow so large and so powerful that delegates could be stopped repeatedly for nuisance security checks? When did a machine become so large and so powerful that even the newsmen were arrested, beaten and maligned when they were only doing their job? When did a machine grow so large and so powerful that only a select few were admitted with banners and materials for the use of only one candidate?

How can a party talk of "joy and happiness" when our individual beliefs must be kept secret for fear of reprisal? As a California delegate stated, "Why the repression of enthusiasm? This convention could stand some enthusiasm!" America is legally and morally obligated to establish justice, insure domestic tranquility, provide for the common defense and promote the general welfare of its people. Guns and billy clubs will not solve our problems. What did the assassinations of President John Kennedy, the Rev. Martin Luther King and Senator Bobby Kennedy prove? Mismanaged federal monies will not solve our problems!!!

Protests and demonstrations will not solve our problems, although it seems the only way to draw the public attention to the wrong or the right of the question. I don't have an answer.

But, how about trying once again fairness and honesty in the dispensing of law and order. We might even try some respect again for God, country, poor ole mom, and flag!

Governor George Wallace

September 12, 1968

It doesn't take any political analyst with facts and figures to tell the average American voter that former Gov. Wallace, of Alabama, is going to draw a large vote in the upcoming election. All one has to do is stand on the street corner or sit in the local restaurants to hear Wallace's name repeated again and again. Wallace personifies the "backlash" against the civil rights movement and the drive for "law and order" in the big cities. Some indicate a strong anti-Semitic element in his campaign.

But a counterattack against his presidential ambitions has been launched recently by several liberal publishers, businessmen, lawyers and a labor leader all from the deep South.

Specifically the group points out that Wallace is not all he appears to be. They mention the high Alabama crime rate and the poor education system under Wallace's administration. Men like Ralph McGill, Pulitzer prize winner and publisher of the Atlanta, Ga. Constitution, points out that Wallace has loaded Alabama's tax structure against the workingman and in favor of the rich and well-to-do

Additionally, the group charges, point-by-point:

He has denied the workingman many real improvements in unemployment compensation laws.

He draws his financial support from some of the biggest union haters in the country.

He has kept Alabama's educational system among the poorest in the nation.

He has lied to the workingman, cheated the workingman and double-crossed the workingman.

All very interesting for a man who advocates establishing a climate for free discussion of public issues! And, if you don't believe him, he'll knock some heads together to prove it.

Cleaning Out My Drawers

September 19, 1968

A person really should let a desk drawer or shelf or two go neglected for a year or two just for the fun of cleaning and discovering a forgotten item, a clipping or an old letter from a friend.

I'm a pack-rat, I don't deny it. I have a terrible habit of tucking away a magazine article, or a newspaper clipping thinking it will come in handy someday. I save complimentary letters (they are so few and far between.) It used to be when the children were small, I saved a sprawling printed valentine or a Mother's Day card or a Bible School drawing. Now it's hard to tell whose work they are… No. 1 or No. 2 son or Daughter.

I even found an empty, elaborate, valentine candy box the other evening. I guess I thought it would come in handy for a party, or dance or luncheon or club meeting decoration sometime or other.

I was delighted to find pictures that had long been misplaced. Then there were negatives of no use whatever. Why I kept unsharpened pencils and out-of-ink pens is beyond me. There were the usual paper clips and rubber bands scattered everywhere…a dried-up bottle of ink and a smidgin of glue. Bridge cards and score pads were in disarray.

Tossed away was a box of complicated jig-saw puzzles, an old copy of Life, clarinet music, broken flashlight, Easter basket grass, old ribbons and bows. Found was my high school diploma and my baby shoe (I always intended to have that bronzed), a 40-year-old local newspaper, unused Christmas cards, and a beautiful gold and white picture frame.

Everything is now safely and neatly put in order. I even got to the trash cans ahead of the family. (The only time to sort and clean is when you're alone, otherwise the family will insist that so-and-so is a cherished relic.) And just think, in the case of my sudden demise, the family will have so much less to sort and toss away!

Short Skirts

September 26, 1968

We, at the Delta, get some of the most interesting telephone calls and some of the most intriguing questions. For instance, an anonymous caller last Friday (they are always anonymous) called to say that the local principals were calling in girls whose skirts were too short. The caller wanted to know where one could buy a skirt that wasn't short. She has a point.

The caller didn't mean she approved of short, short skirts, but thought the principals might start with their secretaries in their own office if there is to be a set hem length.

Now I haven't noticed if the secretary's skirts are too short, but apparently some of the patrons have and are giving fair warning.

But, after a chuckle, I remembered a column someone or other mailed to me this summer. I can't tell from what newspaper it was lifted but the column was written by a Don Daniels.

And here's a man's viewpoint on the skirt controversy:

When I was a juvenile and considerably more delinquent than I am now, it was my good fortune to sometimes spot a sight of thigh and guess it was inspiring. But in those days you had to work for it. I mean you had to drop the pencil in study hall or wait under a bridge.

You shocked?

Nah!...Every unshaven youth in the world plays peekaboo and it didn't start with me.

It might be an indication of approaching antiquity or perhaps my bullish appetites have been satiated over the years...and I take a vitamin pill every day... but for me, mini-skirts are insulting.

Each man, despite his age, is an explorer and discoverer and I think it is a little unfair to put down road maps. I mean if I am to assault a mountain, I want no paths built for me. I got to be pretty old before I discovered a garter belt in action and I have to think that it was part of growing up.

I don't like mini-skirts much.

I mean, a guy goes to a party and here are eight or nine broads sitting around wearing their hems at their earlobes and he doesn't know where to look.

You think I'm kidding?

Not a bit of it, I have been to intimate social functions and spent most of the evening looking at the ceiling because it was the only modest place in the joint. Until lately, the last time I recall seeing a pair of bloomers was on someone's clothesline and that was a far time back.

Now, you can see them every day and they have somehow lost their enchantment. Ladies now wear bloomers not in the case of warmth, but in self defense.

And the lace enhances them not. I would be terribly abashed if I had to sit around with my underwear showing.

Women are abject conformists. If some clown like Givenchy suggests they wear their hemlines at their eyeballs, they must do so. If you aren't like the dame down the street, you are a freak of sorts.

This would surely be a minor league world without women but I wish they would contain something of the mystery. Dames are the most intriguing puzzle a man ever worked on and the solving of same would be a sort of ecstasy. With their skirts at their hairline and their flip top fronts, they have become childish things not worthy of the challenge. When a young man gets to be sixteen today, the best he can ask is "What else is there?" And, there is nothing else.

Carole Lombard, if you can remember, was totally beautiful and she made her captures without revealing a kneecap.

The Great Society Has Arrived

October 3, 1968

Land Ho. The promised land is in sight. The Great Society has arrived. Some months ago, a certain Miss Juanita Sith, 24, an unwed mother of five children, moved to Philadelphia from Delaware. She applied for relief, and was told that Pennsylvania required a year of residence.

This displeased her. She brought suit and a three-judge court then ordered the Pennsylvania Department of Public Welfare to pay her. Thereupon the State called upon Justice William J. Brennan, Jr., who has jurisdiction over Federal courts in Pennsylvania, to delay the effect of the ruling pending an appeal to the Supreme Court. The jurist denied the plea. Without comment. More recently, the US Supreme Court has sanctioned "free love." The Court ruled that a woman and her lover of the moment may engage in a continuing affair without fear of losing the Aid to Dependent Children payments. Now, it appears, no fevered female needs worry about getting carried away some day and marrying the man of the moment. Another judge has opened a third gate. In Brooklyn, New York, a Supreme Court Justice has ruled that the city must pay all expenses involved in procuring a divorce. In New York State, a necessary step in procuring a divorce is the publication of legal notices. That's expensive business. A woman who could not afford to pay for such legal notices applied to the City Finance Department. The department refused to pick up the tab.

An enterprising attorney took her case "to establish a precedent for others."

As a consequence of his effort, the Great Society is now complete. If the precedent stands, the partner to marriage who can't afford the price of a divorce can send the bill to the local government – city, or county – and save the trip to Mexico or Las Vegas. The understanding judge suggested that poor people who want a divorce, and who can prove that they don't have the wherewithal to pay the tab, can trot down to City Hall and deliver the bill. And that completes the possibilities: The taxpayer supports those who don't marry, it supports those who live as if they were married, but aren't: and it finances those who did marry and want a divorce.

Take your choice. You can't lose.

The Value of A Vote

October 31, 1968

Next Tuesday is Election Day throughout this nation. Millions will vote but on the other hand, millions will not. I can only make a suggestion…take a recent phrase quoted by Mayor John Lind and say "Give a damn." I mean vote!

Better yet, for those of you who plan to stay home and then continually gripe about the state of the nation, I can only quote from Sen. Edward Kennedy's eulogy to his brother, Bobby. "Some men see things as they are and say why, I dream things that never were and say why not."

As the population explodes, individuals seem to become less significant.

But are they?

What about the voter and his franchise in a political democracy? Has he become a meaningless grain of sand on the seashore of time?

Let the record speak.

In 1645 Oliver Cromwell was named Lord Protector of Great Britain by the House of Commons. The vote was 91 to 90.

In 1649 King Charles I of England was ordered executed for treason by a nationwide high tribunal of judges. The vote was 68 to 67.

In 1800 Thomas Jefferson was elected President of the United States by the House of Representatives after he and Aaron Burr had received an identical number of votes in the electoral college. The majority he received in Congress was one vote.

In 1839 Marcus Morton, candidate for Governor of Massachusetts, needed 51,034 votes to defeat the rival candidate, Edward Everett. He received exactly that number.

In 1868 an effort was made in the United States Senate to impeach President Andrew Johnson. When the Senate vote was taken the motion to convict received 35 favorable votes, and 19 were opposed. The motion lost because it fell short of the required two-thirds majority by one vote.

In 1876 Rutherford B. Hayes was elected 19th President of the United States over Samuel J. Tilden after a balloting dispute. The electoral college vote was 185 to 184. The electoral commission which settled the dispute decided in favor of the Hayes electors by a vote of 8 to 7 on key issues.

In 1941 a bill to extend military conscription for the duration of the national emergency passed the United States House of Representatives by a vote of 203 to 202. Less than three months later Pearl Harbor was bombed.

Yes, your vote counts because you count.

Christmas Crafts

December 12, 1968

Christmas is supposed to be the most joyous season of the year. For me, it is the most depressing! And all because of those darn Christmas workshops! I'm certainly not noted for my artistic ability…I have the desire, but not the natural tendency. Those workshops just prove my inadequacy.

I mean, one year I went to the YWCA to learn to make decorative mints. Each mint was smoothly cut, neat and precise, and almost with mechanical precision. I tried… each mint was as large and as irregular as the end of a man's thumb. Everyone in the class laughed… but me.

The next year, still undeterred, I tried again. This time we attempted to make 18-inch high Christmas angels, working with mucky paste, strips of newspaper, bits of muslin and gold spray. My angel wasn't the worst in the class but it was the only one with a crooked halo. My halo isn't always so straight either so the angel fitted in nicely with the livingroom décor.

Candles were attempted this year. All looked like those $25 models one buys from Saks of Fifth Avenue. I tried five candles, explicitly followed directions, and every candle was a big "ho-ho." I not even ruined my first attempt, but spilled Mrs. Miller's candle that was hardening on the back porch banister. That's just another indication of my total inadequacy and clumsiness.

Another year at the UW, I tried to make a large wreath with the proper amount of nuts, carefully inserted in a large Styrofoam frame. It didn't look half bad the first year. The next year, it was full of worms…the nuts that is. Another indication of inadequacy… I hadn't properly sprayed the thing.

If I have any natural artistic tendency, it must be deep-seeded. But, if there must be a joker in each class, just call on me. I'm good for a laugh any time!

And, a Merry Christmas to you, too!

Juvenile Crime – The Penalty

December 19, 1968

Because you have no previous conviction, I am permitted to give you parole…But if you never see the inside of a penitentiary, you will not have escaped the penalties of your crime."

These words were said by a judge in Iowa to a convicted 16-year-old felon and were reprinted, along with the judge's other remarks, in the St. Francis (Kan.) Herald and the Kentucky Bar Journal. A reprint of the article came across my desk the other day, and I found the judge's words so penetrating that I decided to use some of them for whatever impression they might make on any young man.

The judge went on to explain to the young parolee the tragic effect of a felony conviction.

Listen:

"The record of your conviction will be here as long as the courthouse stands. No amount of good conduct in the future can erase it…If you are ever called to witness in any court some lawyer will point his finger at you and ask: "Have you ever been convicted of a felony?"…And the question will be asked for the purpose of casting doubt on your testimony. Convicted felons are not believed as readily as other persons.

"It may be that someday…you will apply for a passport. You will not get it… No country will allow you to become a resident.

"Your world is, oh, so much smaller than it was.

"Some day you may seek a position in the civil service… You will find the question: Have you ever been convicted of a felony? Your answer will bar you from examination.

"You may want to take a position of trust, where a surety bond is required. On the application will appear this question: Have you ever been convicted of a felony?

"In a few years you will be 21 and others your age will have the right to vote, but you will not... You will be a citizen of your state and county, but you will have no voice in public affairs.

"Your country is calling men to the colors... But the Army will never accept you, nor will the Navy... You may serve your country in a labor battalion perhaps, but never behind guns. Yours may be the drudgery of war, but never the honor that comes to a soldier.

"I am granting you a parole. A parole is in no sense a pardon. You will report to the men who have accepted your parole as often as they may ask. Your convenience is not a matter of importance. You will answer fully and truthfully any question they may ask. Should they suggest that you refrain from going to certain places or with certain companions, you will follow their suggestions and without grumbling.

"You will also obey your parents...You will perform such tasks as are assigned to you. Your parole is a fragile thing.

"Should the slightest complaint of your conduct reach this court, your parole will be revoked immediately... You will not be brought back here for questioning or explanations. You will be picked up and taken to prison without notice to you and without delay."

Those were the judge's words, said to his friend's young son who stood before him for sentencing.

The judge remains anonymous. So does the young prisoner. But we can imagine, too, that if the young boy had heard or read words like this before he committed his crime, he might have stopped to reconsider.

Perhaps someone else will stop to reconsider. That's why I have passed the words along.

Hospital Expenses

February 6, 1969

Have you been wondering why the cost of hospital care keeps increasing? I think I've found the answer. As a homemaker and housekeeper, how would you like to do 86,355 pounds of laundry a year, or for that matter, 275 pounds of laundry a day.

Sister Mary Herbert in a recent address to members of St. Joseph's Hospital Auxiliary reported just a few facts that might shed some light on increasing hospital costs.

The local St. Joseph's hospital is not tax-supported, nor controlled by the government but by the Sisters of the Pallottine Missionary Society, who continue to do charity work when patients are very poor and with no means to pay the bill. On the other hand, any hospital operates, or tries to operate, in the black. With its income, 55 fulltime and 15 part-time employees must be paid weekly. Interestingly, hospital volunteers of the local auxiliary gave 5, 937 hours of service this past year.

As a housekeeper, how would you like to make up 53 fresh beds each morning and serve 115 meals daily for a total of 42,090 for a year? As a homemaker and hostess, how would you like to greet 1,400 persons as guests in your home? That was the total number of admissions in 1968. The average number of beds occupied per day was 29 or a total of 10,907 beds per year.

Additionally, emergency visits totaled 2,508; outpatient visits 2, 845; 2,735 X-rays were taken and 18,725 laboratory tests were made. While you are making the beds, and serving the meals, and cleaning the premises, and keeping accounts, and coping with emergencies, someplace in the building 350 operations were being performed during the year; 450 anesthetics were given and 225 infants were born.

Total expenses for the past year were $525,996. Salaries comprised 66 percent of the total expenses. And, in addition to the wear and tear, there were eight physicians and five dentists all dashing 'hither and yon' giving efficient care to every patient for every type of illness.

Yes, I think I can better understand the rising cost of hospital care. I've noticed it in my own grocery and maintenance bills this past year.

Student Demonstrations

March 13, 1969

Every time I see a student protest demonstration, I wonder "Where are the parents?" I can just see me continuing to support a son or daughter at college with tuition, board and room, date money, mad money, etc. after they have stepped on my rights or anyone else's rights.

Right now I can hear a reader saying "Her generation gap is showing!" You're darn right my generation gap is showing. I'm old-fashioned. I don't believe in stealing, burning, looting, murder or mayhem. I have rights as does everyone in this country, but just so long as I'm a law-abiding citizen.

If I have a gripe, I write letters. Worse yet, I spill it all in this column. I'm old-fashioned enough to believe that all situations can be clarified, changed and corrected with sensible, peaceful sessions or at the best, peaceful demonstrations. Heaven knows, there are things wrong in this country. Only an ostrich with his head in the sand could be unaware. But, it won't be corrected by fire and smoke. So, it was with jubilation I read recently of Hillsdale College, a small, 125-year-old institution in Michigan whose president has laid it on the line when it comes to student "rebels."

Before enrollment last fall, he mailed a letter to all current students and incoming freshmen with carbon copies sent to parents or guardians, stating that attendance at Hillsdale College was a privilege, and not a right. He also stated that his door was open at all times for new and old ideas… no individual will be denied access to a hearing. But, on the other hand, the college president emphasized that "therefore, let it be known that any act of violence or intimidation, any seizing of property or any unauthorized activity which prevents the normal operation of this college in any way will be considered action sufficient to the suspension or expulsion of students, regardless of the number involved.

"This statement is submitted now in order that any student may still have adequate time to select another college if the above terms are not acceptable."

Hurrah! President J. Donald Phillips, May your tribe increase!

Spray Cans

May 1, 1969

After this past weekend I'm convinced that Americans need not fear the destruction of earth by an atomic bomb. When this old world goes, it will be through the detonation of all the aerosol cans exploding in the city dumps, setting off a chain reaction from one city to the next around the world.

Furthermore, future scientists are puzzled by the enlarged flat index finger on the housewives' right hand. This too can be attributed to the aerosol can.

I reached this simple conclusion after housecleaning my living room, Saturday. You poor wives who are laboring through your spring cleaning probably never stop to think how many times you pick up an aerosol can during the process. For instance, my paneled walls were cleaned and waxed with a convenient spray can. The windows came sparkling clean with a spray preparation from a spray can. The furniture was cleaned and waxed, you guessed it, with a spray can. Upholstery was spot-cleaned, yes again, with a spray can.

The dust cloth and the floor mop were sprayed with a can to end dust. The carpet was sprayed, yep, with a spray can before vacuuming. The drapes were washed and dried automatically, but lo and behold I found myself reaching for the spray starch when I started ironing.

After five hours of this sort of hard labor, I struggled to the bathtub for good, hot bath and would you believe it, I sprayed on after-bath powder, spray deodorant, spray perfume and the final touch, hair spray.

We had French-fried shrimp for dinner and, not liking the odor, I used a spray can of air freshener. For a hurried dessert, I reached into the refrigerator for another spray can, this one with whipped cream. Very convenient.

As I fell into bed Saturday night, totally exhausted, the thought occurred to me that the dog had a bad smell, but my right hand refused to grip another can…I'll spray the "doggie deodorant" tomorrow!

I Hate That Spade

June 12, 1969

There are gifts for mothers, and then there are gifts for mothers! One tries to give appropriate gifts perhaps unusual, and yet usable. On a recent birthday, I got an appropriate gift, and usable… a spade!

It's what I wanted, a lightweight, spadeable spade for use in the flower beds. A spade was an absolute necessity, one that I could wield easily, since both No. 1 and No. 2 sons had fled the nest and were maintaining their own homes and flower beds.

Along with the spade, were gifts of a hose reel, a leaf rake, lawn clippers, and a tool caddy set.

I hate that spade! I haven't had that spade out of my hands since the day I got it! I dug flower beds and flower beds; planted and replanted; dug new dirt to refresh the old; even cleaned up around the trash barrel. One of my neighbors swears that the only reason I want new shrubbery in the front of the house is so I can dig three or four more holes with my new birthday spade.

I hate that appropriate, unusual yet usable spade! The next time one of the kids asks me what I want for my birthday, I won't answer! I'm afraid if I mention a load of manure for the lawn, I'd get it for Christmas!!

Man on the Moon

July 24, 1969

There is a man on the moon, but I can't believe it! I saw the man on the moon, but I still can't comprehend it! None of the adjectives is adequate… we've landed a man on the moon…but who can describe this spectacular and history-making event.

How ingenious is man! How interesting will be the future with its new fabrics, new ceramics, new plastics, new communications, all because they had to be developed on earth before man could go into space.

For a few hours Sunday night, the nations were united, all praying for success in the Apollo XI mission. Yes, humans are ingenious. Now as we reach further into space, let us hope that all mankind will show ingenuity in eradicating hunger, illness and poverty with all the skill, the money and the timetable used in probing the stars.

Neil Armstrong said it…"One small step for man, a giant leap for mankind."

Miss Alta Ice

January 22, 1970

Every once in awhile a person arrives in town quietly and efficiently performs his or her duties without publicity, without fanfare and without the general public really being aware of his or her outstanding community service.

Such a person exists in Buckhannon, working with 35 five-year-olds in the First United Methodist church kindergarten, half of whom are attending on scholarships.

The story of Miss Alta was ably written recently in an issue of the church newspaper. Because the paper is mailed to only church members, it very likely escaped attention of the general public.

Because she quietly and efficiently performs a service without publicity, without fanfare and without public recognition, it seemed to me that her story should be repeated.

When Miss Alta Ice became director-teacher of the weekday kindergarten last fall, she brought with her an infectious smile, many years of experience and a love for children.

These three things alone have assured her of a special place in the hearts of those who know and work with her. But what we didn't know was that she was also bringing her friends with her! We are finding after 40 years of deaconess work, she has a lot of friends.

This is what happened. In Miss Ice's annual Christmas letter to her friends all over the country, she told about her work in the First Methodist kindergarten – about our scholarship program, about the support and concern of the people of this church, and about the struggle sometimes to make ends meet. And that's when Miss Ice's friends rushed into help.

Checks and cash gifts have come from all over the U.S.A., usually accompanied by a note of sincere appreciation for Miss Ice's past work. We have received to date $973 from over 60 persons or groups who knew and worked with Miss Ice in other places.

The Kindergarten policy board is most encouraged. The Kindergarten's future looks very good indeed now. The board and church as a whole express appreciation to Miss Ice and her many friends for this unusual support, and also to the individuals and circles in our own church and community who continue their support with time, money and concern.

Facts you should know about Miss Ice:

- She was ordained Deaconess in 1930 in First United Methodist church right here in Buckhannon by Bishop Leonard.

- She spent her first eight years of service in the Minnie Nay Settlement House, Benwood, West Virginia.

- She has served as Director of Christian Education in churches in Charleston, Parkersburg, Clarksburg (where she worked with our own Charles Godwin), Fredrick, Md., Wichita, Kansas, and Birmingham and Detroit, Mich.

- She served as Director of Children's Work for the Middle Tennessee Conference.

- She started a kindergarten or nursery in every church in which she worked.

- She was Vice President of the Northeastern Jurisdiction Deaconess Association.

- She has traveled in almost every state of the union, including Hawaii and will go on a ten-day tour of Israel this March, 1970.

A Football Dream

January 29, 1970

I had the darndest dream last night… really weird. It seems I was at this state coaches meeting and no matter how much I drilled in and out among the groups of conversation, they couldn't see me.

Being a woman with no football sense, I probably would not have stayed long at a coaches meeting except a couple of men caught my eye because of their animated conversation.

It went something like this :

"Bruiser, you ole' son of a gun. How are ya'?"

"Masher! Gee, it's good to see a friendly face. They've been few and far between this season."

"Things not good, eh?"

"That's a fact, I tell you I've been burned in effigy so many times my suit smells charred. And petitions, I swear, Bruiser, I got confused one day and signed one."

"Losin' season, eh?"

"Yep, four and six. My wife cries all the time, the kids left home and even my mother-in-law doesn't come around anymore."

"Masher, I got the solution for you. Just you tippy toe over to that phone booth right now and call Buckhannon."

"Buckhannon! You out of your mind? The football capital of the state!"

"Now Masher, have I ever steered you wrong? It's the perfect place for you to sit out 'til retirement. That town is so crazy about losers they'll hire you in a minute."

"I don't know Bruiser, three championships in nine years. That doesn't sound like a loser to me."

"That's my point I'm making. Don't win! That's when ya get fired. It's been proven. Now all you got to do is go up there and do a little poor mouthin' about taking three or four seasons to build a team. Each year just win one or two games more than the year before and you'll be alive to retire."

"Doesn't make sense!"

"Nope, but that town is crazy about new coaches and rebuilding. And I swear they must have a pipeline to the U.S. Treasury. You can buy new uniforms and equipment and eat like you've never eaten before. Why they have a booster club up there that all you do is ask and they give. It's a sell-out every game and 5,000 people travel out-of-town just to see a losing game. The gate receipts look like the national debt. Even the mama's like losers. They sell a quarter million pounds of popcorn from that little ole' refreshment stand and they lost count a long time ago on the coffee and pop."

"Sounds like the answers to my prayers."

"It is, it is! Believe me, play it right and you're there for life, and just one bit of advice. Don't have any stars – I mean don't get anyone on all-State. You're treading a thin line there – too much publicity and glory and you'll get your walkin' papers. Good luck and good losin'!"

Middle Age

July 16, 1970

I had a birthday recently. Won't say which one, but it will suffice to say that it meant fat and past forty. Of course, the birthday was duly observed with nice remembrances from family. The point is I have reluctantly reached middle age and it pains me immensely. No amount of nice gifts and prettily phrased cards made it any less painful. I had just gotten over the shock of middle age when a column appeared in a recent state daily newspaper with some observations which made me unhappy all over again.

The column states "Middle age has come when:
"The heels of your shoes become lower each year along with the hems of your dresses;
"You wonder if nightly pin ups are really necessary; "You turn to the obituary page before the comic page; "You are offered a seat on the bus and more doors are held open for you;

"You can't understand why it is more difficult to move around quickly in the morning;
"You think you will want a convertible but you wonder about the draft on your neck;
"You no longer recognize the names of any of the top ten tunes; "You have a feeling of nostalgia when you hear a Guy Lombardo record; "You aren't sure if it's the floor or your knees cracking when you climb stairs;"Your conversation with your friends begins with "Remember when…; "You seek covered shelter instead of an open picnic table; "You supplement your meals with vitamins; "You listen to television commercials that begin:

"Do you have that dragged out feeling?'; "You feel you should buy something red; "You know you'll never adjust to bifocals; "Your scales must need adjusting since they keep weighing heavier; "It doesn't seem so long ago that World War II was 'Current Events';
"You start reading the activities of the Senior Citizens clubs; "Someone replies to you,' Yes, ma'am'; "It's late if you get in after 9 p.m.;
"You go to the elevator instead of the escalator since escalators require more coordination;
"You wear granny gowns instead of waltz length;
"You think in terms of a corset instead of a girdle;
"You recall Russ Columbo and Russ Morgan's orchestra and remember looking on the 78 rpm's to see who was singing with Tommy Dorsey. It was Frank Sinatra."

SNAFU

July 23, 1970

Feeling cheerful today? Out in Lorain, Ohio, a reader tried to remedy that situation by reporting the gist of headlines he found in the newspapers one day on various vital subjects:

Religion – Bishops rebel against the Pope. Catholics and Protestants fight in Ireland. Church attendance dropping.

Health and Welfare – Homicides and suicides up. Crime at its worst. Sickness on increase. Starvation all over the world. Air pollution. Water pollution.

Morals – Television violence warping youngsters. Movies unfit to see. Books filthy. Drugs taking over younger generation.

Patriotism – U.S. flag burned. Draft records destroyed. Public buildings damaged. Respect for nation at low ebb.

Sounds terrible, doesn't it. But don't let your cheerfulness turn to gloom. The world is always in a turmoil. It's sometimes a little better and sometimes a little worse, but never perfect.

Back in World War II there was a word for it, SNAFU, meaning. "Situation, Normal, All Fouled Up."

The best we can do is to keep trying to make the world a better place. In the meantime, keep smiling.

EPILOGUE

Stop The Presses!

Betty Hornbeck once said that it really only happened in the movies, but she loved to tell the story about the one and only time in her life when she actually ran into the back press room with arms flailing and eyes in a panic as she screamed "Stop the Presses, Stop the Presses!"

In addition to reporting on local events, editing breaking news stories, writing the front-page Whirligig column, and performing many other tasks associated with the ongoing production of a weekly newspaper, Betty was also responsible for generating the advertising sales for each edition of the Republican-Delta. It was during the summer of 1964 (as best I can recall) that one of Buckhannon's local clothing stores had decided to run a large display advertisement that was promoting men's short-sleeve knit shirts at what now would be the amazing price of 3 shirts for $8.00 total. At the time of each weekly printing, the local newspaper boys would arrive at the office to pick up bundles of papers for subscriber delivery and to sell a few on the street for extra pocket change. It was an active time, and also the time that Betty would grab a copy of the complete newspaper as it was running through the full press production and lay it out on her desk, wide open, to view the advertisements that she had coordinated for each week's edition.

And there it was! The Big Typo! Boldly displayed in large type as the focal point of the advertisement were the words "KNIT SHITS – 3 for $8".

STOP THE PRESSES! And stop them they did, but not before many of that week's edition had already hit the streets to be proclaimed by all as the best advertising promotion of the century. In fact, sometime later, many business owners were known to have quietly asked Betty if she could "do something like that for me…" I can still visualize that ad and, like many people, I cut it out of the paper and carried it in my wallet for years. But, somewhere along the way, it disappeared. I am waiting to find a copy once more. And the clothing store? They sold out the entire inventory of Knit Shirts.

~Son No.2

Acknowledgements

Nothing happens without a little push here and there. This book took twelve years for Betty Hornbeck to craft the original works, then another twenty years for family and friends to contemplate the historical aspects of collecting and reprinting her stories. Then another ten years to actually begin the initial steps of visiting the archives of the West Virginia Wesleyan Library to locate and capture the appropriate newspaper pages. Then another ten years to coordinate the manual keystroking from original copy to digital documents. Then another two years to organize, edit, layout, and finally take the Whirligig Stories to print.

An overnight success! Only fifty-two years in the making!

There are so many people to thank along the way, a conversation here, a comment there…all lines of thought that eventually connected the dots. But it was Danny Green who opened up the doors to the incredible photo collection of Howard Hiner that added a vision of what the final product could look like. And, even now, I am regretful that the size of the book could not permit a larger trove of photos that would make each story more enlightening. Danny's affable style and his willingness to toss photos and insights my way were a major impetus in driving this project to completion. Thank you, Danny.

To sister Ann, brother David, wife Woody, and Aunt Dot Short, you have my very special thanks for the telling of the stories, for your suggestions toward the work in progress, and for providing me with the energy and the incentive to complete this important task.

To Steve Coonts, childhood friend, prolific New York Times best-selling author of <u>Flight of the Intruder</u> and dozens of additional novels and cooperative works, you have my grateful thanks for your endearing and engaging Foreword to this book. To neighbor Neil McNerney, friend and author of his own publications in the field of family psychology and childhood learning including <u>Homework –A Parent's Guide to Helping Out Without Freaking Out</u> who provided a much needed education in the processes related to taking a book from original thought to actually getting it to materialize on a bookstore shelf. To neighbor Richard Hamilton, a talented graphics designer (r2hcreate.com) who gave of his time and insights to produce the cover design.

Finally, to each of you who lived this life to make these stories true! ~ WRH

Howard Hiner

Howard Hiner was the everyman of photography. He was that superlative character who purposely, or perhaps inadvertently, captured the era of the nineteen-sixties in clear black and white stills of everything that was going on in and around Buckhannon, Upshur County, West Virginia. Betty Hornbeck always called him "Hiner".

Howard Hiner 1914-2002

The newspaper staff wrote the stories, but Hiner captured the vivid images that brought those stories to life. He wasn't an employee of The Delta or any other newspaper or magazine. He was Howard Hiner, owner of Mt. State Photo and Engraving, a free-spirited entrepreneur who seemed to materialize at every activity I can remember, whether a sports event, the school prom, the city council meeting, the big fire…

I really liked Hiner. He had an elfish twinkle in his eye and a deep sense of interest in whatever was of importance to the subject at hand. It seemed as though he always knew what was going to happen, always knew where to position his shot. And there was that half-laugh that became all the larger with his smile. Hiner and wife Mary Margaret were good friends of Betty and often gathered for a table game or cocktails to trade insights and twists to stories of the day; always embedding the conversations with a sense of intrigue. I wish I could sit with them now…

The entire collection of photos is now managed by daughter Ricki and husband Danny Green of Buckhannon. The Howard Hiner Collection is priceless and worthy of the continued efforts to preserve and properly house the reflections of small town life in the mid-twentieth century. The few photos herein include a part of that collection, each of which is a tribute to a very special man.

To those of us who were privileged to have shared this life with him, we are all the better for it.
~WRH

About the Editor

William R. Hornbeck, aka Son No. 2, currently lives with wife Margaret in the Village of Mount Gilead, nestled along a section of the Catoctin Ridge more specifically known as Hogback Mountain, where the eyes are drawn across the valley toward the glorious Blue Ridge Mountains, somewhere near the town of Leesburg, in the County of Loudoun in Virginia.

Bill has lived his life as a technology entrepreneur who has successfully held at bay the aspirations of writing something both publishable and meaningful.

While awaiting the stream of consciousness that would potentially give birth to "the great American novel", he spent many years arranging the transcription and editorial preparation of the more than 370 weekly commentaries published by Betty Hornbeck during her tenure at Buckhannon's Republican-Delta newspaper from 1959 thru 1971.

The resulting publication has enabled a selection of the Whirligig Stories to finally be entered into the digital world and made part of the immortal historical record. This publication has also permitted the editor to place a highly important checkmark on his list of "Things I Must Do But Always Seem to Put Off".

Next checkbox on the list is taking that trip around the world. Please buy this book.

Editor's note: Additional content may be found online at www.WhirligigStories.com

Elizabeth Jane Dutton Hornbeck Van Kirk

April 27, 1925 – January 6, 2009

www.ingramcontent.com/pod-product-compliance
Lightning Source LLC
Chambersburg PA
CBHW080528170426
43195CB00016B/2500